THE 50 BEST
LOW-INVESTMENT,
HIGH-PROFIT
FRANCHISES
ROBERT LAURANCE PERRY

PRENTICE HALL
Englewood Cliffs, New Jersey 0763

8-16-90

Prentice-Hall International (UK) Limited, *London*
Prentice-Hall of Australia Pty. Limited, *Sydney*
Prentice-Hall Canada, Inc., *Toronto*
Prentice-Hall Hispanoamericana, S.A., *Mexico*
Prentice-Hall of India Private Limited, *New Delhi*
Prentice-Hall of Japan, Inc., *Tokyo*
Simon & Schuster Asia Pte. Ltd., *Singapore*
Editora Prentice-Hall do Brasil, Ltda., *Rio de Janeiro*

© 1990 *by*
Robert Laurance Perry

10 9 8 7 6 5 4 3 2 1

Perry, Robert L., [date]
   The fifty best low-investment, high-profit franchises / by Robert
L. Perry.
      p.   cm.
   Includes bibliographical references.
   ISBN 0-13-313529-2
   1. Franchises (Retail trade)—United States.   I. Title.
II. Title: 50 best low-investment, high-profit franchises.
HF5429.235.U5P47   1990
381'.13'0973—dc20   90-31448
                                                                                    CIP

ISBN 0-13-313529-2

PRENTICE HALL
BUSINESS & PROFESSIONAL DIVISION
A division of Simon & Schuster
Englewood Cliffs, New Jersey 07632

Printed in the United States of America

Dedication

In Memory of Daisy

Acknowledgments

Although I cannot list them all individually, I wish to thank the more than 50 franchise sales directors, marketing directors, public relations directors, and assistants who responded to my often urgent demands for information. Without their help, this book could not have been written. I also wish to thank my editor, Tom Power, for his unflagging enthusiasm, patience, understanding, and professionalism. And a special thanks goes to Charles Neighbors for his many years of service as my literary representative. Although many people contributed information to this book, I, of course, remain responsible for its content.

Introduction

A recent advertisement seeking franchisees for frozen yogurt stores stated in no uncertain terms that "financially qualified" individuals had to have a minimum net worth of $200,000, $50,000 in cash assets and $150,000 in other assets. And the cost of the franchise was given as "approximately" $110,000 to $120,000. And that did not include a lot of hidden costs that would surely drive the total cost beyond $135,000 to $150,000.

This is just one example of a disturbing trend in franchising today: the $150,000 franchise. You can not even look at a McDonald's, Burger King, or Wendy's franchise for less than several hundred thousand dollars. Often, they will require total investments in the $1 million-plus range. Look in any directory of franchises and you will see franchise fees in the tens of thousands of dollars for many seemingly innocuous businesses. And the franchise fee is just the beginning of your start-up expenses; these added costs range from travel to company headquarters for training to significant equipment purchases to half a dozen kinds of insurance to increasingly expensive telephone and utility hookup deposits.

In short, more and more often, the middle class simply cannot afford to own the best, most profitable franchises. Or you would have to spend so much money that it would be very hard to make a decent return on your investment for many years. If you borrow money from a bank or the franchise company itself, lease your equipment, and borrow against your personal assets, you could easily have to pay hundreds or thousands of dollars a month in loan payments *before* you can even begin to consider taking a salary, much less make a profit.

Or so it seems. Fortunately for the middle class, not only hope, but plenty of opportunity remains. Of the more than 2,100 franchise companies, many still appeal directly to the middle class. And many of these can provide very profitable enterprises, if not immediately, then within just one or two, but not 10, years. This book presents the 50 best franchises that give you this opportunity.

With low investment, high-profit franchises, you can earn high profits and high returns on your investment by working in the franchise yourself. If you can expect to earn a gross income (income before expenses) of $75,000 a year with an office cleaning franchise, you normally could expect to earn a net income of at least 30 to 40 percent, or $25,000 to $30,000. If you had to pay a manager $20,000 a year to run the business, you would lose almost all of your profit. However, if you work in the franchise and save the management cost, you would trade your labor and increase your return on investment. How this book defines return on investment in several ways is discussed in Chapter 2.

If you are willing to trade your time and work, you can find many lucrative franchises. The fifty in this book were selected from the 200 leading franchises as defined by five sources: *Income Opportunities* magazine; *Franchising Opportunities World* magazine; *Venture* magazine's list of the most profitable franchises; *Entrepreneur* magazine's annual Franchise 500 listings for the past four years; and the U.S. Department of Commerce's annual *The Franchise Opportunities Handbook.*

These companies have consistently proven their leadership in both franchising and their respective industries. And they have shown very effectively that you can still profit from the Great American Dream—franchise style.

Among these fifty, you will find a preponderance of service businesses. Personal service businesses still require far less cash investment than companies selling products, although Subway Sandwiches shows that a well-organized fast food franchise can still be both inexpensive and highly profitable. You won't find any of the major fast food franchises; they are all just too expensive these days and are oriented toward major investors.

But this book is not oriented toward wealthy investors or syndicates. It is dedicated to those millions of average citizens who want to own and prosper in their own businesses, and for whom franchising will remain an excellent way to achieve their personal and financial goals.

How to Use This Book

The first 3 chapters briefly discuss what franchising is and give a step-by-step method by which you can determine which franchise is the best buy for you. The rest of the book discusses each of the 50 franchises in great detail. It is divided into five chapters, each based on a franchise fee range. The chapters are divided like this:

- Franchises with fees of zero to $5,000 (Chapter 4)
- Fees of $5,001 to $10,000 (Chapter 5)
- Fees of $10,001 to $14,999 (Chapter 6)
- Fees of $15,000 to $20,000 (Chapter 7)
- Fees higher than $20,000 (Chapter 8)

The total start-up costs, including all fees, initial investments, and hidden costs for every franchise in this book equal *less than* $100,000. Some franchises state that in some cases, the total costs will exceed $100,000, but they also note that the *average* total cost for their franchises is below $100,000. You certainly can start any of these 50 franchises for less than $100,000, and more than half of them for well under $50,000. This total start-up cost keeps the franchises well within the means of the middle class.

Each franchise holds the potential for high profits. In terms of annual return on investment, an average person can earn—with any of these 50—at least 50 percent during the first two years of operation, according to published reports and reports from existing franchises.

Chapters 5 through 8 are organized on the same format. Each chapter discusses ten individual franchises. Each franchise is described in great detail with pertinent comments about its good and bad points. Each describes a franchise's basic business and structure, and then analyzes the estimated total start-up costs, including fees, required expenses, incidental expenses, and hidden costs, often in an easy-to-read chart. Next, it analyzes the franchisor's package of services, products, and support. Last, but certainly not least, the book describes in specific figures how much money you can expect to earn. You can skip from chapter to chapter to read only the parts that interest you the most. Use this book as a ready reference tool or as a guide to help you select the best franchise for your purposes.

One caveat: No one can guarantee that you will earn similar returns or make as much money as this book hypothesizes. Every franchise company is required by law to tell you that how well you do depends solely on your own efforts. Most refuse to make any earnings projections, so the estimated earnings given in this book are taken from published information, reports from franchisee's, and the author's own financial analyses.

Franchises provide a system of doing business that, if followed correctly, could provide a significant return. These 50 are proven companies with reliable track records, but each year even some of these franchises fail. So do not expect any infallible "get rich quick" schemes in this book; they do not exist in franchising. Your success depends on your efforts as much, if not more than, the franchisor's system. Franchising is an excellent way to build your personal wealth with diligent and intelligent effort. These 50 franchises can simply help you achieve that goal faster than most other businesses.

Contents

Introduction   v

1
Franchising Fundamentals   1

2
Can You Make It on Your Own?   11

3
How to Find the Best Franchise for You   19

4
Franchises with Fees of $5,000 or Less   34

> *Jazzercise, Inc.*
> *Packy the Shipper*
> *Novus Windshield Repair*
> *WOW, Inc. (Wash on Wheels)*
> *Almost Heaven Hot Tubs Ltd.*
> *Perma Ceram Enterprises, Inc.*
> *Sparky Washmobile®*
> *Bathcrest® Porcelain Resurfacing*
> *Bingo Bugle*

5

Franchises with Fees from $5,001 to $10,000   77

Dial-A-Gift, Inc.
Rug Doctor Pro
Chem-Dry Carpet Cleaning
Duraclean International
Subway Sandwiches & Salads
U-Save Auto Rental
Mr. Rooter
Coustic-Glo International Inc.
Mini Maid
Jani-King
Worldwide Refinishing Systems, Inc.

6

Franchises with Fees from $10,001 to $15,000   136

Rainbow International
The Maids International
AAA Employment Franchise, Inc.
Molly Maid, Inc.
Homes & Land Publishing
Servpro Industries, Inc.
RE/MAX International, Inc.
Video Data Services
Century 21 Real Estate Corporation

7

Franchises with Fees from $15,001 to $20,000   179

Decorating Den Systems, Inc.
Management Recruiters International, Inc.
Merry Maids, Inc.
Pak Mail™ Centers of America, Inc.
Adia Personnel Services
Bio-Care, Inc.
Mail Boxes Etc. USA
Haircrafters and Great Expectations Hair Salons
Cost Cutters Family Hair Care Shops
Four Seasons Greenhouses Design & Remodeling Centers

8
Franchises with Fees Greater Than $20,000   234

Tri-Mark Publishing Co., Inc.
Travel Agents International, Inc.
American Advertising Distributors, Inc.
Priority Management Systems, Inc.
Ceiling Doctor International, Inc.
Monograms Plus
General Business Services, Inc.
Uniglobe Travel International, Inc.
ProFusion Systems, Inc.
Press Box News
Dynamark Security Centers, Inc.

Bibliography   288

Index   289

1

Franchising Fundamentals

Visit any highway intersection, shopping center, or shopping mall in the United States and Canada, and you will almost certainly find a familiar name: McDonald's, Midas Muffler, Dunkin' Donuts, Bonanza Steakhouse, Domino's Pizza, Baskin & Robbins, or any of 2,000 more. These names represent an old method of doing business that has developed into the most successful business concept of the second half of the 20th century. This method, of course, is *franchising*.

Since the mid-1950s, franchising has become the most successful retailing concept in the nation. By mid-1989, more than 565,000 establishments founded through some 2,100 different franchise companies were in business. And more than one-third of all U.S. retail sales took place in franchised businesses—in short, over $730 *billion* worth of sales. Moreover, the short-term prospects for franchising appeared rosy as Baby Boomers began to reach an age at which they wanted to leave the corporate world and establish their own businesses.

Yet there was a negative side to this growth, for only 55 huge franchise companies—among them, McDonald's and Burger King—accounted for half those sales. Thus the remaining 2,050 franchises and 90 percent of the units had significantly lower sales *per unit* than the giants. As discussed below, these other franchises were less profitable, but it's important to remember that most franchises do not create millionaires. Properly managed, however, franchises can create comfortable incomes and long-term personal wealth for their buyers.

The Simple Concept

Franchising, as a concept, is very simple. It is a way of marketing a product or service through which the parent company—formally called the

1

franchisor—licenses or gives the right to sell the company's products or services to an independent businessperson.

What franchising *is not* is as important to remember as what it is. Franchising *is not* a dealership, a distributorship, or a chain store business, although it definitely includes elements of all three. Like a chain store, a franchise does have unique signage, logos, registered trademarks, practically identical storefronts, predetermined interior-design schemes, and standard services, products, and procedures. Like a dealership, a franchise is a business that normally sells its products and services to the consumer at retail prices. Like a distributor, a franchise that sells goods, and not services, obtains its products directly from a manufacturer at wholesale prices. But there the similarities end.

Unlike a chain store manager, a franchise operator—formally called the *franchisee*—is one who *owns* his or her business. The franchisee signs a contract with the franchise company and agrees to follow a detailed set of standards and procedures, but the franchise company does not have any ownership rights in the individual operation. The franchisor does, however, retain the ownership of its trademarks, operating manuals, and unique business procedures.

The differences can be difficult to understand, but the basic relationship functions in this way. A franchisee, John Donner, buys a license to operate an XYZ shoe franchise store. He puts up the XYZ sign, installs XYZ fixtures, and follows XYZ company policies and procedures. After a year or two, he becomes dissatisfied and wants to run his own store. After a lengthy discussion, XYZ franchise says, "OK, run your own shoe store, but you can no longer use the XYZ logo. You have to take down the XYZ sign. You can no longer use our fixtures, and you can no longer get the discounts and terms available through XYZ's suppliers. You are on your own."

In a chain store, you would act only as a manager, so you would be fired if you tried to do things your own way. In a franchise, you still would own the business, but upon the cancellation of the franchise contract, you would have to run your own show.

Of course, without the attraction of the franchise company's name, your business may be likely to suffer. By the same token, however, many people who cancel franchise contracts go on to succeed on their own. Moreover, despite the myth to the contrary, franchise companies do go out of business (about 60 per year on average). If you are an unlucky franchisee and this happens, you will be forced to go it alone or fold your tent.

Unlike a dealer, a franchisee usually buys products or offers services only from suppliers whose products or services meet the franchise company's quality and performance standards. As a dealer, you can buy from any manufacturer or distributor you please. As a franchisee, you are constrained by the franchise contract and the franchisor's requirements.

In the past, a franchisor could require you to buy everything from specific suppliers, but federal courts threw out this coercive practice during the 1970s. Franchises can still require you to buy their unique, patented, trademarked, or copyrighted products, but for other products and supplies, franchise companies cannot force you to buy from selected suppliers. However, they can require that you submit to them for approval any products or supplies or services that you may wish to buy from an outside source. The difference is subtle, but legally you retain your "freedom of action."

Unlike a distributor, you maintain a very close relationship with the franchise company. You must file sales and financial reports to them frequently, usually weekly or monthly. The company's representative keeps in close touch with you, both to help you and to make sure you toe the franchisor's line. Under the terms of the contract, both you and the franchisor must also fulfill many conditions that a manufacturer cannot force a distributor or dealer to meet.

Most importantly, dealers and distributors usually have the right to offer competing companies' products *under the suppliers' own brand names,* but a franchisee can only offer products and services under the franchise company's name or those brand names approved by the franchise company. An ice cream parlor can sell anything from Polar Bars to Breyer's, but a Baskin & Robbins can only sell Baskin & Robbins' approved ice cream with the Baskin and Robbins' label on it.

General Types of Franchises

Within this framework, three general types of franchises exist, but this book will mainly be concerned with the first one.

Business format. This is the type now generally recognized as "franchising." According to the International Franchise Association's booklet, *Investigate before Investing,* it means the adoption of an entire retail business operation. Fast-food restaurants, car rentals, unemployment agencies, real estate firms, etc., come under this type.

Selected distribution. This type is an older franchising method, but one that is so well established now that most people do not recognize it as an actual, formal franchise. The type includes automobile dealerships, gasoline and service stations, appliance stores, cosmetic stores, and the like. For example, an independent Amoco station is not allowed to sell Shell gasoline.

Trademark and brand-name franchises. Although widespread, this type is infrequently recognized as a franchise method of licensing manufacturing processes. For example, most soft drink bottlers in the country are franchisees of Coca Cola or Pepsi. The bottler buys syrups and products from the company and makes the soft drinks for local or regional distribution. Although both Coca Cola and Pepsi corporations own some bottlers, most are independently owned and operated and have been for many decades.

Dozens of Business Format Franchises

Within the business format context, practically every type of service business has been turned into a franchise. From mufflers to mailboxes and from burgers to budgies, most retail sales formats have been franchised. Within one of the dozens of categories listed below, you may find a franchise that interests you or one in which you have enough prior experience to enable you to succeed as an independent business owner. The following concise list of these types is based on the categories used by the International Franchise Association and *Entrepreneur* magazine in the former's membership directory and the latter's annual rating guide.

Advertising
Auto and truck rentals
Automotive products and services
Beauty and health aids
Beverages
Bookstores
Business aids and services
Children's services
Clothing and shoes
Computer stores
Construction: materials, services, and remodeling
Dental clinics
Drugstores
Educational products and services
Electronic stores
Employment services
Exercise and studios
Florist shops
Food: baked goods
Food: donut/pastry
Food: grocery and specialty stores
Food: ice cream, snacks, and candy
Food: manufacturers and suppliers

Food: recreation and public facilities

Food: restaurants

Food: specialty stores

Gift stores

Hardware

Home furnishings: retail and services

Insurance

Laundry and dry cleaning

Lawn, garden, and agricultural supplies and services

Liquor, retail

Machinery

Maintenance, cleaning, and sanitation

Medical services

Miscellaneous services

Motels and hotels

Pet shops

Photography and supplies

Printing and photocopying

Printing and publishing: direct-mail advertising, advertising publications

Real estate sales

Recreation: travel, sports, and hobbies

Rentals: equipment and supplies

Retail sales

Sales: Individually owned equipment/property and services

Security systems

Sporting goods

Stained glass and supplies

Storage facilities

Stores: general merchandise

Tools and hardware

Travel agencies

Video specialty stores

Water conditioning

Weight control

This book does not include a franchise from each category, but this does not mean that you cannot find an appropriate and profitable operation in each. For practical reasons, this book is limited to only 50 of the *most* profitable franchises, not the entire universe of more than 2,000.

The Illusive Statistics of Success versus Failure

Franchising has several inherent advantages over starting a business on your own. Franchise companies like to quote government statistics which maintain that fewer than 6 percent of all franchised businesses fail within the first five years of operation as compared to the supposedly terrible failure rate of 65 to 90 percent of regular new businesses.

You should be aware that these statistics quoted may be misleading, although the general conclusion is correct. First, franchise companies have a very strong vested interest in the success of a franchise. Thus they are very unlikely to allow a new franchise to fail. In fact, each franchise contract has a buy-out clause in which the company reserves the right to buy back a franchised operation—together with the lease, the inventory, the fixtures, etc.—and either run the franchise itself or sell it to someone else. When a franchise company buys out a failing or disgruntled franchisee, that business technically has failed, but the franchise company does *not* count it a failure if it takes the franchise over or manages the operation until a new franchisee can be found.

Even so, *Venture* magazine recently highlighted an article in which it was suggested that franchise failure is a significant problem for some types of franchises, particularly for those that depend on converting existing businesses into franchises. Franchise failure is particularly serious, *Venture* noted, when a company tries to grow very rapidly, and its salespeople become overzealous in selling the franchises. In such an atmosphere, salespeople tend to allow poorly qualified prospects to buy a franchise, and they do not make sufficient background checks. Or they may apply high-pressure sales tactics to prospects who do not fit into their mold.

Other problems include the following:

- Individuals with a greater desire for independence and freedom of action than a franchise operation can afford. These individuals tend to rebel against restrictions. They do not follow the system carefully, and often they fail.
- Poor quality and lack of depth in the assistance and service that a franchise company gives to its franchisees. New franchisees who run into difficulty may fail if a rapidly growing or financially strapped franchisor is unable or unwilling to give them the assistance they require.
- A franchise company willing to accept a higher failure rate so that unprofitable franchises are forced out of its "system." *Venture* notes that one

company lost 16 percent of its franchises during a recession. Still, the company's profits fell only 3 percent since the slack economy weeded out its poor performers.

Nonetheless, this survival-of-the-fittest attitude is basically contrary to the stated goal of the franchise world. Most franchise companies base their appeal—and their franchise fees—on how much assistance and guidance they offer the prospective franchisee.

Also keep in mind that a franchise company does not have to give you any money back if you fail. All contracts and disclosure documents clearly state that franchise fees and related charges will not be refunded. You need strong legal reasons—for example, a franchisor's violation of Federal Trade Commission or state regulations—to sue or file arbitration proceedings against a company to get a refund or any of your money back.

It is true that some franchise companies accept relatively high failure rates—in the 15 to 20 percent per year range—because their emphasis is on aggressive selling, but most franchise companies find a high failure rate unacceptable. They find they must sell three new franchises to make up for the loss of time and money that each failure causes. Of the 50 franchises discussed in this book, practically none has a high failure rate, which we define as more than 5 percent of the total franchised units.

In short, when searching for a desirable franchise, consider carefully its failure rate, investigate the reasons for those franchise failures, and analyze what the company's attitude and actions towards them are.

Many other reasons exist for the apparently low rate of franchise failure as compared to the apparently high rate of failures among new small businesses. Many new businesses are "shells" and do not really operate at all; their owners may set them up for short-term reasons of their own and are likely to shut them down quickly after the businesses have served their purpose. Many businesses, particularly high turnover businesses such as fashion and cosmetics, are put into bankruptcy by their owners as a tactic for them to avoid paying creditors. Also, many new businesses that are registered or incorporated simply never get started. Yet when the "non-business" business owners file the paperwork to dissolve them, these businesses are counted among the failures. Thus, government statistics do not consider the *intent* of the person who starts an independent business, and franchise failure statistics do not consider the ways that franchise companies prevent a failure from looking like one.

With these considerations in mind, it still remains mostly true that franchises succeed more often than new independent businesses. This fact may chiefly result from the functioning of several processes:

A franchise company's usually careful weeding out of bad prospects before making franchise agreements. Most franchise companies try to pick the "best beans." They select the candidates who show the best skills and have the best chance to succeed. Many people who get turned down and who have a strong desire to own a business—although they don't have the skills to manage one well—often start their own business anyway. Other rejected applicants never leave their jobs, and still others are accepted by a different franchise company.

The franchise buyer's strong desire to succeed. A franchise buyer, once he or she is culled from many applicants, will be more strongly motivated and put more effort into succeeding than the average person who starts a business.

The amount of preparation and support franchise companies give their franchise buyers. Franchisees do receive far more extensive training and assistance than most new small business owners. It would be interesting to compare the success and failure rates of franchises to independent small businesses whose owners give as much study, preparation, and effort to their concerns as franchise companies give theirs.

Of course, this is one of the chief points that differentiates franchising from do-it-yourself businesses. The franchisee is provided with carefully planned and implemented business procedures that, most often, have been tested on the "field of battle," both by the franchise company and the franchisees themselves. Franchisees do not have to reinvent the wheel as most small business owners do.

Significant Franchise Trends—1990 and Beyond

The world of franchising is rapidly changing. Significant new trends will affect you from now well into the 1990s. Depending on the money you have to invest and your business experience, these trends could help or hurt you.

More and more franchisors are selling "regions" or multiple units or territories to major investors. These agreements are often called "master franchise" or "area development" agreements, and the buyer is often called a *master franchisor.*

In turn, these investors either hire professional management to build, start, and operate their units, or they sometimes sell franchises on their own as "regional representatives" of the franchise company. This approach is primarily used by those companies that want to grow very rapidly and who believe that a state or regional owner better knows what the local market requires than a national headquarters staff. Actually, this is a negative trend; people with limited funds may find themselves priced out of many types of franchises.

Many more women and corporate managers are buying franchises, and franchise companies themselves are seeking out these people. A large group of Baby-Boom-aged women have children who have grown up or are in school most of the time. These women are looking for part-time incomes and opportunities that have a different appeal than the traditional party plan. Exercise franchises, such as Jazzercise, offer them good opportunities to own their businesses. At the same time, a large bulge of Baby Boom middle managers are finding themselves stuck on their rise up the corporate ladder or tossed off entirely. With the wave of mergers and acquisitions during the mid-1980s, tens of thousands of middle managers have been fired. Instead of driving taxicabs, many are taking their nest eggs, retirement funds, separation payments, and the like, and are buying franchises in the hope of building a business over which they have control.

Stricter selection guidelines and "closed shops" are making it more difficult for outsiders to buy franchises. One major fast-food franchise only allows people who have served as store managers for a year to buy into its franchise. Another draws only from it clients. Furthermore, many franchises prefer to sell additional units to existing successful franchises rather than sell to newcomers. And many franchises willingly sell non-competing franchises to investors who already own other franchise territories. This trend represents a serious reduction in opportunity for newcomers to the franchise field.

Major corporations and other franchisors are buying up existing franchises. Pillsbury owns Burger King. Allegis Corporation owns both United Airlines and Hertz. (As of June 1987, Allegis was trying to sell Hertz.) Pepsi owns Wendy's. Government statistics show that more than 100 franchise companies were bought out during 1986. This can be both good and bad news for the potential franchisee. It may be good because it provides more financial backing for a company with a solid concept, but with insufficient resources to assist the franchisees properly. It may be bad because it adds more layers of corporate bureaucracy to the franchise organization—one of the problems most franchisees prefer to avoid. There is no doubt about one thing, however: most franchise companies, properly managed, are very profitable, and so they become enticing lures to potential corporate buyers.

The numbers of franchise consultants, attorneys, brokers, and salespeople are increasing rapidly. These people can help you by showing you the ropes and providing you with assistance in the preparation of a more favorable contract. Or they can hurt you if they represent a franchise company whose tactic is to overwhelm you with high-pressure sales tactics. They also tend to make franchises more expensive. Brokers and salespeople often expect to receive very high up-front commissions. As much as half of your franchise fee could go to pay the commission of a broker, rep, salesperson, "regional manager," distributor, or franchiser.

Far more favorable to potential franchisees is the strong trend towards Franchisee Advisory Councils. The best of the franchise companies—Midas Muffler is one—have long had advisory councils made up of franchisees elected from amongst the membership. These councils represent all the franchisees in discussions conducted with the company about assistance, training, advertising support, product development, marketing, and so forth. A council is a very valuable tool in the franchisee's relationship with the franchise company. Note, however, that many franchisors—even some in this book—name the members of these councils or choose to have only their own executives as members. This defeats the purpose of having an advisory council.

Unfortunately, the day of the truly inexpensive franchise is almost over. Increasingly, franchise fees alone exceed $10,000, and the total initial investment exceeds $50,000 to $100,000. This puts most franchises out of the reach of the blue-collar family and largely makes franchising a white-collar business opportunity.

As important, the higher costs mean that franchise buyers often must use more of their own financial resources, including equity they have in their homes, or borrow large sums of money from finance companies affiliated with a franchise company. So, more and more, franchises are becoming highly leveraged. The franchise buyer can end up paying the bank, the second mortgage lender, and the franchise company for loans, instead of accumulating profits.

There are exceptions to this trend, and this book identifies most of the best. The next chapter discusses how you can determine whether or not you have the qualities it takes to succeed as a franchisee.

2

Can You Make It on Your Own?

The title of this chapter actually begs the question. When you buy a franchise, you are not really on your own. The franchise gives you, in return for your franchise fees and royalties, a complete—and hopefully proven—business structure and method to run a successful operation.

In many ways, you function more like a branch manager for a chain store or an operations manager for a highly decentralized corporation when you run a franchise. Top management, i.e., the franchise company, is mostly concerned about the bottom line, i.e., the profits from your operation. Just as you must follow a chain store's policies and procedures, so must you do with a franchise. The franchise company sets you up, gives you a business format, structures how your business will look, dictates your image, and regulates your products and their quality. Then the company hands you a "bible," tells you how to go forth and multiply, and reminds you to be sure to mail in the royalty checks on time each month.

The principal difference between a franchise and a chain store is that *you* own the business. You simply buy a license from the franchisor to borrow, in effect, his business format. Instead of sending all the profits back to the chain store, you only send the franchisor his royalties. You keep the net profits for yourself. Yet, you also take most of the risks. If a chain store manager does a poor job, he or she is demoted, transferred, retrained, or fired; if your franchise fails, you go out of business.

Perhaps more important, you are required to put up almost all the money. You assume the financial as well as the personal risk. Of course, few, if any, chain store managers are required to invest a significant portion of their financial resources in their employers. In fact, corporations usually give their managers stock option plans and equity ownership to encourage them to do well. Not so franchises. Your gamble is that you can earn a significant return on your investment of time, money, and personal involvement.

11

From the company's viewpoint, selling franchises is the fastest way for it to grow rapidly and with relatively little risk. It is the only business method known in which the managers or operators pay the owners for the privilege of selling the executives' products or services. When you buy a franchise, you not only assume the risk of your own success but you also agree to assume part of the risk of the success of the franchise company itself. Yet, a franchisor's mismanagement, incompetence, or even fraud may destroy your chance to succeed *and* may deprive you of your personal and financial investment—thus, the supreme importance of thoroughly investigating a franchise before you invest and of choosing a franchise carefully.

"Real" Entrepreneurs Need Not Apply

When you buy a franchise license, you trade these risks for the advantages of using a proven business method. In contrast, unlike enthusiastic franchisees, real entrepreneurs want to do things their own way. Most honestly believe—and the successful ones are right—that they can do things better than anyone else. They have a unique vision and an overwhelming desire to make that vision come true. In franchising, the true entrepreneurs *founded* the companies. A man such as the late Roy A. Kroc, who built McDonald's into a colossus, can be considered a "real" entrepreneur. These men do not tend to do well as franchisees. They chafe under the restrictions and find no comfort in running a business the way someone else tells them they must. If you share similar characteristics, if you tend to be a rebel or maverick, it is highly unlikely that you will do well as a franchise owner.

However, if you feel more comfortable with a structured environment, if you work better in an ordered situation, if you respond well to loose controls from an outside source, you can do well as a franchisee.

Advantages of a Franchise

As you begin to consider buying a franchise, you should consider its advantages and disadvantages and also determine how your personality, attitude, and experience fits in.

Listed below are many good reasons why a franchise is preferable to entrepreneurship for the right type of person:

- The strategic and marketing advantages of having the use of a nationally or regionally known trademark and the cumulative positive effect that the trademark has on your growth. Burger King is a more powerful pull than

Sam's Sub Shop in most cases. It's true that Sam's Sub Shop can succeed as well, but usually not to the same extent.

- The marketing advantages of having key information about competition, product demand, customer demographics, etc.
- The purchasing advantage of large discounts and cost savings achieved by buying raw materials and supplies through a central warehousing system. Be aware, however, that many franchise companies receive income from the sales of these products and supplies, so the discounts may not be as great as you think when you compare their prices to those on the open market.
- The additional purchasing advantages of proven sources of supply and service. You do not have to scrounge for new vendors when you get a bad batch of biscuits.
- The sales advantage of having customers already familiar with your product. When you buy an established franchise, your customers usually know its name and reputation. You do not have to sell them just to come in the door. For 40 years, Holiday Inn has promised its customers that they will know exactly what kind of room, food, and service they will receive whether they go to an inn in Alaska or Alabama. Baskin & Robbins Ice Cream, Burger King, Wendy's, McDonald's, and dozens more, all successfully are able to promote this same concept.
- The start-up advantage of a structure that reduces guesswork and problems to a bare minimum. You do not have to reinvent the wheel.
- The start-up advantage of the support of a knowledgeable staff that can give you proven advice on finding a location, assembling capital and financial resources, doing leasehold improvements, and so forth.
- The on-going advantage of tested operating procedures. Most franchises insist that you follow their operations manuals closely, and many franchises state that differing from those procedures will cause trouble.
- The competitive advantage of a franchise's uniform quality of its products and services. You may not get the best hamburger ever made at a fast-food franchise, but you know that it will always maintain a certain standard of acceptable quality. This standardization is acceptable to the vast majority of consumers. The relatively few who insist on gourmet burgers can find them in specialty restaurants and pay $6.95 instead of $1.69.
- The managerial advantage of following established bookkeeping and accounting procedures. For many, using these procedures saves hours or days of pen-and-pencil calculations. In addition, the franchisor knows exactly the state of its and your financial status at a glance, and these tight financial controls almost always help a business succeed.
- The financial advantages of having financial assistance available, either directly from a franchisor or through a franchisor's intervention with your local banker. Some franchises have subsidiaries that make loans to franchisees; most give you a business plan to take to your bank; and some will go to the bank with you.

What It Takes from You

These advantages create an allure for many people who are unsure of whether they can succeed on their own. As noted, people who are middle managers for chain stores or major corporations, or who come from similar backgrounds or have the same "mindsets," tend to do best as franchisees. This is not invariably true however, so it does not preclude anyone from becoming a successful franchisee. Farmers have built very successful mini-chains of commercial cleaning franchises; professionals have opened large territories with fast-food restaurants; and unemployed spouses have become state managers for exercise franchises.

All these people share many or all of certain common characteristics. You need a good combination of these traits and resources to succeed with a franchise.

Money

You must have enough cash, borrowing power, or financial resources to get started. This is absolutely essential. Trying to run a franchise on a shoestring, unless its cost is very low, will simply not work. And starting a franchise, even an inexpensive one, will cost more than you think. The franchise fee is always just the first of your expenses. Listed below are most of the different kinds of expenses that you may have to pay to start a franchise.

There are two different types of expenses you can expect to pay. The first includes the most common expenses, and the second includes expenses often considered "extras" or hidden costs:

A. COMMON COSTS OF STARTING A FRANCHISE

- Franchise fee, paid up-front and non-refundable
- Royalties and advertising fees (on-going after you begin)
- Equipment purchases or leases
- Rents/leases and deposits
- Leasehold improvement costs
- Furniture and fixtures for your outlet
- Training fee—most often included in the franchise fee
- Travel and room and board costs to required training site
- Start-up product inventory—often the highest of your expenses
- Start-up supplies—often included in the franchise fee
- Pre-paid business expenses; i.e., licenses and permits
- Several types of personal and product liability insurance, as well as inventory, plate glass, and other similar coverages

- Utility and security deposits
- Legal, accounting, and professional fees
- Operating expenses, including your own salary, employee payroll, loan payments, business supplies, inventory replenishment, and the like— at least several months' worth
- Grand opening advertising and promotional expenses

In many cases, these are just the beginning expenses. Add-ons may significantly increase your total expenses.

B. HIDDEN OR EXTRA COSTS

- Coupon costs; your revenues may go down if you give away coupons to boost your grand opening sales
- Construction management fees—charged by a franchisor if you hire the company to build your location for you
- Memberships in professional, business, or franchise organizations
- Fluctuating loan repayment schedules with variable interest rates— these may lead to larger payments
- Umbrella or unusual types of liability insurance
- Site selection fees paid to the franchisor if he helps you find a location and negotiate the lease
- Option fees if you wish to buy rights up-front to open additional franchises in your area
- Build-to-suit fees, if the franchisor has to adapt his architectural plans to fit your location
- Excess advertising and marketing costs for your grand opening—these may very significantly from place to place
- Utility connection fees in some states and cities
- Your salary and payroll costs for managers during the construction, training, and pre-Grand-Opening periods.
- Legal expenses for incorporation, lease reviews, negotiations, etc.
- Costs of points and fees for second mortgage or equity loans on your home or real estate if you borrow against them
- Variable costs for rent and lease deposits
- Employment agency fees to hire managers and employees
- Advertising costs to find employees if you do it yourself
- Extra costs for signage if larger than normal, and fees paid to local planning, zoning, architectural review, or sign commissions and boards

If you do not have the financial wherewithal to buy the franchise you want, think again. It is unlikely that a franchise company will allow you to buy a license unless you do. And it is only to your long-term advantage to have adequate funding before you get started. You don't want to flounder and scramble to pay the bills while you're getting started.

PERSONAL COMMITMENT

Even if you buy a part-time franchise, such as Jazzercise, you still must be willing to make the personal commitment of time and energy to succeed. Your success rests on your shoulders, not the franchise company's. When you look into a franchise, carefully consider the demands on your time. For example, an ice cream franchise may be open from 10 A.M. to 10 or 11 P.M. "But," you may think, "I can hire employees to work late at night." What do you do, however, at 6 P.M. on Saturday evening when your teenaged employee calls and says he's "sick," either in actuality or because he doesn't want to miss the big game and the dance? You go do the work, and your plans for a nice evening at the movies, a dinner party, or a night out at a fine restaurant are out the window.

You need to make many personal sacrifices to own and manage a franchise. If you decide after careful consideration that you are unwilling to make these commitments, do something else.

Equally important is the fact that a franchise will place heavy demands on your family. Junior and Jane may not be very thrilled about working in the store on Saturday afternoon when everyone else is at the beach or a movie. Your spouse may not be very happy when you cancel a dinner party or a night out the town at the last minute. Nor may any of them be happy with your long work hours. You must sit down and discuss with them these demands on your time *and their* time, energy, and attention.

At first, you may bring home less money than you did from your last job, so the family budget may be crimped for a few months or even years as you build your business. Is your family willing to make the financial sacrifices, too?

Even if you are just an investor who hires managers to run the show, you must closely watch them. Ask anyone who runs a cash business, which is essentially what most franchises are, and he or she will tell you that controlling the cash register is the most important thing you must do. That's why large franchises have installed automated cash registers. In Mom and Pop sandwich shops, the owner must literally "count the buns," as the phrase goes, to make sure that employees are not stealing. You will need to use automated means and careful accounting procedures to protect yourself.

And this does not include the time, thought, and caring you must invest in the success of your franchise investment.

WILLINGNESS

Willingness means an eagerness to cooperate with the franchise company and to follow its procedures. It also means a desire to learn, a curiosity about how to improve your operations, as well as a willingness to share your knowledge and teach your employees how to better run the franchise. Without it and with an uncooperative attitude instead, you may run into trouble with the franchisor and your employees.

OBEDIENCE

This means having an attitude to do what the franchisor says must be done, meet company deadlines, and follow restrictions. It also means filing your income and payroll tax forms on time, paying your vendors in a timely fashion, and so forth. If you have trouble paying your bills and taxes on time, even when you have the money in the bank, you can expect that owning a franchise will simply make that trait worse.

OUTGOING PERSONALITY

Few curmudgeons or people with skeptical, cynical attitudes can expect to succeed with a franchise. Most franchises rely on good customer service to generate repeat business—the secret to the success of any business. You may have a well-known product of good quality, but if you snarl at or act rudely to the customers, they will not come back. You don't have to be a social butterfly, but you do need to have a genuine like for people.

SKILLS

You don't need to have been a corporate manager or a vice president of marketing or finance for a major corporation to succeed, but you do need good, basic organizational skills. A housewife who consistently gets her kids off to school on time and her husband out to work, one who keeps a relatively tidy house and still has time for volunteer activities, has more than enough organizational skill to manage most franchises successfully.

You also need to have a modicum of employee relations skills. There is no great secret to these skills:

Treat your employees courteously
Praise them when they do well
Scold them gently when they make mistakes
Listen to their problems
Ask for their help

The author of this book has written hundreds of articles about management skills, and all of the advice contained in them can be summarized in the above-stated list of 25 words.

DESIRE

The ambition to succeed can encourage you to learn quickly any skills you do not currently possess. The desire to do so can drive you to work smarter, make better decisions, and put forth the effort that success requires. It can help you overcome the handicap of having limited money available. Bank officers or investors may well be impressed when they sense in you a strong, single-minded desire to succeed. And many believe that deeply felt desire frees creative forces within you. Also remember that the person, team, or organization that has the drive to win or succeed the most almost always conquers the person, team, or organization with less ambition.

PERSISTENCE

From desire comes persistence, which is the ability to overcome any obstacle standing in your way. Persistence enables you to make one more sales call when your previous ten have failed. It motivates you to help a customer try on just one more pair of shoes. It helps you call just one more bank when six have turned down your request for a loan to buy a franchise. It comes from a strong faith in yourself and your goal.

You do not have to be a superperson or possess all these skills and traits in equal measure. In fact, one of the benefits of a franchise is that it allows you to take advantage of the cumulative efforts of a group of dedicated, motivated, knowledgeable, willing, and persistent individuals—those efforts that it took to start the franchise. If you can add your share of these traits to the company's efforts, you can more than likely succeed as a franchise owner.

3

How to Find the Best Franchise for You

Finding the right franchise for you should be a lengthy, detailed process. As Chapter 2 discussed, you must match your personal interests, personality, and financial resources to the available franchises. Understanding your personal "assets" marks only the beginning of your search; use them to lead you in the right direction, but only like a weather vane that tells you which way the wind blows, not as the basis for a final decision.

As the title of this book indicates, these 50 franchises are included because they offer high returns on a relatively low investment. If your goals are primarily financial—that is, you want to run a franchise to maximize your profits and not just to run your own business—then you need to define what the concept of a high return means to you. This chapter explains several ways to define the concept and shows you how to determine the potential return on your investment, even, and especially, when a franchise company cannot or will not give you the detailed information you need to calculate your return. Use these techniques as guide posts to help you identify the best available franchise that meets your other criteria.

This book prefers to define the concept of "return" this way: your return on investment—called ROI by financial experts—is determined by comparing your potential *net income* to your total up-front *cash outlay*. For example, if you invest $100,000 in cash, and if your first year's net income is $10,000 (after all expenses and taxes are subtracted from your gross income), then your return on investment (ROI) is 10 percent. The formula is simple: divide your net income (NI) by your cash outlay (CO) to obtain a percentage; or NI/CO = ROI.

As defined, net income is the amount left after you subtract all your expenses from your gross income. Total cash outlay is defined as the amount of actual money you pay to start your franchise. It does *not* include any expenses you pay after you open your doors and start earning an income. This book also uses the term, *pre-tax net income.* Since your income tax bill is influenced by many factors—such as depreciation on equipment, tax credits, and the like—which are not related to your income, this book does *not* consider your after-tax income. The tax laws are simply too complicated to measure it properly. The terms *net income* and *net profits* are used interchangeably because most franchisees own 100 percent of their businesses and therefore own their profits.

This definition of ROI differs from the classic accounting definition, which usually includes all the money you borrow and the value of assets, such as equipment and furnishings, that you give to the business. Suppose you borrow $25,000 from the bank to get started, and you give to the business a personal computer and some office furniture valued at $5,000. Using the $100,000 example above, your total investment would then equal $130,000, and your ROI would be $10,000 divided by $130,000, or just 7.7 percent.

In this book, we do not include the money you borrow or get from other sources for one simple reason. You are going to pay the loans back out of the income you earn from the business. Measuring that would be analyzing your *net profit,* and the interest you pay in your loan payments would be considered part of your operating expenses.

We also do not include many of the more elaborate accounting concepts, such as depreciation, payback of loan principal, and the like, because we want to keep it simple. Most people want to know the bottom line. A simple ratio, such as the ROI of cash investment compared to net income gives you a clear, concise picture of what the bottom line may be.

There are other ways to measure your return on your investment that you may find meaningful. You can include the amount you borrow and your cash outlays and determine your *return on capital.* In the example given, your return would be 8.25 percent.

In any of these formulas, the key factor is net income. Do not use *gross income*—the total revenues or sales you may earn—because you must pay all your expenses, including your loan payments, out of that amount. Suppose you invested $100,000 in cash and had a first-year gross income of $200,000. You might think, "Wow! I doubled my money." You didn't, however, because your net profit—the amount you put in your pocket at the end of the year— was just $10,000. Your *net margin*—your net income compared to your gross income—was just 5 percent. Heck, you could have invested your $100,000 in a bank savings account and earned more money than this without all the bother.

Another way to look at your return on investment is to compare your cash investment to your net profit *plus* your salary. If you took a salary of $25,000 on a gross income of $200,000 and earned a net profit of $10,000, the formula would show: $35,000 income divided by $100,000 investment for an ROI of 35 percent. A serious drawback to using this method is that you do not give yourself any credit for all of the hours you worked during the year.

If your worked 50 hours a week for 50 weeks and took a salary of $25,000, you would be earning a wage of $10 per hour. The formula would be the $25,000 salary divided by 2,500 hours worked during the year ($25,000/ 2,500 = $10 per hour). You need to determine whether your salary plus a net income will be worth your time, effort, and most importantly, your cash investment.

You must consider these concepts when you begin your search for a low-investment, high-return franchise. Use these formulas and concepts to determine how much net income or net profit you can realistically expect from each franchise.

Investigate, Investigate, Investigate

Finding out the financial details you need to determine a franchise's potential ROI will be difficult. The federal government's strict regulations on earnings projections has caused most franchisors to refuse to publish them. In fact, disputes over projected earnings are the single greatest cause of lawsuits and legal wrangles between franchisors and franchisees.

If a company publishes a statement that you could earn $50,000 a year, and if you bought the franchise yet only earned $15,000, you could sue the company for false and misleading statements. Depending on many other circumstances, you may or may not win your lawsuit. Franchisors, however, want to avoid the expense, trouble, and bad reputation such disputes inevitably cause, so almost all simply will not give you any earnings projections.

You may ask yourself, and rightly, "How then can I determine whether or not I should invest in a franchise if I can't find out how much money I can make?" You can, but now it takes a lot of effort and calculation. The FTC (Federal Trade Commission) rules and state regulations, originally designed to protect the franchise buyer, have actually served to create a practically impenetrable fog that now does more to protect the franchise company. Instead of being able to compare different companies' actual results in an easy way, you now have to do much of the legwork to protect yourself.

Fortunately, the FTC loosened this rule in 1988 and now allows franchisors to make certain earnings claims. Franchisors can now report average franchise earnings, publish the results of all franchise operations, discuss potential earnings ranges, and the like. But most franchise companies do not make earnings claims because franchise buyers can still complain to the FTC if their earnings do not match the companies' claims.

So, you still must do the legwork. This and much other work is absolutely necessary. We repeat what many experts have long said because it is the single most important statement this or any book about franchising can make—investigate, investigate, and investigate some more. All the experts claim that the most common and most dangerous mistake franchise buyers make is that they do not do enough investigation before they buy.

Usually, people become very emotionally involved and get caught up in a fad or a field that suddenly becomes "hot," much like the video stores did during 1984 and 1985, and yogurt franchises during 1986 and 1987. They rush in without a thorough analysis of the situation and often find themselves in a bind after they have already signed a contract. Many back out at the last minute, but many others lose their deposits, if not their entire franchise fee!

At the end of this chapter are several checklists you can use to get the details you need to consider the nonfinancial aspects of the franchises you investigate. Chapter 2 discussed some of these aspects. Be sure to probe deeply behind these questions. They serve as "trail markers" to help you avoid getting lost in the "jungle" of franchise investigation.

Watch for These Warning Signals

Beyond the financial warning signals, you should be wary of franchises for which you develop healthy profit projections, but which also display the following problems:

Rapid growth. Franchises growing very fast may simply not be able to provide you with the support you need to succeed. If your income projections are based on those of the early franchises, they may not be accurate for you and other latecomers. The early bird gets the worm and, in franchising, the most support. Of course, franchisors want their first stores to do very well and build an impressive track record. Franchisees Numbers 1 to 20 may have had the help of the company's top executives or founders. But if you are going to be Franchisee Number 500, you need to determine whether or not you will be receiving the same *quality* of support. In short, thoroughly study the training and local support program. Get to know the local, state, or regional support, and training staff and reps. Make sure you determine whether or not they can adequately help you. Furthermore, obtain information from franchisees that have just opened their doors, as well as from established ones. Ask these franchisees in-depth questions about the kind and quality of support they received as *compared to* what they were promised.

Organizational chart. Each franchise is divided into several basic functions. You need to determine how well each carries out each set of functions. To do this, obtain the franchise's organizational chart and question its executives about how they manage each function. Explore areas related to marketing, grand opening assistance, training, and on-going support and communications. How carefully a franchise controls these functions will largely determine how well it will help you. If a franchisor seems weak in a vital area, such as grand opening methods, compare that weakness to its strengths to consider whether your own expertise can make up for that weakness. If you decide that you cannot, choose another franchise.

Beware of Verbal Projections

It is clear that for the most part the financial projections you need will not be forthcoming—in writing—from any franchise company. But be extremely wary of anyone, especially a zealous salesperson or broker, who makes *verbal* projections. If no one else will back up their verbal statements in writing, watch out. Go elsewhere! This is an absolute rule with no exceptions. And that person who has given you the verbal projections has broken federal regulations and state laws.

How to Dig Up the Numbers You Need

Face it. You are going to have to dig up the information you urgently need to calculate your potential return on investment. There are several ways—each of which requires extensive legwork—for you to get information to make a well-educated guess. None of these ways are foolproof, but you should be able to get enough ballpark figures to do your simple ROI calculations.

First, ask a variety of existing franchisees. In private, many franchisees are willing to discuss—at least, in general terms—their net incomes, returns on investment, and the like. Talk to at least several franchisees in your area, where the actual costs are likely to be similar. For example, the commercial rents for a New York City hamburger franchise will be phenomenally different from the rents for the same amount of space in suburban Pittsburgh. Existing franchisees, of course, can also serve as fonts of valuable information about every aspect of the operation, including on-going support, training, hidden costs, and the like.

Do *not* talk to only those franchisees that the franchisor recommends. Quite naturally, the franchise company is unlikely to suggest that you talk to a disgruntled franchisee. FTC disclosure rules require a franchise to give you a current list of all franchisees. Pick and choose at random from this list.

Second, consider magazine surveys as a means for obtaining general figures. *Venture, Entrepreneur, Income Opportunities,* and others occasionally publish surveys or articles that gauge returns on investment. These surveys, however, are usually based on interviews or data received from a handful of franchisees, so the figures may not be as precise as you would like.

Using the Company's Own Numbers

Third, calculate a rough rate of return from the information in the franchisor's financial statements. This will take some digging, but it will be worth the effort. Franchise companies must include financial statements in their UFOCs (Uniform Franchising Offering Circulars) and disclosure documents. Usually these statements are for the two previous years. To calculate a rate of return in rough terms, do the following:

1. In the income portion of the statement, look for the total annual amount from *royalties.* Usually, the income portion will be divided into franchise fees, royalties, advertising fees, interest earnings, and miscellaneous categories. For example, a company may have a total income of $25 million, of which $10 million comes from royalties.

2. Multiply the franchise's royalty percentage by 100 to produce a multiplication factor. If a franchise has a royalty rate of 5 percent, then the factor will equal 20. (100 multiplied by 5 percent equals 20.)

3. Next, multiply the royalty income by the multiplication factor. In the example given, multiply $10 million by 20 for a total of $200 million. This should approximate the total gross income of *all* the franchises.

Remember to account for advertising fees. If the fees are included in the royalty income category, add the advertising fee percentage to the royalty percentage. If the ad fee was 2 percent in the given example, then you would multiply 100 by 7 percent for a multiplication factor of roughly 14.3. We assume in this example that the ad fee is listed in a separate category.

4. Take the total number of franchises *in operation* during that year. This information will also be given in the UFOC documents. For this example, suppose there are 500 franchises.

5. Divide the estimated gross income of all franchises by the total number of franchisees. In this example, divide $200,000,000 by 500, which gives you an average gross income per franchise of $400,000 per year.

6. Estimate your *desired* net income. If you want to earn a net margin of 20 percent, then you figure your anticipated net income by multiplying your gross income by 20 percent. In this example, $400,000 times 20 percent equals $80,000.

7. Calculate the return on your investment with the same formula given earlier in this chapter: net income divided by cash outlay. In this example, suppose your cash outlay is $500,000 and your net income is $80,000. Your ROI would then be 16 percent.

8. Repeat Steps 6 and 7 to analyze what your net income and ROI would be with different percentages. Use these "what if" estimates to consider whether the potential return is adequate for the required investment.

Use Helpful Breakeven Analysis Tool

Another perhaps easier way to determine whether a franchise will be worth your effort is to do what is called a "breakeven analysis." This is a commonly used accounting technique that tells you a very, very important number: *the minimum amount of gross income you must have to breakeven.* The analysis gives you what its name says: your breakeven point. If you cannot, at the minimum, breakeven on your projected income, you cannot make a profit. Without a profit, you are losing money on your investment. You would not have any ROI, much less one worth considering.

As a financial tool, breakeven analysis will quickly show you how feasible the operation is on a continuing basis. To be able to get these results though, you first need to find out the actual costs of *running* the franchise, which are above and beyond your total start-up costs.

Ask the franchise company for a sample monthly operating budget, an operating statement, a financial statement, an estimated profit and loss statement from an average franchise, or any other related document that shows you the real expenses you will incur in running the franchise. If a franchisor will not give you such a statement, ask franchisees for these figures. You might borrow the information, at least the categories, from the franchisor's accounting manual.

Then follow this simple exercise. First, set up an estimated operating budget that is divided into categories and with two types of costs, fixed and variable.

Simply put, fixed costs are those that you must incur, such as depreciation, insurance, property taxes, salaries for you and your manager, rents and leases, utilities, and so forth. Variable costs are those that fluctuate according to your sales. Inventory, employee payroll, raw materials, and the like, are key variable costs.

Of course, many expenses are "semi-fixed" or "semi-variable," that is, the amount you spend changes with the amount of business you do. Important costs or expenses that can be both fixed and variable include part-time employee wages, supplies, professional fees, shipping costs, advertising, telephone, a portion of utility bills, payroll taxes, maintenance on equipment, training, and so forth. These concepts become very important in figuring out a breakeven point.

Given below is a sample annual expenses budget for an imaginary franchise. The first column lists the specific expense categories. The second and third columns list fixed and variable costs of these expenses. The right-hand column gives the percentage of variable costs as compared to *total sales*.

Go-Go Food Franchise Budget

Total sales = $400,000

Expense Category	Fixed Cost	Variable Cost	Percent (%)
Inventory		$150,000	37.5
Part-time employees		80,000	20.0
Full-time employees	$ 50,000	15,000	3.8
Depreciation	5,000		
Supplies	4,000	1,000	0.3
Utilities	10,000	2,000	0.5
Telephone	500	1,000	0.3
Payroll taxes	6,000	12,000	3.0
Insurance	5,000		
Advertising	10,000	10,000	2.5
Rent	12,500		
Maintenance	2,000	1,000	0.3
Professional fees	1,500	2,000	0.5
Miscellaneous	5,000	5,000	1.3
Totals	$111,500	$279,000	70.0[a]

a. Rounded to nearest 1 percent.

The variable costs of the Go-Go Food Franchise Budget total $279,000 and make up 70 percent of the total budget. To calculate the breakeven point (BE), use the formula given below.

The breakeven point equals the dividend of the total fixed cost (FC) divided by the difference between 100 percent and the percentage of variable costs (VC) of total sales. In the example given, the percentage of variable costs of total sales is 70 percent.

BE = FC / (100% – VC%), or
BE = $111,500 / 30% = $371,667

Thus, your franchise would break even with a gross annual income of $371,667 with that budget, but this leaves you with a net income of just $28,333. Now, to figure out your net profit margin, divide your net income of $28,333 by your gross income of $400,000. This gives you a net profit of just 7.1 percent.

To figure out your potential return on investment, divide your net income of $28,333 by your total cash investment. If your total cash investment is $250,000, then your projected cash ROI would be 11.3 percent, which is not bad, but not great, either.

Do a similar breakeven analysis for *every* franchise you investigate. It may seem tedious, but it is a very valuable and revealing way to find out exactly what you are getting into.

You may wonder how you can develop an estimated budget similar to the one above. You can estimate many of these numbers from the start-up budgets that the companies must list in their Uniform Franchise Offering Circulars (UFOC) or disclosure documents. For expenses they do not list, you will just have to dig up the figures for yourself or by asking existing franchisees. Obtain the insurance estimates from your own insurance agent or broker. Estimate your own salary levels and those of any full-time employees you plan to hire. Call utility companies and ask for average monthly expenses for a similarly sized amount of retail space. Call commercial real estate brokers for estimated rents. Ask your accountant and attorney for estimates of annual fees for tax returns, bookkeeping, and legal services.

And be sure to use estimates on the high end. Testing these formulas with low estimates will artificially raise your net profit margins and ROIs and so mislead you. High estimated expenses will tend to reflect more realistically what will happen. Remember Murphy's Law: Whatever can go wrong will go wrong and at the worst possible moment. Therefore you can expect that your on-going expenses will almost always be higher than you anticipate.

If your estimates turn out to be too high, that is all to the good. If your actual expenses are less, your actual ROI will be higher, and you will benefit all the more.

After you have used several breakeven analyses to test your choice of franchises, you can more easily decide which one will make you the best potential return on your investment.

Develop a Business Plan

If you consider that laying the groundwork in buying a franchise is like an obstacle course or a steeplechase you must win before you get the "prize," you will have the correct attitude. If you are not willing to put forth great amounts of time and effort that are required for you to make a wise decision, you will sharply increase the chances that you will squander your investment. If you are not willing to do some relatively simple things yourself, such as conducting a site location search or survey, you may not have the desire and drive to make your franchise a success. To pick the right franchise, you really do have to "wear out shoe leather" in gathering information, visiting franchises, talking to helpful professionals, and the like.

In addition to doing breakeven or ROI analyses, you also need to develop a thorough business plan. Many franchises will give you a prepared one when you go to the bank for a loan, but this type of plan is not the one we mean. Before you sign any agreement, you should prepare a business plan for yourself. Doing so will give you a complete understanding of exactly what you are getting into when you buy any particular franchise.

Given below is a proven outline of a business plan. It incorporates much of the information you will already have gathered and developed if you followed the recommended steps above in this and earlier chapters. You can obtain much of the remaining information that you need from the UFOC. The key idea in writing out the business plan is that it serves to clarify for you each specific aspect of the franchise operation. It provides you with what actions you must take both before and after you buy and open your franchise outlet.

BUSINESS PLAN OUTLINE

A. Capsule Summary

List key features, and describe the franchise opportunity.

B. The Franchise

1. Describe what the franchise is, its products and services, and its customer base and potential markets.

2. Discuss how you became interested in this franchise.

3. Discuss the industry in which the franchise operates and the business background of the franchise company and its management.

C. Products and Services

Describe each type you will offer.

D. The Market

1. Describe who your customers are likely to be and where, how, and why you are likely to find them.

2. Discuss how large the total potential market can be in your area, and consider how large a share of that total you can expect to have.

3. Discuss the actual and potential competition and both its and your position.

E. The Marketing Plan

1. Define your annual and quarterly sales goals for the first two or three years.

2. Explain your selling, customer service, advertising, public relations, and promotion methods and strategies.

3. List your marketing strategies, that is, your orderly plan for reaching potential customers.

4. Define how much you plan to charge for your products and services, and compare and contrast your prices to your competitors'.

5. List your sales methods, service policies, and procedures.

F. Operations

1. Examine your location and why you plan to put your franchise there.

2. Discuss the equipment you will need to buy or lease to run the operation, how much it will cost, and from whom you will get it.

3. Describe your product production procedures or service delivery methods.

4. List your potential sources of supply.

5. Describe how many employees you need, from what groups they will be hired, what kinds of help you need (full-time, part-time, sales reps, etc.), and the training and/or experience required.

G. The Management

1. Discuss who your managers will be and how you and they will work on a daily basis.

2. Explain management salary and bonus structure.

3. Describe any needed or required management training.

4. List your outside professional support team (for example, accountants, attorneys, ad agency, banks, etc.).

H. Grand Opening Schedule

1. List the steps you must take to get your outlet under way.

2. Give deadlines and projected completion dates for each step.

I. Anticipated Problems

Discuss the likely situations that could delay or affect your planned grand opening.

J. Financial Outlook

1. Discuss your accounting procedures.

2. Include an estimated profit and loss statement for the first two or three years.

3. Provide a cash flow forecast for the first two years.

4. Do balance sheets of potential assets and liabilities.

K. Projected Financing

1. Review your total estimated start-up and operating costs, discuss your financial requirements, and where you plan to get the money (i.e., your own resources, friends and family, bank loans, private investors, etc.).

2. Discuss how the financing (cash, bank loans, donated assets, etc.) will be used.

Doing this complete business plan is the best way to protect yourself, and it enables you to make the wisest possible choice in acquiring a franchise.

A Final Rule of Thumb

Now that you know how to calculate a ROI, net profit margins, and similar key financial facts, you need to know how to determine when you should go ahead with a purchase. Follow this simple rule of thumb: if the ROI will be three to five times greater than you can earn with a "passive" investment (bank certificate of deposit, municipal bonds, common stocks, mutual funds, Treasury bills, etc.), then you can feel fairly confident about buying a franchise.

For example, long-term Treasury bills were paying about 9.00 percent interest in mid-1989. For a franchise really to have been worthwhile at this time, you would have needed to earn a ROI of 27 to 45 percent per year. If you expected an ROI of only 10 to 12 percent, why would you have bothered to buy the franchise? You could have invested your cash outlay in T-bills and sat back and collected checks for 20 or 30 years. You could have worked for someone else, earned a living, and not have had all the trouble of being your own boss.

Of course, you can willingly accept a lower ROI at first if you plan to build a chain of franchises in your area. You can feel comfortable in the fact that your future gain will far outstrip what you could earn in T-bills or the stock market. Or, you can anticipate the personal, business, and tax advantages of owning a cash business. Perhaps you prefer to earn a salary from your own business and not have a significant concern about the size of your return on investment.

All these considerations are legitimate ones. If your primary concern is the return on your investment, however, then the rule of thumb given above is a good one to follow. In fact, the best franchises usually produce ROIs of between 35 and 50 percent per year. The fifty franchises described in the second part of this book have shown consistently that you can earn similar or even better ROIs with them.

CHECKLIST: Key Questions for Careful Consideration

Investment

1. What is the franchise fee, and what products and services do you receive in exchange for your fee?
2. What other costs does the franchise *require* you to make for equipment, supplies, start-up inventory, training, etc.?

3. What outside costs, such as lease deposits, professional fees, etc., will you incur to get started?
4. What are the "hidden" costs?
5. How are you restricted in your choice of suppliers, and how does this affect your costs?

Operating Costs

1. What are your monthly operating expenses?
2. What are the franchisor's royalty rates and advertising fees?
3. Are there any additional fees for extra training for new managers or employees, for on-going consultations, and so forth?
4. What are the likely total costs of bank loans, franchisor's financing arrangements, paybacks to investors, and the like?
5. What occasional or unanticipated expenses are likely to occur?

Site Selection

1. How is your territory defined?
2. What are the actual boundaries of your territory?
3. What no-compete clauses does the franchise offer and what do they mean?
4. Are you confined to operating within this territory?
5. Does the franchisor provide assistance in choosing a site? If so, how deep and broad is this support, and do you have to pay for it?
6. Who is directly responsible for finding a site and negotiating a lease or purchase?
7. Is your right to the franchise license dependent upon a particular location or lease?
8. Does the franchisor provide constructions services, and if so, at what cost to you?
9. Does the franchisor provide prepared architectural plans for construction? Do changes cost more?

Restrictions and Controls

1. What specific quality control standards does the franchisor place on your operation?

2. What approval procedures does the franchisor have for reviewing alternate sources of supply or vendors that you choose?

3. How long can the franchisor delay a decision on alternate vendors?

4. What restrictions are placed on your day-to-day operations?

5. What kind of training are you given and where? How long does it last and who pays for related room, board, and transportation?

6. What additional training and support does the franchisor provide, and what does it cost?

7. In what required advertising and promotional programs must you participate?

8. What kind of national or regional advertising program does the franchisor offer?

9. What continuing management assistance do you receive, and what specifically does it include?

10. Do you have to run the business yourself or can you hire managers? What restrictions are placed on their activities?

11. What kinds of equipment, fixtures, furnishing, etc., must you install and according to what specifications?

12. What are the bookkeeping and accounting reporting systems?

13. Who furnishes and pays for these reports?

14. Are you restricted concerning the types and styles of products and services you can offer?

15. Does the franchisor derive income from the sale or lease of equipment, supplies, raw materials, and products to you?

16. Does the agreement guarantee you will receive the benefit of any discounts or quantity purchase agreements?

Cancellation/Termination

1. Under what circumstances can you terminate the contract?

2. Under what circumstances can the franchisor terminate the contract?

3. What is the duration of the license, and what are the terms for renewal?

4. What actual practices does the franchisor follow in terminating contracts?

5. How many franchisees have been terminated and for what reasons?

6. In what kinds of litigation concerning cancellation has the franchisor been involved?

7. Does your family or spouse inherit the contract upon your death?

8. If not, how does the franchisor handle the sale or transfer of the franchise after your death?

9. Can you sell to someone else, mortgage, or transfer your franchise license? What conditions and restrictions are placed on your right to sell or transfer your license?

Add these questions to the questions and concerns discussed in Chapter 2 about the franchisor's management team and background to develop a complete and clear picture of how the franchise works.

4

Franchises with Fees of $5,000 or Less

Jazzercise, Inc.
Packy the Shipper
Novus Windshield Repair
WOW, Inc. (Wash on Wheels)
Almost Heaven Hot Tubs Ltd.

Perma Ceram Enterprises, Inc.
Sparky Washmobile®
Bathcrest® Porcelain Resurfacing
Bingo Bugle

JAZZERCISE, INC.

Jazzercise, Inc.
2808 Roosevelt St.
Carlsbad, CA 92008
1-800-FIT-ISIT (348-4748)
(619) 434-2101

Jazzercise, Inc., offers the single best opportunity to invest in a low-cost, high-profit franchise. For total start-up costs of less than $2,500, you can earn net profit margins of 55 percent or more, but you literally have to sweat for it as a Jazzercise dance and fitness instructor.

Jazzercise, Inc., is the leading dance fitness and exercise franchise in the country, with more than 4,000 franchised instructors around the country by early 1990. Since it began franchising in 1982, Jazzercise has been among the fastest growing franchisors, yet it also has a reputation as one of the best.

Simply put, franchisees offer exercise classes to anyone who wants to attend. As a franchisee, you do not get involved in establishing storefront health clubs, spas, or fitness centers. Instead, you give hour-long "dancercise" classes at community centers, school gymnasiums, or in similar facilities that you rent at low cost on a per use or leased basis.

Jazzercise classes are aimed at a predominantly female audience who want to do relatively light workouts in the mornings or after work to keep their bodies trim and in shape. Jazzercise specifically avoids the heavy-duty workouts favored by other companies. Therefore, it tends to attract a broad group of people, ranging in age from their teens to their 60s, with most "students," as they are called, in their late 20s and early 30s.

You make money in two basic ways: you charge a per class fee, and you earn commissions on the sale of Jazzercise items and exercise clothing carrying the Jazzertogs® label. You don't sell clothing or stock inventory, however. Your students buy directly from catalogs that you hand out, and you earn a commission from these orders.

How Much It Costs

Jazzercise has a very low franchise fee, just $500. You pay $250 when you are accepted for a training workshop, and $250 more within six months of your opening classes. In other words, you can pay half the fee from your cash flow.

Your total start-up costs are minimal as compared to most franchises. They include the following charges:

Record player and microphone. For a cost between $800 and $1,000, you must buy a record player and microphone that meet Jazzercise's specs. Unlike most franchises, however, Jazzercise does not sell the equipment, so you can buy it from any approved supplier.

Videotape player. You must also own a VHS videotape player, but you don't need to buy another if you already own one. Buying a new videotape player ranges from $200 to $500 for appropriate models.

Routine packet. Jazzercise gives you a free start-up package of videotapes and printed choreography sheets of exercise routines. Then, every two months, Jazzercise sends you a new tape of routines. You must buy 45 rpm records of the songs that the dances are for, which are on the videotape. You do not have to buy the records from Jazzercise, however. You probably can find them at a local record store, or you can buy them from a Jazzercise-recommended company, Ritter Records. It is unlikely you can find better prices than those that Ritter offers because it sells record packets to all Jazzercise instructors at a sizable discount.

Apparel. Add $100 to $150 for athletic shoes, leotards, and exercise apparel. Again, you don't have to buy Jazzercise clothes if you don't want to, but the company's 30 to 40 percent discounts probably mean better prices than you may find elsewhere.

Business cards and stationery. Add $25 to $50 for a start-up supply of receipts, accounting system forms, and brochures. You are required to buy

Jazzercise's accounting system and receipt books. However, Jazzercise gives you many brochures, flyers, fitness pamphlets, newsletters, and the like.

Liability and related insurance. You must pay $100 per year for your minimum coverage of $1 million for various kinds of personal, employer, and professional liability insurance—an excellent price. Or, if you can obtain less expensive insurance, you can buy it from an outside source.

Total start-up costs equals the amount shown in the table below.

	Minimum	**Maximum**
Franchise fee	$ 500	
Equipment	1,000	1,500
Records packet	50	55
Apparel	100	150
Business cards	25	50
Insurance	100	
Rent/lease fees	100	500
Total	$1,875	$2,755

Jazzercise estimates that rent or lease of facilities from schools or community groups will average 20 percent of your total gross income, with the actual costs ranging from free to 35 percent, or an average of $0 to $50 per class session. The $100 to $500 estimate is given to cover one month's operating costs, but you will probably be able to pay for this out of your operating income. Also remember that half the franchise fee can be paid after you get started, thereby reducing your start-up cash investment anywhere from $350 to $750.

Additional costs include travel and room and board when you travel to the company's four-day training workshop. These are held four to six times a year in different regions. For example, training sessions for the State of Florida are often held in Tampa, so potential franchisees must travel there to take the course.

If the facility you rent does not have a raised platform, you may need to buy one at a cost of $100 to $150. This is unlikely in most situations, however.

On-Going Expenses

Your on-going expenses will not be heavy either, but will include the following items:

- A royalty of *20 percent* of your gross student enrollment fees. This may seem high; in fact, it is one of the highest royalty rates in franchising. But, look more closely. It means that you pay Jazzercise only about 80 cents per student per class. With minor exceptions, this is all that you pay.
- New routine packets, including tapes, written choreography, and optional record purchases at a cost of $50 to $55 every two months. Since you *own* the packets you bought in the past, you may, as many established Jazzercise instructors do, mix "oldies" with new routines. This satisfies students who like particular exercises and yet want variety and something new.
- About $100 per *year* in advertising and promotional materials, such as flyers, brochures, handouts, etc. You can buy more, and Jazzercise itself offers a variety of local and district ad and marketing programs to help you build "traffic."
- Optional exercise apparel, books, vitamins, jewelry, etc., from Jazzercise. As noted, instructors buy at a big discount.
- Auto and gas expenses of commuting to and from your local community facility where you give classes.
- Performance payments for the use of the songs and records played at Jazzercise classes. Under copyright laws and agreements with various entertainment unions and associations, the singing group or artist whose songs you play gets paid a small fee every time a song is played. Jazzercise signs a blanket agreement, and it bills you for your proportional share of these payments. Your share reflects a complex formula calculated by the number of students in each class and the number of times you play a song.

All in all, these expenses and on-going charges are very low for a franchise.

How Much Can You Make?

Now the good news. On his or her initial investment, a Jazzercise franchisee can easily earn a net return of *1,000 percent* during the first year. Here's how it works. You charge a per class fee to each person, which averages $2.25 to $6.00 per class. You also offer special discounts to students for signing up for many classes. For example, you might charge a student $20 for eight classes, or $60 for three months. This brings the average fee per student down, but it sharply improves your cash flow.

The average class size is about 30, and it can range from 10 to 100. The size depends largely on how well you and your area manager promote your classes. On average, this will mean that each class brings in $90. Of this amount, you must pay Jazzercise $22.50, and the rent should cost you about $18. This leaves you with a gross profit of $49.50.

If you hold 10 classes a week, an average of two one-hour classes five days a week, you can earn a gross profit of $495 per week, or $24,750 during a 50-week year, allowing for a week off around Christmas and another week during the summer.

You can arrange your Jazzercise schedule the way you want to aim for the income you desire. You can offer more discounts, charge higher prices, do promotions, or participate in special events held at football games or community festivals. Engaging in these activities will help boost your income. You could also become an area manager and receive income from Jazzercise for training and managing local franchises.

In short, if you are an intelligent, fitness-minded person and particularly if you want a superior part-time income while your children may be attending school, Jazzercise is probably the best available opportunity.

PACKY THE SHIPPER

Packy the Shipper
PNS, Inc.
409 Main St.
Racine, WI 53403
(414) 633-9540
(800) 547-2259

Packy the Shipper® is a very inexpensive preparation and shipping franchise with a unique twist. It is largely sold as an add-on service that serves to help an existing retail store build more foot traffic. It is not designed to function as a store's only or even major source of income, but as an adjunct to a complementary activity, such as a card shop. In fact, Packy the Shipper outlets can be found practically anywhere—in florists, bicycle shops, hardware stores, office supply houses, variety stores, newsstands, etc.

By late 1989, there were more than 1,300 locations in 48 states. The company's unique twist is this: you collect the shipping and handling costs from the customer, but the company does all the rest. It pays the carrier, such as UPS, from a centralized billing system. It assumes liability and insurance costs for lost or damaged packages, and it absorbs all service and correction fees charged by the shippers. The company also provides a sophisticated, legal trading scale, and it notifies you of the changes in postal and shipping rates when they occur.

In return, you pay the company an 85-cent per package maintenance to accept the package, charge your customers an additional handling fee of

$2.00, and make sure the carrier picks up the package at the appointed time. The $2.00 per package is your profit.

According to the company vice president of finance, here is how Packy the Shipper works: You pay a very low franchise fee of just $395. You receive a training and operations manual, a stock of business forms and supplies, signage, banners, and a training videotape. The nationally approved, guaranteed legal scale—a $1,000 item—is loaned free of charge to you, but the franchisor retains ownership. The company also provides free the necessary business forms.

How You Make Money

You charge each customer a handling fee of $2.85 per package. Your only expense is the 85-cent per package fee to the franchisor, so your net profit on each package is $2.00. The company estimates that the average franchisee handles 1,300 packages per year for a net income of $2,600 per year.

This doesn't seem like much, but remember that it equals a 329 percent return on investment during the first year. You can significantly boost your profits in three other ways.

1. *Sell packaging services.* You can offer to pack the items for your customers and charge them for this extra service. Other pack-and-ship franchises emphasize this service, but Packy the Shipper encourages you to do it on your own. You can charge an average of $6.00 per package, with jobs ranging from as low as $1.00 to more than $100 for elaborate boxes used for shipping furniture and equipment. Of course, you need the space and materials to provide this service, but the back room of a card, or florist shop more than accommodates the supplies you need.

2. *Sell packaging materials.* You can sell new and used boxes, tape, wrapping paper, stuffing material, marking pencils, and more. You can earn gross mark-ups well in excess of 100 percent for this service.

3. *Build foot traffic for ancillary products.* You can stock ancillary products in your store, or rearrange your shelves and your merchandise to lead your customers to your items. For example, a florist could coordinate a flower-sending service or a card shop could coordinate stationery and pens with the package shipping.

Of course, as the Packy the Shipper executive notes, these figures are averages and may vary according to your location, attitude towards the business, hours that your business is open, parking availability, local competition from private packing services or other franchises, and so forth.

What You Get

The company offers a variety of benefits for its franchisees:

- An indefinite franchise agreement that lasts until you either go out of business or give the company 30 days notice that you want to end the agreement.
- Operations manual, supplies, videotape, unique four-part business forms, packing labels, and advertising materials.
- Payments to United Parcel Service are made through the national franchisor, so you do not have to worry about them.
- Complete accounting and administrative services through which you send your shipping forms each week to company headquarters. The company processes your forms and sends you a master invoice list, a transaction history, and a profit and loss statement—in short, complete store records.
- Handling of COD (cash on delivery) transactions.
- Protection from the Interstate Commerce Commission. As a franchisee, you are exempt from ICC's jurisdiction, so you do not have to worry about meeting federal regulations or acting as a shipping broker.
- Toll-free WATS lines for tracing information and filing claims, getting shipping and packaging information, and getting reports and advertising information.

Packy the Shipper is an easy-to-start franchise and is easy to manage. It fits in well as an add-on business with a wide variety of retail operations. It can be combined with a full-blown packaging, crating, and preparation business, and you can increase your net income to the $15,000 to $20,000 range by offering these kinds of services. Note, however, that this field has become very competitive with several other franchises and numerous do-it-yourself operations, with more on the horizon. Be aware, also, that this is a seasonal business with peak times during the Christmas and Thanksgiving holidays and around Easter. At these times, you may need part-time help to accommodate the rush. Company officials say you can expect to average about 20 shipments per week for 11 months a year, but 100 per week during the holiday seasons.

You will also need to promote your franchise as a reliable, nationally proven alternative to standing in line at the Post Office or at your local competition counter. All in all, the company offers a very inexpensive franchise that delivers on its promises.

NOVUS WINDSHIELD REPAIR

Novus Franchising, Inc.
10425 Hampshire Ave. South
Minneapolis, MN 55438
(612) 944-8000
(800) 328-1117

Novus Franchising is the largest, lowest-cost and simplest windshield and commercial plate-glass repair and scratch removal franchise in the U.S. By late 1989, the company had almost 700 franchises in all 50 states, and 1,500 dealers in 30 international countries. During 1988, the dealers reported $30 million in gross sales for an average of $13,636 each, but the franchisees reported gross sales above $30,000.

During 1986, the company had 564 open franchises and closed 28. During 1987, the company opened 122 new franchises, but closed 92, leaving a total of 565. During 1988, it opened 179 new ones and closed 78, leaving a total of 666 active franchises on January 1, 1989. By the beginning of 1990, that total had increased above 700. The company plans to sell at least one franchise in each state during 1990 and in each year beyond.

Novus also makes and distributes its own polishes, which remove scratches and haze from plastic surfaces. These products give you a second profit center.

Most Novus franchisees aim their efforts at local vehicle fleet owners and branches of major fleet owners, such as major rental car firms, telephone companies, delivery services, and so forth. Novus estimates that its dealers could repair up to 75 percent of the eight million cars and trucks whose damaged or broken windshields are replaced each year. This creates a tremendous market for this simple, inexpensive, and profitable service.

Many Novus franchisees also repair plate glass in commercial buildings, retail stores, offices, warehouses, and factories.

Novus's key selling point is this: insurance companies, vehicle owners, and merchants find it much cheaper to repair a damaged windshield or window for less than $50 as compared to replacing these items for, at the least, several hundred dollars. In fact, most major insurance companies now waive the broken windshield or plate-glass deductible and pay the full cost of repairing them. Commercial plate-glass repair also saves the cost of new glass, new signage or sign lettering, alarm system rewiring, and weather stripping.

How It Works

Novus is an excellent low-cost, home-based franchise. Once you become a franchisee, you receive five days' training at Novus's Minnesota headquarters. Most importantly, the training emphasizes how to sell your services. The repair processes are very simple to learn. To succeed, however, you must recognize that you have to sell your services to the best possible markets—local fleet owners and managers, major automobile dealerships and used car dealers, rental car agencies, insurance agencies, and similar companies who can provide numerous windshields for you to repair. You set up regular repair visits with these customers; in turn, you give them substantial discounts for volume business. But you save so much from the increased volume that your profits increase dramatically.

How Much It Costs

The entire Novus package costs just $5,990: a $2,900 franchise fee; a $990 training fee; and $2,100 for a complete equipment package, which provides you with enough repair supplies to earn you more than $15,000 in gross sales.

You have two franchise program choices: a complete windshield and scratch removal service, or a windshield-only repair service. The size of your franchise is limited to not more than one person doing windshield repair and one person doing scratch removal services. No price difference exists between the two programs; the franchise fee equals $2,900 for one or both.

The one chief difference between the two programs is the following: if you choose windshield repair only and then decide later to add scratch removal, you must sign the then-current franchise agreement and pay the then-current service fee. You therefore take the risk that the service fee (really a royalty) might be higher in the future.

You can use your own vehicle, even a small car, so you save the expense of purchasing or leasing. Although you must have a separate telephone, with someone answering "Novus" when it rings, you can use a home telephone. You can either ask your spouse to answer it in a business-like way or have the phone hooked up to an answering machine. Another option for you to consider is an answering service, for which you may have to obtain a local occupational license at a cost of up to $100. This requirement varies from town to town.

After your begin, you must pay Novus a service fee equal to 6 percent of your monthly gross sales, or a minimum of $185 per month, whichever is greater. However, Novus waives the $185 minimum for the first nine months, although you still must pay the 6 percent royalty. For example, if you earn $1,000 your first month, you pay Novus $60, not the $185 minimum.

Although it does not now charge an advertising fee, Novus's contract does allow the company to charge a 2 percent ad fee upon 90 days' notice.

You can lease the windshield repair equipment package (WSR) at a cost of $33 per month for 60 months (five years), which totals $1,980, and the scratch removal package (SRS) at a cost of $60 per month for 60 months (five years), which totals $3,600.

Novus estimates total start-up costs as shown below in the table. This under-$10,000 start-up cost is a very reasonable and even liberal estimate.

Item	WSR & SRS Package	WSR Package
Franchise fee	$2,900	$2,900
Training	990	990
Materials	420	195[a]
Equipment	1,390	785[b]
Maintenance kit	115	0
Ad materials	175	175
Working capital	1,000	1,000
Insurance/misc.	2,600	2,600[c]
TOTAL	**$9,590**	**$8,645**

a. Windshield repair = $195; scratch removal = $225
b. Windshield repair = $785; scratch removal = $605
c. Includes training travel cost estimate, $400 for insurance, and a deposit for a separate phone line, although not necessarily a business phone.

You must also obtain replacement supplies and equipment from Novus. Only Novus makes the scratch removal equipment, although you can obtain the windshield repair equipment from other approved suppliers.

What You Get

For your franchise, training, and equipment fee, you receive a five-day training session at Novus's headquarters, a complete operations manual, the right to use Novus's name, trademarks, and service marks, etc.

Most importantly, Novus gives you the benefit of its 18 years of experience in the windshield repair business. Chairman Gerald Keinath is the "founding father" of the low-cost windshield repair industry, and his expertise is head and shoulders above the others in the field. Moreover, Novus provides you with promotional and advertising materials, as well as advice.

Novus does *not* grant exclusive territories, however. Novus's UFOC does state the company does not intend to open more than one franchise per 50,000 population, but it reserves the right to change this policy.

You receive a five-year agreement with the right to renew it for two additional five-year terms. You do not have to pay a new franchise fee to renew, but you must pay the then-current service fee percentages, advertising fees, or other charges.

The Sears Bonus

In an appealing arrangement, you can establish a Novus franchise at a local Sears Auto Store as a means of rapidly building your volume and profits. You might benefit greatly from the combination of the Sears and Novus names. The catch is that you have to pay Sears a 15 percent royalty of your gross sales, as well as Novus's 6 percent royalty. The difference in volume, however, should more than make up for the additional fees. You get to use Sears's premises and cash register to conduct business—a very fair trade.

Note, however, that Sears has the right to select the stores in which the Novus franchises go. Sears determines the locations by size and volume of its local auto center, territory population, and number of vehicles in the area.

How Much Can You Make?

From Novus's 1988 financial statements, one can calculate that its franchisees earned a total of $24.5 million, or an average of $36,800 each. Novus executives report that many franchisees go to the extra expense of opening free-standing offices in warehouse locations. With these fixed locations and with numerous employees, they apparently build a high-volume, high-profit traffic. Even on average, this means you could earn a gross ROI of more than 350 percent within two years, if you do the labor.

You earn by charging flat fees to repair a windshield. These fees range from $20 to $50 per repair, with the average about $35. Since the cost of materials is only 4 percent, and the service fee equals 6 percent, you earn 90 percent gross profit margins. The rest is gross profit, from which you subtract your very low overhead expenses and a salary for yourself.

Of course, if you do much fleet business, your average revenues will decrease somewhat, probably to the $25 to $35 range, but the volume increase will save you your most valuable asset—time—and your travel and selling costs. Repeat business is almost always more profitable than new business!

After you subtract your overhead and expenses, you should expect an average net profit before taxes of $20,000 to $30,000. This could equal a net ROI of about 250 percent by the end of the second year—a healthy return and a good business for a person interested in working with cars and trucks and in owning a business.

WOW, INC. (WASH ON WHEELS)

WOW, Inc.
5401 South Bryant Ave.
Sanford, FL 32771
(800) 345-1969
(800) 432-7088, Florida
(407) 321-4010

Wash on Wheels (WOW) is a 22-year-old pressure cleaning franchise with 104 operating franchisees. Owned by the same man since the company began as a distributor of exterior pressure cleaning systems, WOW offers an inexpensive, home-based franchise, from which people who like working outside can earn profit margins in the 50 to 80 percent range. WOW is a member of Women in Franchising, Inc., a leading advocate for women franchise owners, and also encourages couples to operate a franchise together.

Typically, one partner sells the service and does the pressure cleaning work, while the other manages the business, makes appointments, and sells the service.

As a WOW franchisee, you offer your services from a special trailer, which you must purchase from the company. This expense is your greatest cost. If you work from home, you have very little overhead, and so your gross margins are extremely high.

WOW offers three franchise programs and significant discounts to those who buy all three. WOW claims to be the only service franchise that combines exterior maintenance, interior and ceiling cleaning, and carpet, upholstery, and drapery cleaning, all in one business.

During the mid-1980s, WOW experienced serious financial difficulty, but founder George Louser turned the company's fortunes around during 1988. The company seems to be on a dramatic upswing again. Louser originally concentrated on the pressure cleaning side, but he found that the demand for this single service did not enable his franchisees to make long-term significant profits. So, he added the indoor cleaning and carpet cleaning services. It is this combination of services that has appealed to franchisees. He sold 40 combination franchises during the first six months of the new company program.

From selling WOW systems as dealerships, Louser says he has learned that the secret to business success is three-fold: cash flow, cash flow, cash flow! Not only is the secret true for WOW's corporate success, but it holds true for your success, too.

WOW's triple-thrust combination includes the following:

- *WOW Pressure Cleaning.* It provides service for buildings, windows, factory walls, patios, pools, and practically any other exterior service. It has recently developed a lucrative market in the exterior cleaning and restoration of old and historic buildings, as well as other structures that range from houses to government buildings.
- *WOW Indoor Clean.* It offers cleaning services for acoustical tile and blown (popcorn) ceilings, as well as for vinyl walls and ceilings, vinyl upholstery, and painted surfaces. It provides these services to hospitals, restaurants, kitchens, convenience stores, apartment complexes, bars, offices, and to government buildings. WOW Indoor Clean seeks to capitalize on the success that Ceiling Doctor and Coustic-Glo have found in the ceiling and interior wall cleaning services field.
- *WOW VAC II Franchise.* It offers cleaning services using a *dry cleaning* system for carpets, upholstery, and drapes. This system differs significantly from that of most other carpet cleaning franchises since they use steam or wet cleaning processes.

You can expect 40 percent of your business from residential customers, but 60 percent from commercial customers. The commercial side usually proves more profitable since you often can sign long-term contracts with business firms, and this provides you with steady cash flow. On the other hand, you usually sell the residential jobs one at a time, and this "onesy-twosy" approach is time-consuming and expensive.

How Much It Costs

WOW charges a very low $3,500 franchise fee for each of its three franchises, but gives substantial discounts—probably up to 50 percent—if you buy all three. For each franchise, however, you must buy a different equipment package:

Pressure Cleaning
- Hot Water Trailer: $24,995 for a complete van-based system, with enough supplies and chemicals to earn $14,400 in sales.
- Cold Water Trailer: $18,195 for complete trailer-mounted unit and all components.

- Indoor Clean: $9,495 for complete ceiling tile cleaning system, with enough chemicals to earn between $15,000 and $20,000 (140,000 square feet at between 11 and 14.3 cents per foot).
- VAC II: $9,995 for complete carpet, upholstery, and drapery cleaning system.

Of course, you can buy just one of these franchises and also buy an option for the other two. You can expect total start-up costs to range from $17,000 to $72,000, or somewhat more. The table below gives you a sample breakdown of these costs.

	Cost
Pressure Cleaning	
Franchise fee	$ 3,500
Hot water trailer	24,995
Cold water trailer	18,195
Training travel	1,000
Start-up expenses	1,500
Working capital	2,500
TOTAL	$51,690
Indoor Clean	
Franchise fee	$ 3,500
Cleaning system	9,495
Training travel	1,000
Start-up expenses	1,500
Working capital	2,500
TOTAL	$17,995
VAC II	
Franchise Fee	$ 3,500
Cleaning system	9,995
Training travel	1,000
Start-up expenses	1,500
Working capital	2,500
TOTAL	$19,495

Combinations will bring discounted franchise fees with little, if any, additional start-up costs, so you could start all three at the same time for about $52,000 to $60,000. Fortunately, WOW offers liberal financing programs, which are determined franchisee by franchisee.

WOW also charges a relatively low 3 percent royalty on the first $6,000 of gross sales; this amount declines to 2 percent, thereby encouraging you to grow rapidly and preserve more of your profits with the lower royalty. WOW also charges a 1 percent advertising fee. And you may buy most of your chemicals and supplies from WOW as well.

What You Get

Most importantly, you receive a protected territory, which is based on county boundaries or adjacent zip codes of major metropolitan areas.

If you buy the pressure cleaning franchise, you get the WOW hot and cold water trailers, so you must have a pickup truck or van to pull them. If you buy the indoor cleaning or carpet cleaning franchises, you simply will need your own truck or van. WOW also requires you to have its decals and signage put on your truck or van.

The Secret to WOW

The five-day training session at WOW's Florida or Pennsylvania headquarters is more important for your success than your tangible equipment. WOW officials say that the company's five-day training not only teaches you how to use the equipment but it also emphasizes direct selling techniques. These are the secret of your success Day in and day out, you must sell your services and make cold calls to new prospects as you travel around your territory. Direct selling requires consistent effort and the use of good techniques. WOW affirms that direct selling can be a "minefield." This author has sold his services directly for 12 years and can also affirm that being successful at making sales takes persistence, self-confidence, and also doing it day after day. The importance of direct selling also points to the significant advantage in having commercial contracts: once you develop a steady clientele, you won't have to spend so many hours selling. Instead, you spend most of your time working and making money.

Ideally, you will grow rapidly and, as a consequence, have more options. For example, if you enjoy selling, you can sell while your hired technician does the cleaning. Or your spouse may enjoy selling while you do the cleaning work.

WOW also doesn't leave you out in the cold after the training. It supports you with an impressive direct response campaign that WOW's Louser says earns 5 percent returns, which means that, for every 100 direct mail letters, you get five responses. This rate is 10 times (1,000 percent) better than the national average for direct response advertisings, which is one-half of 1 percent.

And WOW has a multiple-listing Yellow Pages advertising program. The way it works is that you put a small advertisement in each appropriate Yellow Pages section, which refers prospective customers, in turn, to a master advertisement. Although this approach is relatively expensive, it is necessary. After all, most customers find these cleaning services in one of three ways: by word of mouth or referrals, through the Yellow Pages, and by direct mail.

How Much Can You Make?

WOW emphasizes that franchisees should strive to *gross* $500 per day with its "triple thrust" marketing plan of offering three types of cleaning services to every commercial establishment: exterior cleaning, such as masonry cleaning; interior cleaning, such as degreasing an exhaust system; and the cleaning of carpets and upholstery.

That $500 a day multiplied by five or six days a week equals substantial gross revenues that will range between $130,000 and $156,000 per year. To achieve this level, you may need to hire a technician while you concentrate on sales. Another alternative is for both you and your spouse to work actively in the business every day. You can expect a net income in excess of $65,000 per year before taxes, and perhaps more if you do the labor.

Assuming that you do the labor, you can realistically expect to gross about $80,000 to $100,000 per year during the first two years, and net in the $30,000 to $40,000 range if you buy the pressure cleaning and one of the other cleaning franchises of WOW. You should expect to begin to realize significant ROIs on your total investment by the end of the second year.

If you finance a substantial proportion of your start-up costs, you can expect your cash ROIs to be very high—in the 50 percent range—by the end of the second year. As we have stated previously, however, be careful, and avoid taking on more debt and monthly payments to WOW than you can afford. Remember that you also have to provide for your living expenses.

In summary, WOW's "triple thrust" approach appears to provide a strong chance for people who want an inexpensive, but active, franchise. Louser relates that a father/son combination makes up one of WOW's successful franchisees. The father is a 38-year-old former grocery store meat-department manager, and the son is an 18-year-old high school graduate who lives at home. This father/son duo bought into WOW for $15,000 cash and financed the remainder of about $35,000. WOW's Louser prefers families to work together and says they have the greatest potential for success.

ALMOST HEAVEN HOT TUBS LTD.

Almost Heaven Hot Tubs Ltd.
Route 408
Renick, WV 24966
(304) 497-3163

Almost Heaven Hot Tubs Ltd. is a significantly different type of franchisor. It does *not* charge a franchise fee; in fact, there are no fees of any kind for any "intangible" as, for example, even the use of the Almost Heaven Hot Tubs name. The company combines franchising and selling through distributors.

For as little as $265 for a sales and technical instruction package, you can start selling the company's products under the Almost Heaven Hot Tubs name. Its product line includes a very wide range of types and sizes of hot tubs, spas, saunas, steam baths, whirlpool baths, indoor and outdoor wood furniture, and architectural woodwork, such as cornices.

With this package, you essentially can begin selling hot tubs and spas from your home on a part-time basis. Company executives say that some of their most successful franchisees began selling from their homes. These franchisees sell directly, both wholesale to contractors, architects, developers, and interior designers, and retail to consumers. Almost Heaven executives cite as an example a woman in Connecticut whose physician husband encouraged her to start selling Almost Heaven Hot Tubs to their friends. It happened after the couple had bought a hot tub for themselves. Soon, they found that many of their friends and neighbors were besieging them with questions about their tub and where they could buy one, and so the wife decided to sell hot tubs. Within two years, her business had grown so rapidly that she decided to open a retail store. She sold out about two years later at a profit measured in the hundreds of percent.

How Much It Costs

Almost Heaven Hot Tubs notes that you can set up the business in a separate location where you can install Almost Heaven store fixtures and sample tubs and spas. Doing so will increase your costs, however. Almost Heaven is very up-front about these costs as well as your prospects for success if you try to sell from your home.

Almost Heaven store fixtures cost from about $3,000 to about $10,000 if you buy several hot tubs for display. The company estimates that your first-year start-up expenses will total range from $10,000 to $30,000 or more, depending on the costs of leases, payroll, advertising, etc.

If you do open with a location, Almost Heaven will give you an exclusive territory, and it will refer to you all inquiries—wholesale and retail—

that it receives from the territory. In planning for a location, consider an inexpensive warehouse-type facility with ample, secure storage space that is in an area populated with similar companies: plumbers, carpenters, cabinet makers, awning builders, and other building trades firms. Inexpensive, yet copious, space can often be found in old storage lofts that have been converted to inexpensive, small-scale industrial or wholesale trade outlets.

On the other hand, Almost Heaven executives say that regional mall locations make very significant profits because their sales volume grows so much more rapidly than the volume one may sell from home or at a warehouse location.

Here's another option that you may wish to consider: take the money you would spend for a retail location and put it into advertising in the Yellow Pages and in promotions directed at local and regional builders, architects, and interior designers. The families or individuals who want to buy a hot tub will probably find you through the Yellow pages or a reference from Almost Heaven's national advertising campaign in slick home-and-garden magazines. The company does have a liberal cooperative advertising policy, which pays up to half your advertising costs and of which you should take advantage. Of course, you can reduce your actual cash investment by generating income to pay for start-up expenses.

Go for Volume Business

You may think that your business will come primarily from homeowners putting hot tubs and spas in their backyards or replacing an old bath tub with a new Jacuzzi®-equipped spa or tub. You would be wrong; the company emphasizes that your greatest profit potential comes from the wholesale market, i.e., from selling large numbers of Jacuzzi®-equipped spas and tubs to building contractors, plumbers, developers, apartment building renovators, architects, and designers. The onesy-twosy selling approach may take as much time as selling a contract for 100 tubs to a builder developing a new subdivision, and the latter may bring you a gross profit in the hundreds of thousands of dollars.

Almost Heaven also advertises in the building trades magazines but, most importantly, it takes the largest single insertion—28 color pages—in all editions of *Sweet's Directory,* the "bible" for U.S. contractors, designers, and architects.

How Much Can You Make?

Almost Heaven gives a 40 percent discount on all its products, which range in price from as low as $1,395 retail to as high as $7,855, *before* adding and costs for accessories and ancillary items. Its most popular model, a 5-foot by 3-foot hot tub, retails for $2,845. It has all Jacuzzi® equipment. Additional accessories, chemical, and ancillary items sell for, on average, $1,000. Almost Heaven executives note that selling hot tubs is like selling autos: you make more profit from the add-ons than from selling the basic models.

From the price given above, you earn a gross profit of $1,707. You can also anticipate a 40 percent net profit before taxes, or a net profit of $683 from an average sale to an individual. You need to sell 500 to 600 of these units per year to earn an appreciable net income.

It would appear that you need a sizable territory of upper middle class and affluent homes or residential buildings to reach this sales volume, preferably in an area with strong growth in new housing starts and residential building activity. You can sell retrofit whirlpool baths, and the like, to hotels and motels in your area as well.

A Better Way

You can do appreciably better by acting as a distributor. Your gross margins will average 65 to 67 percent. To become a distributor, all you have to do is place an order for just *two* complete tubs, spas, saunas, or whirlpool baths, or you can order one tub or sauna for display at the dealer price. If you do so, you get distributor pricing on any future orders.

If you decide to act as a distributor and sell primarily to the wholesale market, you will then have to pass on some of your discount to the contractors. Consider, however, that they would absorb the installation costs; or you could increase your margins as a distributor by offering installation services, service contracts, and the like.

Watch for Competition

Although you should not fear competition—it often means that a thriving market exists for the tubs and spas already—you should be aware that the market for these products is very competitive. Almost Heaven helps you combat the competition in several ways. It has—

- Better retail prices compared to its leading competitor;
- Higher quality, more feature-filled products;
- Better product guarantees; and, most importantly,
- The Jacuzzi® name.

Almost Heaven has exclusive use of Jacuzzi® whirlpool pumps, suction jets, and many other Jacuzzi® products. The name, of course, is as generic a term in whirlpool baths as is Kleenex® in facial tissues or Coke® in beverages. Jacuzzi® also has an extensive national advertising campaign of its own, so you stand to benefit from two very powerful names.

Almost Heaven is the oldest of the hot tub franchisors, and it currently has almost 1,500 dealer/distributor/franchisees around the country. Its name is very well known and respected in the wholesale building trades and among architects and designers.

PERMA CERAM ENTERPRISES, INC.

Mr. Joseph Tumolo, President
Perma Ceram Enterprises, Inc.
327 Village Place
Wyckoff, NJ 07481
(201) 670-8379
(800) 645-5039

Perma Ceram is one of the nation's largest bathtub, sink, and wall tile resurfacing franchises. By the end of 1989, more than 125 Perma Ceram specialists were in business—a steady, although not spectacular, increase of about 25 percent since 1984. Perma Ceram offers a unique spray-on "porcelaincote" resurfacing process that provides the same strength and durability as an original porcelain finish.

The marketing advantage that you sell is that refinishing or resurfacing a tub costs half or less than the cost of a new tub. And the cost of resurfacing—and changing the color of—the bathtub, the sink, and the wall tile ranges from $250 to $600 as compared to between $2,500 and $7,000 to remodel a bathroom completely. Although you might think your market would be cost-conscious consumers, it appears that your best repeat customers come from hotel/motel chains, apartment management firms, home improvement contractors, fire insurance adjustors, plumbers, and bathroom remodeling contractors.

How Much It Costs

Perma Ceram was selected for this book because it has no franchise fee and no royalties. Perma Ceram charges you a flat fee of $24,500 for all equipment and supplies, five days of training, transportation to and from an established Perma Ceram location, operating, technical and business manuals, and business and advertising materials.

The company, Perma Ceram Enterprises, makes its profits by selling the equipment and services and then from sales of "porcelaincote" and related materials that you need to do the job. Perma Ceram is the only source for these materials, and it charges a normal mark-up.

Perma Ceram is a very interesting franchise; you can work at it part- or full-time. You can work out of your home, basement, or garage; and you can haul your simple equipment and supplies in a van, truck, or station wagon. The repair business itself is easy to learn and carry out. You can concentrate on high-volume, repeat business with commercial accounts, and build the business far faster than you could by just relying on direct sales to individual homeowners.

What You Get

For the total $24,500 payment to Perma Ceram, you receive the following:

- Five days of training, including on-the-job work with an existing franchisee.
- A non-exclusive territory determined by the potential market size. You will need to negotiate the territory issues carefully because the disclosure statement and company literature do not give many details.
- Payment for your transportation to and from the nearest training location and four days' room and board for one person. You must pay for additional trainees.
- Marketing, advertising, and business management manuals, which you learn how to use during your training period.
- Enough equipment and supplies to do about 75 bathrooms. The equipment and materials should enable you to earn between $15,000 and $20,000, depending on how much you can charge per job. The company's reprints of published articles show that Perma Ceram franchisees charge between $250 and $600 per job.
- On-going assistance and support from the company's technical support team.

The Market

The market for the service will grow as the cost of redoing bathrooms continues to rise. Rising prices and the desire to reduce costs make Perma Ceram very attractive to commercial customers. Your residential customers will be those families who need to redo their bathrooms, but who cannot afford the $2,500 to $7,000 to do so. They might more easily find the $600 you would charge them.

Another good market is old house restoration. Old tubs are undoubtedly of better quality than today's, and people who restore or preserve old homes usually preserve or restore the old, claw-footed porcelain tubs. You might offer your services to antique stores and large yards that specialize in old furniture, fixtures, and plumbing furnishings. These businesses may have many old tubs in their yards, and your process could easily and dramatically increase their value.

You reach these markets by direct sales—knocking on doors, visiting contractors, etc.—by direct mail to residences and to business accounts, and by Yellow Pages advertising under plumbing or bathroom furnishing listings. Much of your business will come through referrals and word of mouth, but you need to establish repeat business as quickly as possible to reduce your selling time and expenses. An average job takes four hours, so if you had to sell as well as do the work, you could only do one job a day.

Start-Up and Operating Expenses

The $24,500 you pay Perma Ceram does not include a range of ordinary start-up and operating expenses you must pay. You'll need transportation, unless you own an appropriate van, truck, or wagon. If you do have one, you can begin to amortize that portion of the cost of the vehicle that you use for business. For example, if you use a van 65 percent for business and 35 percent for personal use, and it costs $10,000, then under a five-year straight line depreciation schedule, you can deduct $1,300 per year (65 percent of $2,000 value per year for 5 years) as a business expense. You can also deduct mileage charges for all business miles you drive.

Other expenses include insurances—commercial vehicle, personal, business and product liability—business telephone deposits, Yellow Pages or other advertising costs, answering service or paging service, and—especially—working capital, meaning your living expenses until you establish the business as a going concern.

To obtain a total start-up cost estimate, add from $5,000 to $10,000 to the $24,500 fee. This revised total ranges between $29,500 and $34,500.

Start-Up Strategy

There are several ways to approach this franchise. You can start it part-time, working on weekends, nights, and afternoons until you establish the business. You might want to involve your spouse as a salesperson, as someone to answer the business phone, or as someone who performs many functions while you continue in your full-time job. You could reverse the roles and go it alone full-time while your spouse works full- or part-time to supplement your income. Or you could reduce your cash investment as low as possible by borrowing the money. Perma Ceram makes information available about how to finance your franchise, which includes leasing the equipment and borrowing the money from F & F (friends and family) or the bank.

If you are confident that you can make enough to pay off an installment loan, and your credit rating is good, you should try to reduce your up-front cash investment as much as possible. That is how you gain a larger return on your cash investment (ROI) as quickly as possible.

How Much Can You Make?

The dollars and cents of this franchise are attractive if you play the right strategies. Simply put, sell for repeat customers and volume business, and offer all the services you can at prices about half the cost of buying and installing new plumbing fixtures. During 1989, existing Perma Ceram franchisees were charging between $300 and $600 for standard-sized bathtubs, and about $5 per square foot for regrouting, resealing, and resurfacing ceramic tile. An average bathroom has about 65 square feet of ceramic tiles just around the tub, and far more if the bathroom is completely tiled, so you can earn $250 to $350 for redoing the tile. Many Perma Ceram franchisees do not like to do sinks unless they are old, since sinks can be replaced more cheaply than they usually can be repaired for. Of course, you charge extra for colors and additional services. Profitable additional services include porcelain stoves, washers, dryers, refrigerators—that is, any interior surface originally covered with porcelain or fiberglass.

If you charge $300 for a standard tub, you should earn a net profit—after overhead and amortizing your initial investment—of between $150 to $180, or net margins of 50 to 60 percent. This means that, to earn a net income of $25,000 per year, you have to do 166 tubs per year, or more than three per week in a 50-week year. Also, most of your work will be concentrated in the warmer months of the year, so you will need to do more advertising and marketing during the off-season, whenever that occurs in your area.

Fortunately, these numbers are not impossible, or even very difficult, to achieve. Clearly, if you can build the business to where you have one or two two-person crews doing 12 to 20 tubs or bathrooms per week, you can earn a substantial net income while you supervise the crews and sell your services. You could also involve family members in office administration, direct sales, or in other ways.

If you are interested in working with your hands or capitalizing on your experience in the building or plumbing trades, Perma Ceram presents a good opportunity to explore.

SPARKY WASHMOBILE®

Sparky Coin-Operated Washmobile®
E.P.I. Inc.
P.O. Box 543
Longboat Key, FL 34228
(813) 377-8320

Who would not want to own a franchise in which your customers pay you $1.00 every 12 minutes and use their own labor in using your service? Most people would, and Sparky Washmobile is about the best franchise you can find that does this. Sparky Washmobile was selected as *Entrepreneur's* highest-rated car wash franchise in the magazine's Franchise 500 report. The franchise offers outstanding cash flow potential. The company has grown steadily since 1948; it now has more than 170 franchises, and it grows about 10 percent per year. It is not a fancy company, nor does it try to overwhelm you with fancy literature or sales presentations. What it does offer you is a plain, straightforward arrangement.

Sparky Washmobile is a portable, self-service, coin-operated car wash and wax system. You install it at service stations, car dealerships, shopping centers, car washes, at airports for planes and vehicles, and at garages and in the lots of auto/truck fleet owners. Other possible locations are mobile home parks, garages, motels, campgrounds, marinas for boats and vehicles, convenience stores with gasoline pumps, auto and truck rental agencies, apartment buildings, etc.

You provide the water hookups and the Washmobile, and the customers insert their quarters for three minutes of do-it-yourself wash and wax. Most customers will use it for longer than three minutes, so they will continue to insert their quarters. And since it's portable, you can move it as you wish to a more profitable or promising location.

The Wash "Works"

The equipment consists of an automatic water-, detergent-, and wax-dispensing system that is housed in stainless steel. You can add many options to the basic unit, including window brushes, a high velocity dryer, a wheel washer, a spray wax system, a vacuum cleaner, towel dispensers, etc.

The parent company, E.P.I., also offers an optional "Designer" coin-operated vacuum island with two automatic vacuums. There are many self-service auto vacuum units around, but this one has an advantage; it is factory pre-wired for a single connection, unlike many others, which require on-site wiring by licensed electricians. The Designer costs about $10,000, but your income from it is almost pure profit.

Company executives also note that E.P.I. offers a full line of brushless and "touchless" tunnel-type, full-service automobile washing equipment. This equipment costs about $180,000, so starting a complete free-standing car wash would cost at least $250,000, perhaps more. Still, if you have the money, this operation can prove to be very lucrative.

How Much It Costs

The catch to this conceivable pot of gold is its price: $45,900 for the complete Sparky Washmobile unit. Note, however, that Sparky Washmobile has no franchise fees and no royalty payments. Essentially, you purchase the equipment, and you receive some exclusive territory rights.

The franchise is expensive because it is operated in a way that is similar to laundromats. All your proceeds are cash—hundreds and thousands of quarters. The benefits of this positive cash flow and equipment depreciations schedules make this franchise more valuable than a service- or labor-intensive franchise.

Like a laundromat owner, you need to cope with two basic problems:

Theft from your coin boxes

Equipment malfunctions or damage

Security is important for your equipment; and if you don't keep the unit working, you can't make any money. The parent company claims that its solid-state equipment virtually never breaks down. Still, since it is so important to you that the equipment not malfunction, it may be desirable for you to locate a repair service should you need it, or at least learn to repair and maintain the unit yourself.

Moreover, you will need to ensure that the dispensers stay full of soap, wax, wheel cleaner fluid, and the like. These machine servicing needs are why most Sparky Washmobiles are located in or near service stations and other similar locations. If you set up a free-standing unit, you will need to visit it twice a day or hire someone part-time to collect the coins and do routine service.

If you decide to invest a great deal of money, you could set up a four-bay self-service car wash with four Washmobiles and also hire an attendant at a low salary. This set-up requires much effort and about $225,000. And you would need zoning approvals, construction funds, water permits, waste-water clearances, and the like.

How Much Can You Make?

To make significant profits in this business requires that you lease or finance your equipment purchase. Instead of paying cash and waiting for a three-year ROI, you make payments on the equipment and fund it from your cash flow. Sparky Washmobile's president, W. C. Koppel, claims to have founded the car wash industry back in 1948. He says that an average Sparky Washmobile owner can expect to earn a 40 percent "net net" margin, that is, net profits before taxes.

He warns, however, that the secret to success can be counted in terms of three priorities: "The first priority is location; the second is location; and the third priority is location." He advises you to avoid shopping centers and to look for locations adjacent to or behind service stations since these businesses usually sit on fairly large and mostly vacant land parcels.

You should lease or finance the equipment for a five-year period, make monthly payments, and deduct the costs with a five-year depreciation schedule ($9,100 per year on a straight line method). By reducing your up-front cash investment, you generate positive cash flow and a small tax shelter.

On a five-year lease, with $9,000 down, your monthly payments amount to about $700. Adding your expenses for land or space rental, water, operating expenses, and the like, your breakeven point equals only 350 washes per month, or only about 12 per day. Koppel suggests that, with a good location, an average of three times that number will use your service daily. Your location should be open 7 days a week, and 24 hours per day.

An even better profit center is the vacuum system, which costs much less than the Washmobile. With practically no operating expenses, such as for water or soap, you generate additional cash flow at a much faster pace. Most customers will use both services if they are available. Some 90 to 95 percent of every 50 cents that customers insert into the vacuum is pure profit.

Koppel also suggests that you might want to consider establishing an auto detailing service in an abandoned service station or in any similar location on a main thoroughfare. For a total investment of $86,000—$45,900 for a Washmobile and the rest for the auto detailing location—you can earn equally significant net profits. A 25-minute wax job can cost $50; your costs include minimum-wage labor and your overhead, leaving you a gross profit of about $40 to $45 per job. Of course, your lease or rental costs, your advertising expenses, and the like, will reduce your net net margins to the 30 to 50 percent range, depending on the variable costs.

The standard Sparky Washmobile operation is not necessarily a business for someone who wants a full-time business; rather, it may be, at best, an additional profit opportunity for someone with an existing, related business who wants to improve his or her cash flow and take advantage of financing and depreciation deductions.

BATHCREST® PORCELAIN RESURFACING

Bathcrest, Inc.®
2425 South Progress Drive
Salt Lake City, UT 84119
(800) 826-6790
(801) 972-1110
(801) 977-0328 FAX

Bathcrest, Inc.®, is the largest porcelain refinishing franchise in the U.S., with about 200 franchisees. It offers a highly professional approach to this relatively lucrative, hands-on business. *Entrepreneur* magazine has ranked it among the 200 fastest growing franchises during the late 1980s as well, according to company executives.

Bathcrest® encourages its franchisees to emphasize commercial accounts, including property managers, interior designers, contractors, universities, and government housing agencies. But it also encourages you to mix residential and commercial account sales.

Bathcrest's® refinishing process, called Glazecote™, is a synthetic porcelain finish that chemically bonds to an original surface, according to company literature. The quality of this material allows you to give a standard five-year warranty, the best in the industry. As important and different from its competitors is the fact that Bathcrest® promotes ancillary profit centers, which include bathroom trim, accessories, modern plumbing fixtures, and fixtures for antique baths and pedestal sinks. You make 50 percent gross profit margins on these products.

Bathcrest's® marketing emphasizes a very professional look and approach to its sales literature, with glossy brochures for direct response mailings and even slick doorknob hanging pamphlets. The company provides telephone support and newsletters through which other franchisees share their successful marketing and work techniques and discuss their problems.

During 1990, Bathcrest® is introducing a new product line for acrylic repairs that expands the size of your potential market by almost half. Bathcrest® executives say that before the company developed this new repair technique, no refinishing firm was willing to warrant its acrylic repair process. Now, Bathcrest's® process allows you to offer an unmatched one-year warranty, a significant competitive advantage.

Bathcrest® took a cautious approach to this new product introduction; it required all franchisees who wanted to use this new product to take company training and receive company certification. Bathcrest® offered this training at its early 1990 national convention and continued to offer this training, thereafter, at its regular training school.

Getting Started

The author suggests that you start in this business doing the work yourself. Have your spouse or family member help you by answering the phone, making telemarketing calls, keeping the books, and so forth. You do not need an employee to start, but you will need at least one, perhaps two, technicians if you plan to grow rapidly. You tend to grow most rapidly if one or two people do the work, and one person sells and markets the service.

Bathcrest® executives say that its franchisees' experience shows that you do better if you have a small showroom and office through which you can display your products for your customers. Your business seems more professional that way, so you probably want to plow your initial profits back into your business to follow the company's advice.

How Much It Costs

Potential franchisees must pay Bathcrest® $24,500, but unlike most franchises, that total includes all of the costs of training travel—airfare, hotel, and meals—for two people. And the franchise fee equals only $3,500. Bathcrest® generally divides your $24,500 payments like this:

Category	Amount
Franchise fee	$ 3,500
Equipment/supplies	8,085
Company commissions/expenses	4,200
Training	2,500
Dealer procurement	2,300
Banner, signs, printing	1,325
Training travel	1,100
Legal fees (Bathcrest's)	990
Dealer manual, sales aids	500
TOTAL	$24,500

Other Start-Up Costs

In addition to the required payment, Bathcrest® estimates your start-up costs will range from about $2,650 to $8,500. This estimate *does* include relatively small amounts for opening a 500- to 1,000-square-foot, warehouse-type office. But Bathcrest® notes that you can easily start this business from your home; the author encourages you to do so to reduce your expenses. Nor do you need a truck or van, although having one or a station wagon would make carrying and storing materials easier.

The following table combines both Bathcrest's® and the author's estimates of start-up costs:

Category	Low End	High End
Bathcrest® payment	$24,500	$24,500
Licenses[a]	50	200
Insurance[b]	300	500
Rental space[c]	200	1,000
Furniture, fixtures[d]	500	2,000
Vehicle[e]	1,000	2,000
Supplies[f]	*	*
Equipment[g]	*	*
Travel expenses[h]	*	100
Operating expenses[i]	500	5,000
TOTAL	$27,050	$35,300

a. Business or occupational licenses.
b. Required liability policies; more if you hire employees.
c. The low end is too low for any adequate space.
d. If you open an office, you'll need a desk or two, chairs, file cabinets, and the like. These estimates seem to run high.
e. Author includes down payment on a light truck or van.
f. Start-up supplies included in Bathcrest® payment, but you do have to make minimum, required purchases from Bathcrest®.
g. Also included in franchise fee.
h. Included in franchise fee, except for personal expenses.
i. Includes everything from utility deposits for a business phone to working capital to pay living expenses for three months. The high estimate seems more appropriate to cover your operating expenses for about 60 days.

Other Required Payments

Although Bathcrest® does not charge either a royalty or advertising fee, it does charge you a $1,200 annual renewal fee. You pay the same renewal fee for the first three years of the agreement, but after the third year, Bathcrest® may increase the fee up to 10 percent per year. This fee is a reasonable amount; it helps you reduce the impact of the fee as you work hard to increase your income. This approach appears much more profitable for you than a percentage royalty.

However, unlike strictly service franchises, Bathcrest® makes most of its profits by selling you refinishing chemicals, materials, equipment, and supplies. You must buy from Bathcrest®, the sole supplier, six kinds of supplies, including Glazecote™, filler, reducer, and etching compounds.

The company requires you to buy "5 quarts of Glazecote™ per week averaged over a three-month period and starting six months after you complete training," the company's offering circular states. If you do not meet these minimum purchases, Bathcrest® considers you inactive and will resell your territory. You must spend about $150 to $200 per week for this material.

The company estimates that these required purchases will equal about 50 percent of your total material and supplies purchases. Bathcrest® notes that it receives a 20 percent profit from these supplies. And it acknowledges that it receives payments from the suppliers of its ancillary lines of bathtub fixtures.

Those cited above make up all the payments you make to the company—not an unreasonable arrangement for this industry.

What You Get

Bathcrest® offers one unusual incentive: after you pay a small deposit, you do not pay the remainder of the $24,500 until after your first day of training. If you do not want to proceed, Bathcrest® refunds your deposit, and you leave with no other obligation. Of course, if you leave, you have to pay your own travel expenses. If you choose to stay, you give the company the remainder and sign the franchise agreement at the end of the first day.

The author endorses this approach for several reasons. First, the author has experienced over-eager (and poorly financed) franchisors who take checks for tens of thousands of dollars when franchisees sign the franchise agreement. Then, the franchisors fail to deliver on their promises; in effect, they take the money and fade away. New franchisees tend to be very "starry-eyed" about their prospects and often second-guess themselves after it is too late. The FTC disclosure rule does not give you a cooling off period *after* you sign the agreement. You have a 10-day cooling off period between the time you receive the UFOC disclosure document and the day you sign the agreement.

Second, for most franchisees, the trip to headquarters for training is their first contact with actual company personnel. Franchisees often deal with brokers in their own towns and have little or no contact with the company, so sometimes they find they don't like the company, its culture, or its people. With most franchises, however, the franchisee is stuck with the situation after he or she signs the agreement.

Last, the training session should reveal whether you really want to commit yourself to the real work involved in this franchise. Porcelain resurfacing and refinishing is not a cream-puff business; it takes work to apply the finishes, and it takes someone with both technical and selling skills to do well.

After the first day's training, if you decide to continue with Bathcrest®, you receive the following:

Paid training. You receive one-week training in Salt Lake City, which includes both classroom instruction and hands-on training. Bathcrest® has operated a company-owned franchise since 1979 and knows this business well.

Exclusive territory. You receive a substantial territory, with a population of 300,000 people. Make sure your territory includes many potential business customers, such as hotels and motels, apartment buildings, and many other businesses with lots of bathtubs that people may be likely to damage often.

Company support. You receive support through telephone hot lines, newsletters, advertising and promotional materials, a continuing research program (such as the new acrylic finishing process), regional meetings, an annual national convention, visits from company representatives, and so forth.

Adequate materials. Your original materials supply, the company says, will enable you to almost recoup your initial investment. One quart of Glazecote™, the company says, will bring you gross profits of $350 retail; you receive 60 quarts, for a potential income of $21,000. You also receive set quantities of other materials that boost your potential income before you are required to order more supplies. The supply should last three to six months.

Easy termination. You can drop out of the system easily with just 60 days' notice to the company. Although the company does not want a right to repurchase, it does reserve a right of first refusal if you want to sell your franchise to someone else. However, few franchises have terminated their agreements. Nor has the company terminated many agreements. The UFOC shows that Bathcrest® cancelled only four agreements between 1986 and 1988 for not complying with the agreement and minimum purchase requirements.

How Much Can You Make?

Bathcrest® reports that its franchisees earn an average of $350 for each combined bathtub and bathroom sink resurfacing job. It suggests the following retail prices for your services; these prices vary from region to region:

Tub/sink combination	$350
Bathtub in color	295
Bathtub in white	275
Sink only	95
Ceramic tile[a]	300

a. Average tile surround equals 50 square feet, and with a suggested price of $6 per square foot.

The company gives the following expenses and gross profit margins:

	Percentage
Applicator labor[a]	20
Materials	20
Overhead[b]	10
Overhead[c]	30
Expenses	50 to 70
Net pre-tax profit[d]	70 to 30

a. Your salary if you do the work.
b. If you work from home.
c. If you work from an office.
d. 70 percent if you do the work yourself.

The company estimates that one applicator can do two jobs per day, each of which takes three to four hours. This means that if you do the work yourself, you can do 5 to 10 jobs per week, for a potential weekly gross income ranging from a low of $1,375 (5 white tubs at $275 each) to as much as $3,500 per week (10 combination jobs at $350 each).

So, your gross annual income can range from about $60,000— including two weeks' vacation and days you have no work—to as high as $175,000. Realistically, you would need to hire at least one, perhaps two, applicators if you were doing 10 jobs per week.

At the low end, you could expect net profits of about $30,000, while at the high end and with one applicator and an office, you can expect to net between $50,000 and $75,000 by the end of your second year. In short, you can breakeven within the first year and start turning ROIs of 200 percent or more by the end of your second year.

A company newsletter notes that a Winter Haven, Florida, franchisee started part-time, but did so well that, after just a few months, he quit his job and began working full-time. The newsletter also reported that a Seattle, Washington, franchisee earned $20,000 annual gross income doing simple repairs of small chips in sinks and bathtubs. The materials cost him only $300 and left him with a fantastic gross profit margin. And the company reports that some of its franchisees earn gross incomes of as much as $20,000 per month or $240,000, or more, per year.

Clearly, Bathcrest® provides an excellent way to earn very high ROIs in a low-cost, easy-to-learn business.

BINGO BUGLE

Bingo Bugle
K & O Publishing
7522 20th Northeast
Seattle, WA 98115
(206) 527-4958

Bingo is the fourth most popular leisure activity after swimming, bicycling, and camping. It is the second largest legal, commercial gambling game after state-run lotteries; people wagered more than $5 billion per year on bingo during 1989, according to surveys by various federal and state commissions. And bingo players are unusually active in their game; almost 90 percent of active bingo fans play at least once a month, and about 15 percent play at least once a week. They participate far more often and actively than other gamblers or sports enthusiasts.

Since bingo is a form of gambling, it is not legal in all states. Moreover, some states do not allow advertising publications about gambling even though it may be legal. And in some quarters, bingo has a negative reputation. You do best to investigate the laws and regulations in your state and consider whether you have any personal objections to promoting this type of enterprise actively.

What does bingo have to do with franchising? Although no one has yet franchised bingo parlors, K&O Publishing, Seattle, has franchised an intriguing and potentially lucrative adjunct to bingo games: free, give-away monthly magazines that publish bingo advertising and local bingo news and information. Called Bingo Bugle, this franchised publication is distributed through local bingo halls (some 95 percent of the copies), convenience stores, supermarkets, or in news racks.

By late 1989, Bingo Bugle had about 40 franchises in 21 states and one Canadian province, with plans to open franchises in 10 more states and six more Canadian provinces during late 1989 and 1990. Bingo Bugle was the 18th best low-investment franchise in the 1989 *Entrepreneur* magazine listing of the Top 500 franchises.

In essence, you become publisher of a local edition of a nationally known bingo publication. As a franchisee in a major metropolitan area, you license the right to use the Bingo Bugle name. You sell local advertising primarily to bingo halls, local restaurants, and bingo support-service companies. You become a full-fledged editor, publisher, and reporter for your own magazine. You—or a family member, employee, or freelance writer—also write local news and feature stories about bingo halls, bingo topics, and bingo players.

Unlike other advertising publications, Bingo Bugle allows you to hire local printers to prepare your publication. Most other franchised ad publications make most of their profits by printing and distributing your publication for you. Bingo Bugle's approach puts more responsibility on your shoulders, but you gain greater flexibility and the power to do competitive bidding among many local printers.

You can do very well with this franchise. Bingo Bugle is very forthcoming about its franchisees' actual results. It has published each franchise's reported monthly gross revenues for every year since 1983. During 1989, some 40 Bingo Bugle franchisees reported system-wide revenues of about $2.5 million, or an average of $62,500 per year. That includes figures from 10 franchises less than a year old. At the end of this discussion, you will find a complete list of Bingo Bugle's franchisees' gross monthly income for 1987, 1988, and the first 10 months of 1989. You will find that gross income ranges from as low as $15,000 per year to more than $333,000 per year. The median or average exceeds $78,000 per year with individual franchisees netting average incomes between $30,000 and $50,000 per year.

Many Bingo Bugle franchisees are retired newspaper editors, active advertising salespeople, and retired military. The only prerequisites for success with this franchise are a willingness to work hard, a strong liking for people, and—at the least—an acceptance of the bingo culture. The most successful franchisees spend many hours each week visiting bingo parlors, talking to players, managers, and owners, and distributing their publications.

You start small with an initial circulation of 5,000 papers and an eight-page publication. How large you grow depends on your territory and your efforts. In California, the most successful Bingo Bugle franchisees have exceeded circulation of 30,000 copies and 50 pages per month.

You can start from your home part-time or work with a spouse or family member and thereby reduce your start-up costs to a very small amount. You are required to participate in the operation.

How Much It Costs

Bingo Bugle is a very inexpensive operation with a franchise fee as low as $1,500. The highest franchise fee ever charged, company executives say, was

$6,000 and resulted from three existing franchisees having a bidding war on the resale of a lucrative territory in California.

The franchise fee, usually about $1,500, varies according to size of the metropolitan area, the number of area bingo games, population territory, and state regulations.

Your total start-up costs should not exceed $12,000, making this one of the least expensive, yet most lucrative, franchises available. The table shown below gives an estimated range of start-up costs:

Category	Low End	High End
Franchise fee	$1,500	$ 6,000
Equipment[a]	0	2,000
Travel training	400	1,000
Prize money[b]	100	200
Promotional containers	35	60
Working capital[c]	1,500	3,000
TOTAL	$3,535	$12,260

a. If you already own a car, typewriter or personal computer, camera, telephone, automobile, etc., you will not need any equipment.
b. You increase reader interest with a monthly contest and a small prize, usually $100, and you must fund your first issue's prize.
c. This includes your initial printing costs, license fees, legal fees, and living expenses. If you have a full- or part-time job, money in the bank, or a retirement income, you can use those resources to help you make the transition.

Royalties and Other Costs

You pay Bingo Bugle a 10 percent monthly royalty. This seems high, but Bingo Bugle executives note that your royalties are their primary income source. Bingo Bugle also sells national advertising which it has the right to insert into your publication free of charge, but the franchise agreement limits Bingo Bugle's national ads to no more than 5 percent of any issue, or one page out of every 20, or one-half page out of every 10. And you must pay the company a 15 percent commission if Bingo Bugle sells a national or regional ad which it places in multiple local editions of Bingo Bugle.

You also must pay other franchisees a 30 percent commission if they sell regional advertising that appears in your edition. This is a fair arrangement that works both ways. It encourages all franchisees to cooperate and seek out major accounts, such as restaurant chains, resorts, casinos, and the like, and it can only strengthen the system's long-term financial health and reputation.

You can expect mechanical reproduction costs to range between 30 and 40 percent, and printing costs to range between 30 and 45 percent of your local *operating costs,* not your gross income. If you buy a desktop publishing system (about $7,000 to $9,000), you can eliminate the need for typesetters and layout artists and thereby save thousands of dollars per year.

In short, Bingo Bugle makes a very inexpensive start-up operation. Because you take deposits on every ad you sell, and you don't publish your first issue until you sell enough ads to fill an eight-page magazine, your clients help pay most of your initial printing costs.

However, Bingo Bugle also requires you to earn gross advertising revenues each month of a minimum of $1,000. If you don't fulfill this quota, Bingo Bugle has the option to cancel your agreement. Although several franchisees did occasionally fail to meet this quota during 1988, Bingo Bugle did not cancel all these agreements; instead, the company helped the franchisees improve their results or sell the franchises to someone else. During the same year, however, two franchises were cancelled because they failed to meet the quota.

What You Get

For your franchise fee, you get a range of services and support:

Exclusive territory. You get rights to a major metropolitan area or a significant portion of one. Company executives note that Orange County, California—which includes San Diego—is a one-franchise territory. The State of New York, they feel, will support five or six territories. This company policy means that you will have a more than adequate territory to develop your business.

Significant agreement term. The initial agreement lasts five years, but you can easily renew for five more years without paying another franchise fee. After 10 years, the agreement is renewed from year to year.

Editorial package. Each month, the company gives you a package of news, bingo information, crosswords, games, features, and illustrations which you supplement with local news and features. Some 35 percent of each issue is editorial material.

Training. You receive two days of training in the basics at Bingo Bugle headquarters. This is a relatively brief training session for a relatively complex subject: selling advertising and putting together a publication. Still, the company provides continuing support with telephone hot lines, regional support representatives, and regional and national conventions.

Sales materials. You receive an operations manual, rate cards, and billing forms.

For the low franchise fee and monthly royalty income, Bingo Bugle does provide a solid support program.

How Much Can You Make?

Bingo Bugle executives say that you should have net pre-tax profit margins of about 55 percent of your gross revenues if you do not hire a full-time salesperson. If you hire a full-time ad salesperson, you will need to pay commissions ranging from 15 to 35 percent of his or her gross sales. If you sell the ads, distribute the paper, and use freelancers to do the writing, your income will depend solely on how well you cultivate your market.

The Colorado Springs franchisee reported in *Editor & Publisher* magazine that his start-up costs equalled $8,000, and his monthly gross income ranges from $7,000 to $8,500 per *month*. The Tampa franchisee reported averages of a 36-page magazine with a gross income of $11,000 per month, and a net monthly income of about $5,000 before taxes.

The appended tables show the actual monthly results for all of Bingo Bugle's franchisees during 1987, 1988, and the first ten months of 1989. The latter shows that, during 1989, system-wide revenues averaged more than $260,000 per month, or about $6,500 per franchise, including ten start-ups. The ten-month figures show that the lowest revenues for a franchise in business all year was only $13,250, but the highest equalled $333,000, with seven franchises exceeding $100,000, or $10,000 per month. The median, all-year franchise exceeded $55,000, or $5,500 per month.

Clearly, for an investment of less than $10,000, you can break even during your first three months, and turn a net ROI exceeding 300 percent during your first year. If you like gaming action and mingling with people, Bingo Bugle can prove a very lucrative enterprise.

1987 Bingo Bugle Revenues

Actual Monthly Results ($)

	Jan.	Feb.	March	April	May	June	July	August	Sept.	Oct.	Nov.	Dec.
South Bay	9,638	11,759	13,309	13,408	11,834	10,763	11,708	11,975	12,548	12,733	12,306	11,633
South Sound	5,920	5,940	5,900	6,030	5,946	5,945	6,135	6,435	5,850	6,670	6,110	6,040
Columbia Riv.	6,948	6,643	6,242	7,168	6,831	6,696	6,776	6,930	7,036	6,901	7,393	7,034
Willamette	1,673	1,510	1,510	1,583	1,684	1,684	1,729	1,339	1,394	1,394	1,569	1,394
Can-Am	8,054	9,200	7,200	7,900	8,150	8,900	10,200	11,300	11,450	12,400	15,200	17,000
New Mexico	—	1,703	1,567	2,810	1,750	2,250	1,297	1,573	631	897	1,186	1,033
San Diego	14,927	14,270	15,012	14,902	14,723	12,900	12,871	13,729	14,020	15,181	15,073	14,664
East Bay	12,174	11,554	12,651	13,556	13,796	13,172	15,152	13,141	14,268	14,369	14,472	13,652
Golden Gate	9,098	9,615	10,487	13,066	11,207	10,211	10,191	10,686	11,578	11,495	10,323	9,426
Orange Co.	13,607	12,265	14,310	13,590	14,982	14,494	14,059	14,118	14,315	14,622	15,424	13,969
LA I & II	32,000	32,000	32,300	32,300	32,480	33,000	33,000	33,000	32,000	31,000	31,000	31,000
North Bay	7,400	7,160	7,360	8,027	7,966	7,842	6,884	7,035	6,400	6,997	6,789	6,423
Central Cal.	5,524	7,886	7,054	8,154	8,157	8,143	10,408	9,776	10,567	8,910	7,640	8,566
Houston G.	11,130	10,965	12,735	14,564	13,955	11,194	14,328	15,070	14,390	15,626	14,629	15,091
Lone Star	—	1,405	1,240	1,883	1,017	1,504	2,204	1,674	1,285	950	1,000	1,000
Windy City	3,509	3,500	4,510	4,250	4,300	3,450	3,400	3,145	3,230	3,275	3,200	3,200
Sacramento	7,617	8,005	9,134	7,786	7,970	7,835	10,846	9,173	9,885	10,724	8,704	8,186
San Bern.	3,325	3,127	3,850	6,594	5,322	3,383	3,652	3,400	5,757	5,971	2,554	2,461
Arizona	3,237	3,072	3,372	3,566	2,942	3,172	3,879	4,121	3,299	3,482	3,514	3,569

1987 Bingo Bugle Revenues *(Continued)*

	Jan.	Feb.	March	April	May	June	July	August	Sept.	Oct.	Nov.	Dec.
Wash. DC	3,425	3,580	3,605	3,479	2,615	2,721	2,240	1,975	1,655	2,335	2,340	2,750
Santa Barb	3,435	3,710	3,998	5,594	3,977	4,730	4,170	6,432	6,357	7,281	5,768	4,953
Gr. Michigan	—	—	2,160	2,700	3,016	3,305	3,998	4,170	4,362	5,002	5,307	5,300
N. Central Ill.	990	752	1,114	1,790	1,215	1,409	1,495	1,296	1,297	1,387	1,699	1,631
Gr. Boston	3,640	3,245	3,010	3,610	3,320	3,690	2,890	2,595	3,105	3,135	2,690	2,515
Central MA	1,465	1,110	1,662	1,923	1,890	1,280	1,575	1,215	1,200	1,560	1,700	2,400
Beaumont/ G. Tri.	2,950	2,950	3,100	3,755	2,850	2,885	3,381	3,311	3,405	4,037	3,500	3,695
Richmond VA	2,990	2,075	2,183	3,119	2,020	2,931	4,245	5,073	4,070	4,560	4,010	5,085
Gr. Prairie	575	1,055	940	950	1,100	710	—	—	—	—	—	—
Tampa Bay	4,695	3,933	4,470	5,234	5,498	5,365	6,570	4,327	5,095	6,683	9,362	8,940
S. Anton./ Austin	1,280	2,300	2,400	*2,500	2,200	2,790	2,700	2,750	*2,700	*2,700	*2,750	*3,000
Las Vegas	3,558	3,508	3,785	4,057	4,070	3,453	3,863	4,059	3,865	4,257	5,274	5,206
Denver	2,150	2,957	4,206	4,599	5,117	6,076	7,209	6,812	6,037	6,701	8,616	8,414
New York	—	—	—	—	—	—	1,100	1,145	1,295	1,200	1,100	1,100
Oklahoma	—	—	—	—	—	—	3,752	5,690	6,120	7,882	7,692	8,655
Tulsa	—	—	—	—	—	—	—	—	—	2,780	—	3,407
Tucson	—	—	—	—	—	—	—	—	732	732	762	1,317

* indicates estimate.

1988 Bingo Bugle Revenues

Actual Monthly Results ($)

	Jan.	Feb.	March	April	May	June	July	August	Sept.	Oct.	Nov.	Dec.
South Bay	10,543	9,933	11,567	11,591	12,458	11,457	10,098	10,053	11,265	10,774	10,480	10,650
South Sound	6,285	6,195	6,210	6,326	6,390	6,530	6,285	6,330	6,250	7,190	6,450	6,485
Columbia Riv.	7,204	6,981	7,948	8,966	7,598	7,565	8,560	8,475	9,225	9,076	8,941	8,961
Willamette	1,394	1,095	1,095	1,095	1,384	1,600	1,555	1,555	1,690	2,100	2,920	2,525
Can-Am	12,214	9,429	11,730	8,790	7,740	6,740	10,300	8,800	9,200	9,000	9,000	*9,000
San Diego	12,882	13,255	13,844	13,605	14,182	14,233	15,424	14,868	13,723	15,525	15,324	14,945
East Bay	13,571	13,000	13,508	14,822	14,596	14,429	13,886	14,759	15,338	17,868	18,374	19,593
Golden Gate	9,314	9,500	11,257	12,282	11,652	9,932	8,512	9,387	9,797	9,898	9,857	10,328
Orange Co.	15,379	14,574	14,525	14,194	14,019	12,990	12,808	12,892	14,362	14,928	15,633	17,357
LA I & II	32,000	33,000	31,000	31,000	33,000	31,000	31,000	31,000	31,100	31,000	31,000	32,000
North Bay	6,928	6,553	6,834	6,811	6,751	6,614	6,859	6,519	6,697	7,350	7,037	6,237
Central Cal.	8,992	9,003	8,433	9,642	9,441	8,511	10,270	9,089	9,847	9,243	8,821	8,892
Houston G.	14,020	13,231	13,400	12,300	12,438	13,667	12,423	14,184	15,651	16,280	14,656	12,260
Lone Star	1,234	1,110	1,123	1,110	1,800	1,203	1,370	1,055	2,578	2,096	2,194	2,366
Windy City	3,200	3,250	3,100	3,625	3,560	3,525	3,500	3,764	4,308	4,869	4,054	4,224
Sacramento	8,062	7,447	7,878	12,003	8,916	9,780	9,288	9,712	9,956	10,007	10,795	*10,000
Arizona	4,468	3,988	4,638	4,213	5,103	5,145	5,860	5,349	6,055	6,372	6,302	6,312
Tucson	1,140	1,350	1,167	1,160	1,745	1,012	925	930	1,135	1,590	1,600	1,685
Wash. DC	2,063	3,019	3,447	3,119	2,459	2,461	2,363	2,629	2,738	2,759	2,443	2,278

1988 Bingo Bugle Revenues (Continued)

	Jan.	Feb.	March	April	May	June	July	August	Sept.	Oct.	Nov.	Dec.
Santa Barb.	4,987	5,452	4,956	6,046	6,911	6,949	7,042	8,010	6,396	6,159	7,197	7,064
Gr. Michigan	5,641	5,484	5,446	5,245	5,241	5,136	4,946	4,922	5,061	6,050	5,349	4,699
N. Centr. Ill.	1,697	1,514	1,302	1,194	1,381	1,595	1,500	1,247	1,679	2,330	1,697	1,956
Gr. Boston	2,299	2,972	2,700	2,539	2,650	2,465	2,125	2,096	2,642	2,940	4,000	*3,100
Central Ma.	2,295	2,305	2,319	2,402	2,638	2,682	2,355	2,335	2,285	2,220	1,930	2,110
Golden Tri. TX	3,260	3,225	2,203	1,850	1,800	—	—	—	—	—	—	—
Richmond	4,298	3,873	3,484	3,544	3,902	4,188	4,490	3,863	4,100	4,645	5,207	4,630
Tampa Bay	8,424	6,677	6,634	6,199	6,297	6,052	5,206	6,598	5,548	7,437	6,753	6,691
San Anton./ Austin	2,650	2,875	2,730	3,180	3,525	3,250	3,675	2,825	2,991	*2,900	—	—
Las Vegas	3,556	4,910	6,332	5,720	5,300	5,295	4,350	4,628	5,003	5,977	5,776	5,902
Denver	6,857	7,278	8,914	9,645	8,544	8,600	7,305	9,425	9,390	10,305	10,390	11,000
Oklahoma C.	6,401	6,689	7,097	7,652	6,499	7,070	9,986	7,190	6,548	5,273	5,940	*6,000
Tulsa	—	2,732	2,799	2,546	2,248	2,350	2,324	2,793	2,568	2,705	*2,700	*2,710
Pittsburgh	1,492	1,840	2,113	—	2,200	780	780	—	—	—	—	—
New Mexico	1,033	1,704	1,527	863	1,553	896	900	850	—	—	—	—
Gr. Prairie	—	—	—	—	—	3,469	3,195	3,835	3,845	5,373	5,790	6,763
Colorado S.	—	—	—	—	—	—	—	—	1,285	1,450	1,400	*1,495
Kansas C.	—	—	—	—	—	—	—	—	—	—	1,282	1,409
San Bern.	—	—	—	—	—	—	—	—	—	—	1,642	1,786

* indicates estimate.

1989 Bingo Bugle Revenues

Actual Monthly Results ($)

	Jan.	Feb.	March	April	May	June	July	August	Sept.	Oct.	Nov./Dec.	Total
South Bay	10,278	8,686	10,381	9,730	10,332	10,338	10,400	9,980	10,000	10,123	—	100,248
South Sound	6,890	6,440	6,500	6,415	6,295	6,100	6,200	6,750	6,900	6,990	—	65,480
Olympic Penn.	—	3,100	3,150	2,550	2,700	2,800	2,880	2,715	2,800	2,889	—	25,584
Columbia Riv.	9,501	9,185	10,381	10,011	9,520	9,055	9,100	9,715	9,800	9,812	—	96,080
Willamette	2,155	2,415	2,565	2,797	3,527	3,115	3,700	3,715	3,600	3,679	—	31,268
San Diego	15,887	14,463	15,209	13,755	15,457	13,858	14,100	14,200	14,500	14,320	—	145,749
Phoenix	6,741	6,867	7,011	7,396	7,771	7,709	9,442	9,454	7,583	8,213	—	78,187
Tucson	1,521	1,636	1,637	1,802	1,787	2,102	2,302	2,270	1,997	1,847	—	18,901
Central Cal.	8,649	8,782	9,563	9,500	9,547	9,483	9,952	9,252	10,390	10,100	—	95,218
San Bern.	2,967	3,130	3,450	3,770	4,600	4,270	4,300	3,450	3,660	3,760	—	37,357
East Bay	19,793	17,023	18,310	19,291	18,317	18,516	18,553	18,224	18,224	18,770	—	185,021
Golden Gate	9,060	8,011	8,827	9,050	9,452	7,982	7,302	7,276	8,441	9,561	—	84,962
LA I & II	32,000	32,000	33,000	35,000	32,000	33,000	36,000	33,000	34,000	33,000	—	333,000
North Bay	7,414	6,616	6,956	6,695	6,832	6,557	6,890	6,380	6,517	6,607	—	67,464
Orange Co.	16,215	16,243	16,185	16,000	15,969	18,310	16,352	15,825	17,267	18,925	—	167,291
Sacramento	7,637	8,562	8,401	8,990	9,175	10,130	8,681	9,100	8,500	8,500	—	87,676
Stockton	1,511	2,196	1,461	1,666	1,607	3,026	—	2,980	3,000	3,000	—	20,447
Santa Barb.	7,290	6,435	6,510	5,976	6,568	6,770	6,909	7,112	7,377	7,512	—	68,459
Denver	11,450	10,685	10,999	10,607	13,865	11,119	11,335	13,345	12,860	13,234	—	119,499
Colorado Sp.	1,999	—	2,749	3,552	3,271	2,804	2,105	1,544	—	—	—	18,024
Wash. DC	1,994	2,715	2,619	2,869	2,800	1,945	1,705	1,995	2,510	2,105	—	23,257
Florida	5,600	5,627	5,060	5,870	5,767	5,767	5,587	4,792	4,497	4,500	—	53,067
Windy City	3,740	4,289	4,064	4,109	4,614	4,055	3,969	4,300	4,819	4,019	—	41,978
N. Central	942	1,823	1,309	1,406	871	1,422	1,249	1,337	1,592	1,300	—	13,251

1989 Bingo Bugle Revenues (Continued)

	Jan.	Feb.	March	April	May	June	July	August	Sept.	Oct.	Nov./Dec.	Total
Gr. Boston	4,065	3,515	3,890	3,705	3,337	2,756	2,436	2,543	2,340	2,430	—	31,017
Central MA.	1,793	1,434	1,350	1,615	1,902	1,930	1,765	1,815	—	—	—	13,604
Gr. Michigan	5,495	5,244	5,415	5,520	5,235	5,600	5,495	5,445	5,430	6,320	—	55,199
Las Vegas	5,332	5,134	5,114	4,509	7,274	6,797	6,311	5,543	4,733	6,207	—	56,954
New Mexico	1,715	2,950	2,273	2,331	2,296	1,591	1,700	1,645	1,580	2,303	—	20,384
Gr. Prairie	5,698	6,305	5,435	5,470	5,430	6,995	5,400	5,543	5,400	5,400	—	57,076
Kansas	2,632	1,968	3,085	2,275	2,805	2,947	3,326	3,305	3,040	3,690	—	29,073
Oklahoma	6,000	5,000	5,000	5,000	6,695	5,385	5,945	5,075	4,875	4,900	—	53,875
Tulsa	3,000	3,000	2,500	1,526	1,743	1,525	1,500	—	—	—	—	14,794
Houston	16,030	15,653	15,037	12,544	17,384	16,429	18,801	18,557	15,370	17,037	—	162,842
Lone Star	2,212	1,714	1,783	1,511	1,704	1,783	1,669	1,514	1,470	1,631	—	16,991
Richmond	3,956	3,205	3,422	5,159	4,273	4,153	3,563	3,970	2,885	3,795	—	38,381
Fort Myers	953	1,239	1,309	1,190	1,610	1,970	2,050	2,010	2,310	2,290	—	16,931
N. Carolina	—	—	—	1,402	1,625	1,671	1,885	1,665	1,755	1,865	—	11,868
Miami	—	—	223	370	1,303	1,543	2,046	2,050	1,236	1,280	—	10,051
San Antonio	—	—	565	1,170	1,835	3,239	3,725	3,750	2,280	1,845	—	18,409
Orlando	—	—	—	—	—	—	913	947	1,398	1,218	—	4,476
Buffalo	—	—	—	—	—	2,648	3,429	3,570	4,170	4,290	—	18,107
S. Carolina	—	—	—	—	—	—	—	—	—	—	—	0
Corpus Chris.	—	—	—	—	—	—	1,502	1,520	2,827	2,800	—	8,649
Lubbock	—	—	—	—	—	—	—	—	—	3,795	—	3,795
Annapolis	—	—	—	—	—	—	—	—	—	3,550	—	3,550
Palm Beach	—	—	—	—	—	—	—	—	760	800	—	1,560
Atlanta	—	—	—	—	—	—	—	—	—	—	—	0
Total	250,115	243,290	252,698	254,104	269,095	269,195	272,474	269,178				2,080,149

5

Franchises with Fees of $5,001 to $10,000

Dial-A-Gift, Inc.
Rug Doctor Pro
Chem-Dry Carpet Cleaning
Duraclean International
Subway Sandwiches & Salads
U-Save Auto Rental

Mr. Rooter
Coustic-Glo International Inc.
Mini Maid
Jani-King
Worldwide Refinishing Systems, Inc.

DIAL-A-GIFT, INC.

Dial-A-Gift, Inc.
2265 East 4800 South
Salt Lake City, UT 84117
(801) 278-0413

What FTD and Teleflora have done for sending flowers, Dial-A-Gift is doing for sending an incredible variety of gift baskets and gifts. Dial-A-Gift is an international gift-basket-by-phone system that works the way FTD works with a local florist. If you want to send a gift to someone in your city, you call Dial-A-Gift, and the local franchisee prepares and delivers it. If you want to send a gift to someone across the country—to Canada, the United Kingdom, Switzerland, most Caribbean countries, or Japan—you call or visit your local Dial-A-Gift store and order your gift. The store makes all the arrangements either with another Dial-A-Gift store or with an affiliated gift-basket dealer in the recipient's area.

Dial-A-Gift has been rated one of the top 100 franchises for women by *Women's Enterprise* magazine and one of the top 100 by *Venture*. Its system-wide sales increased 38 percent during both 1988 and 1989, and company executives expect this expansion rate to continue through the next several years. Dial-A-Gift excels, the company executives state, in the two fastest growing segments of the gift-giving market: catalog sales and gift baskets.

Dial-A-Gift has a relatively inexpensive, straightforward, and simple structure, as well as an easy-to-understand disclosure statement and contract. By late 1989, more than 130 Dial-A-Gift franchisees worked with more than 4,000 affiliated dealers around the world. The company has a goal of 2,000 franchisees within five years, which is a very ambitious expansion plan. It has grown sluggishly since mid-1987 when it had 112 franchises, and moreover it did not meet its target of adding 200 more franchises during that year.

The short-term success secret of Dial-A-Gift is the promotion of local gift-basket delivery business, a concept that has become very popular during the past several years. A potential franchisee, however, faces very stiff competition from many already well-established competitors: florists who are "branching out" (pun intended) into balloon delivery, gift baskets, and the like; independent gift delivery service businesses; retail gift shops adding their own delivery service; mail order catalog gift houses; etc.

The long-term success of Dial-A-Gift rests on the growth of the established network. FTD and Teleflora succeed because practically every florist in the country belongs to one or both of these networks. Dial-A-Gift, on the other hand, is selling franchises, the total start-up costs of which average $30,000. Dial-A-Gift also works with independent gift services to widen its geographic coverage, but the costs and nature of the franchise probably prevents its network from growing as rapidly as the teleflorists' ones.

Company executives say they aim to strengthen Dial-A-Gift's national identification and standards and make Dial-A-Gift as well known as the household-name teleflorists.

Dial-A-Gift is currently an excellent opportunity because its start-up cost is relatively low for a retail operation, and its marketplace should continue to grow very rapidly. In affluent areas of the country, gift-giving for social, charitable, and business affairs is very serious business, and people are always looking for a new and different gift to give an important friend, a business client or associate, or a relative—not to mention spouse and lovers.

Dial-A-Gift appears to be responding well to the rapidly changing trends in gift-giving, for it recognizes how gift-giving differs from region to region. The company encourages franchisees to develop their own baskets that will appeal to a local audience, as well as to follow the company's national standards. Dial-A-Gift's selections now include the traditional fresh fruit baskets, bouquets of balloons, gourmet food baskets, cheese cake, popcorn, smoked ham and turkey, wines and champagnes, meats, cheese, cakes, fruit cakes, and even cookie bouquets, with cookies arranged so that they look like flowers at the end of long stems with silk leaves. The cookie bouquet was adopted nationally after several local stores tested the concept and found it to be a winner. During 1989, a "beauty basket" of soaps, sachets, perfume, body lotions, and the like, became a top seller.

How Much It Costs

As noted, the average total start-up costs for a Dial-A-Gift franchise are about $30,000. This amount can vary, depending largely on the retail space you lease. You may find a space that needs little work to make it attractive, or you may have to "build out" a retail space from scratch. Listed below is a good estimate of the costs involved.

Start-Up Costs

	Minimum	Maximum	Comments
Franchise fee	$10,000	$10,000	Up to 100,000 population
Rent	1,200	1,200	Estimate higher if more deposits required
Build-out costs	1,000	20,000	Varies widely
Workroom equipment	3,500	3,500	
Beginning inventory	4,000	10,000	Some opt for more
Sign[a]	1,100	1,100	
Insurance	250	250	Required liability
Total	$21,050	$51,050	

a. Sign cost may be higher, depending on local contractor, lease requirements, and local zoning code requirements.

These amounts do not include the following costs, which you also will undoubtedly incur.

	Minimum	Maximum	Comments
Business and license fees	$ 250	$ 500	Especially for beer/wine, and occupational or business licenses
Utility deposits	300	750	Phone, electric, gas
Delivery vehicle	200	1,000	If leased or bought; not required
Yellow Page ads	30	150	Per month; may have up-front payment
Miscellaneous	250	500	For Murphy's Law
Additional Total	$1,030	$2,900	

You therefore can reasonably expect your costs to range from a minimum of $22,080 to a high of $53,950. The amount will be higher if you choose to purchase an optional $2,000 computer hardware and software system for your cash register, ordering, and inventory system.

Royalties and Fees

After you start your service, you pay Dial-A-Gift a monthly royalty of 4 percent of your gross sales and a $100 per month flat advertising fee. Dial-A-Gift also takes 10 percent of all long-distance orders you make or receive, and the franchise with which you place the long-distance order also gets 10 percent. Therefore, you receive about 76 percent of each long-distance order, but you keep 96 percent of all local orders that your arrange and deliver.

Potential Operating Costs

Your likely operating costs include $40 to $100 per month utility bills; $200 to $400 per month for telephone and Yellow Pages ad; and monthly rent ranging from $600 to $1,200 for totals between $849 and $1,700. Local taxes are not included in these costs. Usually, partners, spouses, and family members work in a store, so the business most often has no added labor costs. If you hire part-time workers, expect to pay $4 to $6 per hour. Your supply and inventory costs should equal about 30 percent of your gross sales.

What You Get

As a Dial-A-Gift franchisee, you get a good package of benefits and assistance from the franchisor.

Exclusive territory. This is granted when the franchise fee of $10,000 is paid. Dial-A-Gift suggests a minimum territory with 100,000 population. The boundaries are delineated by zip code. Several Dial-A-Gift franchisees have discovered this boundary secret. If you are the first one in your area, grab the zip codes with the most affluent neighborhoods, first, and the most up-scale business, corporate parks, and office areas, second.

National network and clearing house. The thrust, of course, is to strengthen and broaden the company's national ordering network. To reinforce this concept, the company has agreements with 4,000 dealers who will make deliveries in areas where Dial-A-Gift franchises are not located.

List of suggested suppliers. You would expect to receive this list, but keep in mind that your success depends more than many other franchises on your purchasing quality item products from reliable suppliers.

Training sessions. It is one of the few franchises that *pays* the round-trip air fare for you to go to its Salt Lake City, Utah, headquarters for training. The training sessions last one to two weeks, and they include both classroom study and hands-on training in an active Dial-A-Gift store.

National advertising campaign. Dial-A-Gift advertises in many up-scale national magazines, including *Food & Wine, Bon Appetit,* prominent business publications, and the *AT&T 800 Toll-Free Directory.* This exposure is essential to establish a national identification for the franchise, build network traffic, and enhance franchisee local credibility.

Location, location. The company provides you with assistance in finding a good location. It strongly recommends that you rent a small retail outlet of from 600 to 1,200 square feet near, but not in, a major mall. The company recommends strip centers to save money, but these do, however, provide ample parking. Some franchises have chosen to go into higher traffic and more expensive malls or centers, and they report that the increase in sales volume usually compensates for the increased costs. The choice is ultimately yours, however, since the company does not dictate nor is responsible for finding you a location.

Other assistance. Dial-A-Gift, as a matter of course, provides you with an operations manual, start-up help, training, and advice on local ad programs, newsletters, and so forth. It also provides you with a six-month supply of business and accounting forms.

How Much Can You Make?

In local newspaper and magazine articles, several franchisees have reported that their sales exceeded $2,000 per month or more in less than a year. The company reports that its top franchisee had $980,000 in gross income during 1988, and an analysis of the franchise's potential estimates that franchises can reach $150,000 in gross sales by the end of the second year. An accountant's more conservative estimate, quoted in a business newspaper article, cites that, on the basis of a $10,000 franchise fee, one should anticipate a $15,000 to $20,000 profit during the first year.

Dial-A-Gift is clearly designed to earn gross margins of 50 percent of total sales. To date, franchisees report that an average sales is a $42 basket, so your average gross profit after costs of sales and fees for each basket will be $21. To turn a first-year net profit of $20,000 requires sales of 953 baskets, about three per day.

Keep in mind also that gift-giving is a very seasonal business, with most sales peaking during the holidays and at Valentine's Day. Franchisees must work hard to promote birthday, anniversary, special occasion, and corporate gift-giving to smooth out the business's peaks and valleys.

By 1989, somewhat more than 15 percent of a store's business was coming through its national orders, but the company expects this business to grow to between 30 and 50 percent as the network grows.

Dial-A-Gift is definitely not a get-rich-quick scheme. However, its two-year payoff on a relatively low initial investment puts it in the range of many people's pocketbooks. Of course, you can borrow most of the money from various sources and thereby reduce your own cash outlays even more. The long-term potential for the franchise is excellent since there are few better ways to make money than by helping make people happy.

RUG DOCTOR PRO

Rug Doctor, L.P.
2788 North Larkin Ave.
P.O. Box 7750
Fresno, CA 93747
(800) 678-7844
(209) 291-5511
(209) 291-9963 FAX

Rug Doctor Pro, "the new kid on the block" among mobile van-based carpet cleaning franchises, offers a very competitive franchise arrangement. It seeks to grow rapidly and compete effectively against several large and well-established, even venerable, franchises: Servicemaster, Duraclean International, and Servpro. These three competitors are discussed in other sections of this book.

As the company executives rightly note, Rug Doctor Pro has one essential difference over its competitors, which it offers to a prospective buyer; it gives you the chance to buy the best available territories anywhere in the country. With well-established franchises, finding a quality territory may be much more difficult unless you buy an established franchise. That road may be much more expensive than starting fresh.

Rug Doctor Pro is not included in this book just because it is new. Of primary importance is the fact that Rug Doctor Pro is itself a subsidiary of a nationally known company, Rug Doctor, Inc., which for many years has been the leading supplier of rental carpet cleaning equipment through grocery stores, hardware stores, and similar outlets. Company executives say they have entered the carpet and upholstery cleaning franchise business for one simple reason—their market situation. The demand for rented carpet cleaners is declining about 5 percent per year, but the demand for carpet cleaning services is growing by more than 5 percent per year. Rug Doctor's rental business continues to grow, the executives say, but they realize that they are taking a greater share of business from their competitors and not benefitting from an expanding market.

Therefore, Rug Doctor has decided to go to where the money is going—to the franchised carpet and upholstery cleaning services. Rug Doctor Pro faces very stiff competition from the three leading franchises and many others, but its executives are determined to serve the same targeted consumer market segment—higher income families, and two-income professional families and couples who do not have the time or desire to clean their own carpets.

Rug Doctor Pro Differences

Most interestingly, Rug Doctor has taken a "new, fresh approach" with its territories. First and unlike the majors, you are allowed to accept jobs from *outside* your territory through direct mail, telephone Yellow Pages, or advertisements in local newspapers. Advertising media that overlap territories—newspapers that serve a metropolitan area, for example—can be used by any or all franchisees who own the territory in that area.

Rug Doctor Pro executives say this course is a desirable one because franchisees build the business with referral and word-of-mouth advertising. It is only fair, they believe, to let franchisees who do a good job take advantage of their success, regardless of their territories' boundaries.

On the negative side, this policy could eventually lead to conflict among adjacent franchisees. It also could result in their working together in cooperative advertising programs and share the cost of advertising in the regional Yellow Pages, metropolitan daily newspapers, and the like. The latter case is much more likely.

Territory Size and Boundaries

To support this principle, Rug Doctor Pro has a new way of determining franchise boundaries. The new approach is based on defining territories with a minimum population of 50,000 people. The company makes use of zip codes and charges franchise buyers only for the exact population within these zip codes. As a franchisee, you have the opportunity to identify and buy the zip code territories with the most affluent population in your area. You can readily identify these areas by asking for census and zip code information from the business reference librarian at your local municipal or college library.

Unique Professional Image Marketing Approach

To support its up-scale territory emphasis, Rug Doctor has developed a unique marketing plan that, for the first time, creates a very professional image for carpet cleaning franchises. Called a "multiple impression program," it is designed to show your customers repeatedly that you present a professional image and do a thorough, high-quality job.

To reinforce this concept, it is necessary for you to adhere to the company program. First, you wear a tie, a step that immediately sets you apart from the jeans-and-sneakers carpet cleaning crew. Second, you put a mat down on the carpet at the front door before you step into the house. Third, you wipe everything you touch with a white cloth. Fourth and after each job, you give a mail-in report card to the homeowner so that he or she can write down comments in privacy and mail the card at his or her convenience. Last and after completing a job, you send a "thank you" card and telephone the customer to make sure that he or she is happy with your performance.

The goal of these multiple steps is to make carpet cleaning not a run-of-the-mill service to the customer, but a pleasant experience. Rug Doctor executives say their goal is to make the experience so comfortable and pleasing that the customer not only ever again thinks about calling any other service but also feels compelled to tell friends about how well Rug Doctor Pro does its job.

Furthermore, Rug Doctor Pro correctly realizes that most carpet cleaning franchisees may be good technicians, but few of them are good salespeople. Therefore, the company has largely taken the selling out of the technician's hands.

Instead, the company offers a high-quality videotape. When you go into someone's home, you immediately hand over a check sheet and ask the customer to watch the videotape while you are setting up your equipment. The video shows and explains the complete range of services you offer—your profit centers—such as upholstery cleaning, pressure washing, and even Rug Doctor's unique mattress cleaning service.

Rug Doctor executives stress that the idea is for you to extract as much potential income as you can while you are extracting dirt from the customer's carpet. This is the correct business approach; once your foot is in the door, you should do your best to maximize your effort. It is also the most efficient way for you to make sales. Spending money on any form of advertising always carries much more risk and far lower returns than making additional sales to an established customer. You are much more likely to generate repeat business if you leave the customer with a clear idea of exactly what services you offer.

Last, but not least, Rug Doctor Pro has developed distinct marketing campaigns and direct response solicitations to appeal to your three primary market segments: commercial, consumer, and insurance (for damage restoration services). Each type is a professional-quality, three-color brochure/mailer, to which you can add your own special offer.

Rug Doctor Pro is raising the quality of marketing campaigns for carpet cleaning and related services to a new higher level.

How Much It Costs

To encourage rapid growth, Rug Doctor Pro charges a low franchise fee of $1,000 per 10,000 population, with a $5,000 and 50,000-population minimum. You can buy more population in groups of 10,000 for the same $1,000 amount. In addition, Rug Doctor Pro offers several substantial discount programs to existing businesses that want to convert to Rug Doctor Pro franchises and offers the following methods for doing so:

Carpet cleaning service. There is a reduction in the franchise fee and royalty rate during the first two years that is based on the service's existing gross annual revenues. For each $10,000 of "exempt revenues," primarily those from an existing business, you receive a 10 percent reduction in the initial franchise fee, up to 80 percent. And you pay a smaller royalty fee: the greater amount of either a $200 monthly minimum or declining-scale percentage royalties as described below.

Existing Rug Doctor rental license. There are substantial royalty reductions and a full 80 percent (four-fifths) reduction in the initial franchise fee, and no royalty payments on what are called "exempt revenues" for two years. Exempt revenues are those derived from their existing or continuing businesses.

Royalty Fee Scale

Although it offers a very low initial minimum royalty rate to encourage your success, Rug Doctor Pro's normal royalty fee structure equals the *greater* (higher dollar total) of the following minimums based, first, on monthly gross revenues or, second, on territory population. The following minimums apply to monthly gross revenues:

Monthly Revenues	Royalty Rate (%)
$0 to $9,999	6
$10,000 to $19,999	4
$20,000 or more	3

The minimum fixed-dollar royalty rates are based on population and are equal to the following amounts:

Population Size	Monthly Payment (per 1,000)
0 to 49,999	$5.00
50,000 to 99,999	$4.00
100,000 to 199,999	$3.00
$200,000 or more	$2.50

Low Start-Up Minimum Royalty

A great benefit to you, however, is that Rug Doctor reduces the minimum royalty during the first two years, with the scale shown in the following table:

Minimum Royalty (%)	Length of Time
0	First 6 months (0–6)
25	Second 6 months (7–12)
50	Third 6 months (13–18)
75	Fourth 6 months (19–24)

The royalty rate only reaches its full rate during the first month of your third year in operation. The royalty rate system is a very good one from your point of view. It gives you plenty of time to build a sizable business without the worry of losing your first profits to royalty payments.

The company does charge and collect a 2 percent advertising fee, which goes into a separate advertising fund. In its UFOC (Uniform Franchising Offering Circulars), Rug Doctor Pro also notes that it will not spend more than 15 percent of the ad fund for its internal advertising costs, such as for its advertising department overhead and administrative costs. This appears to be a reasonable rate.

Additional Up-Front Costs

Besides the relatively low fee, Rug Doctor Pro offers several different equipment packages. You choose one based on your territory's size and your operation's scope. The following table lists these packages and their related costs:

Equipment Package	Costs
Starter Package[a]	$ 6,454
Portable Package[b]	11,890
Electric Truck-Mount Package[c]	18,232
Gas-Powered Truck-Mount Package[d]	22,137

a. All materials to do most carpet, upholstery, Scotchgard®, and repair services, but not drapery and upholstery dry cleaning or damage restoration. *Note that you must buy* dry cleaning and damage restoration equipment within one year.
b. Adds trailer-based cleaning equipment to start-up package.
c. Adds truck- or van-mounted power source for heavy-duty work and steam cleaning.
d. Uses natural gas-powered source for heavy-duty cleaning.

Total Start-Up Costs

Rug Doctor Pro also provides the estimated total investment ranges that are shown in the table below. Its estimates include training travel costs and initial working capital. But they assume that you will start your franchise from your home or an existing office. If you do not, you must add the estimated costs of renting office or warehouse space, office furniture, business telephone lines, and the like.

Expense	Range	
	High	**Low**
Franchise fee	$25,000[a]	$ 5,000
Equipment package	40,615[b]	10,200
Supply inventory	1,200	900
Insurance, deposits	1,500	325
Working capital	10,000	4,000
Total	$78,315	$20,425
Added expenses	5,000[c]	2,500
Total	$83,315	$22,925

a. Based on 250,000 population.
b. $16,000 for new van and cost of advanced equipment package and tools.
c. If you choose to open an office.

Financing Arrangements

Rug Doctor Pro goes out of its way to offer financing arrangements. Through its own subsidiary or two other companies, it offers to finance a portion of your franchise fee and up to 50 percent of your equipment package for a maximum 48-month term. The financing programs offered by Bush & Cook Leasing and Finance America, Inc., (current as of January 1, 1990) follow.

BUSH & COOK LEASING

Equipment Only

$ 6,453.55	Starter Package A
171.66	Monthly (plus sales tax) for 60 months
645.36	Residual (10% buyout)
968.32	Down = (15%)
$11,890.05	Portable Package B
316.28	Monthly (plus sales tax) for 60 months
1,189.00	Residual (10% buyout)
1,783.06	Down = (15%)
$22,137.05	Gas Truck-Mount Package D
588.85	Monthly (plus sales tax) for 60 months
2,213.71	Residual (10% buyout)
3,320.56	Down = (15%)

Equipment and New Van

$20,453.55	Starter Package A with new van
520.00	Monthly (plus sales tax) for 60 months
2,045.36	Residual (10% buyout)
2,045.36	Down = (10%)
$25,890.05	Portable Package B
658.00	Monthly (plus sales tax) for 60 months
2,589.00	Residual (10%)
2,589	Down = (10%)
$36,137.05	Gas Truck-Mount Package D
918.00	Monthly (plus sales tax) for 60 months
3,613.71	Residual (10%)
3,613.71	Down = (10%)

Contact: Bush & Cook Leasing, Inc.
1600 West Main St.
Wilmington, Ohio 45177
1-800-342-4784
1-513-382-5150

FINANCE AMERICA, INC.

Lease and Purchase Information

New Equipment Only

$ 6,453.55	Starter Package A
200.71	Monthly (plus sales tax) for 48 months
645.36	Residual (10% buyout)
401.42	Down (first and last payment in advance)

$11,890.05	Portable Package B
317.23	Monthly (plus sales tax) for 60 months
1,189.00	Residual (10% buyout)
634.46	Down (first and last payments in advance)

$22,137.05	Gas Truck-Mount Package D
562.95	Monthly (plus sales tax) for 60 months
2,213.71	Residual (10% buyout)
1,125.90	Down (first and last payment in advance)

New Van [a] and Equipment

$21,453.55	Starter Package A and New Van
479.70	Monthly (plus sales tax) for 60 months
4,505.25	Residual [b] (21% buyout)
479.70	Down (first payment in advance)

$26,890.05	Portable Package B and New Van
601.26	Monthly (plus sales tax) for 60 months
5,646.91	Residual [b] (21% buyout)
601.26	Down (first payment in advance)

$37,137.05	Gas Truck-Mount Package D and New Van
830.38	Monthly (plus sales tax) for 60 months
7,798.78	Residual [b] (21% buyout)
830.38	Down (first payment in advance)

a. The new van is a 3/4 ton, long wheel base cargo van and is figured at approximately $14,000.

b. Residual amount can be re-leased for another year, at no interest, to get the additional benefit of the write-off. The customer does not have to come up with *any* cash at the end of the lease term. However, the customer may wish to cash buyout at this time.

Financing is available with 10% down and 13.5% to 15% interest on trucks and equipment packages.

Prices and interest rates may change without notice.

Note: The last two years of income tax records may be needed.

Phone: 800-338-5220   Mass. (413) 583-8224 and 800-252-4112
FAX: 413-589-9344

What You Get

In addition to the exclusive territory and unique marketing approaches described above, you receive an exceptionally generous five-day training program at Rug Doctor Pro's headquarters. Company officials say that its training program is the only one offered by a carpet cleaning franchise that is certified by the International Institute of Carpet and Upholstery Certification, a prestigious industry association. Company executives extol their training program: "We tell the truth. We give them five different cleaning methods. We train them in how to turn commercial accounts into appearance management programs through which regular cleaning schedules are set up. We teach them how we get our customers, how we treat them well, and how we help our franchisees succeed."

The training program is divided into two parts: technical and equipment training, and business management training. During the latter part, you are taught to use the company's unique marketing approach, as well as accounting and reporting methods.

Besides the territory, marketing, and training, you receive the benefits of Rug Doctor's long- and well-established national reputation and name recognition. This established name can be of some help to you, but remember that you are competing against the leading companies in the field.

How Much Can You Make?

Rug Doctor Pro does not release or give estimates on how much you can expect to earn. Fred Thompson, a company executive and director of marketing, states that, as a high school dropout and before he joined Rug Doctor Pro, he started his own successful cleaning service on a shoestring. He adds, "I lost a bank customer because the bank president was upset that I made more money than he did. I made more than $50,000 a year in a small city in Tennessee. If you know the state, you know that is a lot of money. And I sold the business for $80,000 to work for Rug Doctor."

If you do the work yourself, you can expect to realize gross profit margins of 70 to 80 percent. You should break even after the first month and be able to earn a living and draw some cash from the business by the end of the second month.

Your ROI on your cash investment largely depends on how much of your costs you finance. If you finance your van purchase, half of your starter package, and part of your franchise fee, you lower your cash investment by about half, but you add a very substantial debt load with severe monthly payments to meet from the first month on. Not having to pay the full royalty amount for two years helps significantly, but be very careful about assuming too much debt. With $1,000 per month in debt payments, you may have to do about 10 to 15 jobs just to pay for your van and equipment before you can start earning a living and making a profit.

With Rug Doctor's marketing program, a clear-cut opportunity, and rising demand for your services, however, you at least have a very good chance to succeed. You can expect to net $20,000 to $30,000 as your earnings or wages (if you do the work yourself and your spouse or family helps manage the business side) during the first year. By the end of your second year, your cash ROI could equal 30 to 50 percent or more.

CHEM-DRY CARPET CLEANING

Chem-Dry Carpet Cleaning
Harris Research, Inc.
3330 Cameron Park Drive
Suite 700
Cameron Park, CA 95682
(800) 841-6583
(916) 677-0231
(800) 821-3240, in California

Chem-Dry Carpet Cleaning is undoubtedly one of the best and most profitable carpet, upholstery, and drapery cleaning franchises in the country. Its founder, Robert Harris, has patented a unique carbonated cleaning method that gives his carpet cleaning process many advantages over its competitors: (a) the product gets rid of very difficult stains, including red dyes and pet stains; (b) dries very quickly; (c) does not leave soapy or sticky residues; and (d) the service offers a money-back guarantee. These are clear advantages over the products and services offered by most other carpet cleaning franchises.

Chem-Dry has grown very rapidly since its founding in 1978. It now numbers more than 3,500 franchises in all 50 states and 18 foreign countries, and its plan is to have a total of 5,000 franchises worldwide by 1993. In the United States, Chem-Dry plans to grant up to 400 new franchises each year for the next several years and up to 1,000 international franchises within two years.

The company was selected for this book because it has a very low total initial investment as compared to most of it competitors and offers a very reasonable package of services and benefits. It appears to be a very good opportunity for people who do not have a lot of money, but who do have the time, energy, and effort to build their businesses. Chem-Dry encourages its franchisees to start from their homes and keep their expenses low. Not by any stretch of the imagination is Chem-Dry a "get-rich-quick" scheme. As the figures listed below show, however, you can build a very substantial and profitable business in a few years, but you do have to work hard at it. Fortunately, Chem-Dry helps you do this in many ways.

Defining the Territory

Chem-Dry gives its franchisees a *non-exclusive* territory with an average population of 60,000 and a maximum population of 110,000. Chem-Dry is one of the few franchises that defines territory boundaries, but which does not grant an *exclusive* territory. Its territory definitions are very specific and may be considered the only area in which the company can be seen as hard-nosed. The three factors that it uses to define territories are the following:

1. County boundaries and population characteristics.
2. Telephone directory coverage. Yellow Pages are used to prevent overlapping between two Chem-Dry marketing areas.
3. *Rand McNally Marketing Atlas and Guide.* This reference source provides statistical information and interpretation of business, economic, and geographic information about a given area.

Chem-Dry's parent company, Harris Research, takes a given population area and divides that area by about 60,000. The result determines the number of franchises Chem-Dry will grant in the area.

You can make a franchise territory *exclusive* by becoming a master franchisor in any one given area. If you buy all the franchises of the area, you retain your exclusivity regardless of sales volumes or market penetration. However, if you buy an area and the population grows beyond the maximum set for that area, your gross sales volume will be used to determine whether you will be allowed to purchase an additional franchise and so maintain your exclusive rights. If your gross sales volume exceeds $5,000 per month for three consecutive months in an area with an excess population, you are given first option to purchase an additional franchise for that area. The fee equals the same amount as the initial franchise fee, and you pay for it under the same terms.

Although Chem-Dry does not charge a percentage-based royalty or advertising fee (substituting a fixed monthly payment), it clearly seeks to capitalize on your growth with its strict territory controls.

Chem-Dry also requires you to buy its patented cleaning chemicals. It earns a 40 percent profit margin on the chemicals, but this is reasonable since it is Chem-Dry's unique product that offers you a competitive advantage.

How Much It Costs

More than offsetting its territory rules are Chem-Dry's low start-up costs, which are the following:

Paid to Chem-Dry

$ 7,600	Franchise fee
2,300	Advertising, chemical, and equipment package
$ 9,900	Total required by Chem-Dry/Harris Research
3,995	*Optional* water damage extraction package
4,050	*Optional* drapery and upholstery cleaning package
2,495	*Optional* computer software (about $6,000 for hardware and software turnkey system)

Start-Up Expenses

$ 5,000	Vehicle, telephone deposit, working capital, licenses. This is Chem-Dry's estimate.

$14,900 to $28,945   Total initial investment range

The actual range will vary because you probably will incur additional expenses that Chem-Dry does not mention. Chem-Dry managers remind buyers that they need only start with the basic package and their start-up expenses. You can add the options later as your business grows and pay for them out of cash flow. Chem-Dry divides the start-up expenses in one way, but does not include the cost of renting commercial space or higher than estimated costs.

Listed below is a somewhat different range of start-up costs as compared to Chem-Dry's estimates:

	Chem-Dry	**Scenario #2**
Vehicle purchase	$1,500	$2,000[a]
Vehicle insurance	200	500[b]
Business phone deposit	100	350[c]
Business licenses	100	200[d]
Working capital	2,000	3,000[e]
Insurance premiums	100	150[f]
Legal/accounting fees	500	1,000[g]
Training travel, etc.	500	1,000[h]
Commercial space	0	1,000[i]
Total	$5,000	$9,200

Notes:

a. If you already own a van, station wagon, or truck, you can eliminate this expense.

b. Varies with driving record. This expense should be considered a down payment on commercial vehicle insurance. Fund the rest from cash flow.

c. $100 is far too low for even a residential phone deposit and installation expenses in most of the country.

d. Even many small cities charge $100 or more. Large cities may charge far more.

e. Depends on whether or not another family member keeps working for a full-time, adequate income while you start the Chem-Dry business. If you and your spouse start the franchise together, give yourself a much heftier financial cushion of at least three months' living expenses for your necessities—home mortgage, car payments and insurance, food and clothing, etc.

f. Soaring costs all over the country for liability, business contents, and the like, make this figure more reasonable.

g. You really should have a competent attorney or accountant review the franchise contract and help with negotiations.

h. Chem-Dry pays for the training, but as usual you pay for your transportation and room and board for the two-day training session. The session is *not* required. You can buy a $200 set of videotapes and try to teach yourself, but self-training is not recommended by the author or by Chem-Dry. The $1,000 estimate may be high if you live close to Chem-Dry's California headquarters, but may be low if you and a manager or spouse fly from the East to the West Coast.

i. Scenario #2 includes this amount for commercial space rental or leasehold improvements if you are compelled by zoning restrictions or space limitations to take this step. If possible, start from your home and save this expense.

A more sensible range for your total investment would therefore fall between $19,100 and $25,000, which is still a very reasonable figure for this business.

Deferred Payments

Fortunately, Chem-Dry helps you with a very liberal, interest-free payment plan for two-thirds (67%) of the required initial payments. Of the $9,900 total for the fee and package, you must pay $3,300 down, but you can take up to 60 months to pay the remaining $6,600, or $110 per month.

Chem-Dry adds another benefit as well. Your monthly franchise fee equals just $104—no percentage royalties or ad fees—regardless of how much money you earn for two years after you buy the franchise. This very beneficial royalty structure goes a long way to help you start your business and keep your expenses low. The fee cannot be increased, except for an increase based on the government's official cost-of-living index, which the company reviews annually. Looking back, the fee has increased since 1978 from as low as approximately $17 per month to its current level, but it has only increased 4% between 1986 and 1989.

What You Get

In exchange for the franchise fee and the package, you get the territory rights described above, a complete equipment and start-up package (equipment is shipped freight free, another savings), five days of training, semi-annual seminars, regional meetings and annual conference, on-going telephone and newsletter support, and so forth. In the materials package, you receive enough supplies to clean a minimum of $15,000 worth of carpet, almost enough to recoup your initial investment.

How Much Can You Make?

Chem-Dry does not publish earnings estimates, but you can talk to successful franchisees, and they can give you a clear idea of how much you can expect to earn. The business, like most services, is labor-intensive and has very low materials and overhead costs. Therefore, you need to consider how much you want to earn per hour for your labor and how much net profit margin or percentage you wish to make to decide whether Chem-Dry is a satisfactory investment for you.

You earn income by charging by the square foot for your service. Depending on the competition's intensity, your price per square foot may range from as low as 10 cents (for major commercial projects) to as high as 25 cents, with 16 cents to 18 cents considered an average range. Chem-Dry does not determine your prices, but it does advise on how best to set your prices. On this basis, you would charge between $240 and $270 for an average 1,500 square foot home with wall-to-wall carpet. In competitive areas or during peak seasons, you may have to charge less.

Chem-Dry managers say that an average crew can clean four 1,000-square-foot homes per day, for which they earn gross sales of $720 per day ($180 times four homes). Even better, Chem-Dry franchisees report that they receive net margins of 40 to 60% *after* all expenses, which include labor. If your crew is busy six days per week, you can earn a gross income of about $225,000 and a net income (before taxes) of between $89,900 and $135,000. Not bad at all for a family business!

The many competitors in this business, including several other excellent franchises, could drive down your prices. You may also have to offer many special discounts, seasonal promotions, and the like, especially when you compete for residential businesses. Most Chem-Dry franchisees learn that selling their services to commercial establishments (apartment management companies, commercial building owners and cleaning companies, real estate management companies, etc.) enables them to do more volume work in less time than residential work.

At first, this estimate may seem an unreasonably high expectation. Chem-Dry's existing franchisees report that reaching these levels takes from two to five years. For example, Golden State Chem-Dry soared from $12,572 gross sales in 1981 to $359,554 in 1986, a very successful growth record. In 1986, it was a Top 10 franchisee, but by 1989, it had dropped out of the Top 20, although its sales had continued to increase steadily.

P&G Chem-Dry, the oldest Chem-Dry franchise and the top franchise for 1986, exceeded $1 million in total sales during its first nine years, an average of about $111,000 per year. Moreover, P&G took only three years to reach a two-million-dollar total, with an average of $333,000 per year between 1987 and 1989.

Good Profits and Strong Equity

With 30 to 60 percent net profit margins, you can easily build annual net profits ranging from $25,000 to $100,00 over a period of time. Perhaps more importantly, Chem-Dry is one franchise in which you can build substantial equity. Some Chem-Dry franchises have sold for as much as $375,000, with an average exceeding $100,000.

These figures mean that you can earn ROIs, figured in several ways, in the hundreds of percent in just three to five years. Not bad at all for cleaning carpets!

Furthermore, Chem-Dry/Harris Research is a financially strong, but very tightly managed, company. It spends substantial amounts of money on research and new product development, and it plans to continue its technological leadership. This will help ensure a franchisee's future success.

DURACLEAN INTERNATIONAL

Duraclean International
2151 Waukegan Road
Deerfield, IL 60015
(708) 945-2000

Duraclean is one of the oldest, most profitable, and best-established carpet and upholstery cleaning franchises in the country. During 1989, Duraclean had more than 600 active franchises in the U.S. and Canada, as well as in 17 countries overseas. It has been in business since 1930 and is one of the oldest franchises in continuous and successful existence. Ownership of the parent company remains in the founding family, and the son of the founder, Irl H. Marshall, now runs the company.

Duraclean encourages its franchises to appeal both to commercial and residential markets, with a heavy concentration at first on cooperative retailer prospects. These are service businesses that offer complementary services with whom you can share leads to new business.

How Much It Costs

Duraclean is included in this chapter because the portion of its total package cost allocated to franchise fees is less than $10,000. Most of the cost of each of the company's three packages is accounted for by equipment, materials, and supplies.

Duraclean offers three different franchise packages: Freedom Franchise; Advantage Franchise; and Contract Management Franchise.

Freedom Franchise. This franchise enables a dealer to provide carpet and rug cleaning, furniture cleaning, deep-suction vacuuming, stain/soil repellent and removal, soil retarding, and static electricity control services. You receive $5,400 worth of equipment, tools, supplies, and accessories, including the portable Extractovactor II carpet cleaner, the Duralizer high-suction vacuum, and a Spraymaster II sprayer with Durashield Plus for stain removal, static control, and soil retardation.

The standard dealership costs $10,900, but can be financed with a down payment of $3,900. You make $177 per month payments for 60 months on the difference, for total outlays of $14,520. The annual percentage rate for all three packages is 17.9 percent.

Advantage Franchise. To the Freedom Franchise, this franchise adds a Fabricrafter, a machine to provide an additional service for on-location drapery cleaning, plus an "Automatic" Extractovator for carpet cleaning. The latter piece of machinery is automatic and lends itself to both commercial and residential carpet cleaning, so it can be an important addition to the services you offer. This franchise equipment package is oriented more towards the full-time, best-efforts business and is worth $11,600.

The franchise costs $19,800, which can be financed for $6,900 down and with monthly payments of $378 for 48 months, for a total cost of $25,044.

Contract Management Franchise. This franchise is designed to capture the professional maintenance service market. As a Contract Management franchisee, you will offer cleaning maintenance service to building owners, managers, and tenants. The contracts include various services for systematic cleaning and maintenance, as well as related services that may be performed project by project. This franchise offers individuals with management skills a system to capture a meaningful share of this growth market.

The franchise includes training, equipment, chemicals, and business-building materials for an investment cost of $22,800. You can make a $9,900 down payment with financing of minimum payments of $377 for 48 months. On this basis, the total franchise cost would equal $27,996, but this amount does not include the cost of buying or leasing a van.

Duraclean does provide decals for your van as part of the package, but your vehicle must also have the approved colors. This could lead to an additional auto painting cost.

You can expect the van to cost between $10,000 and $15,000, with down payments in the $1,000 to $2,000 range. If you lease the van, your payments may range from $200 to $275 per month. Duraclean does help you to make arrangements both for the van and the equipment leasing, but does not lease anything itself. Nor does it receive any income from the leasing companies.

Additional Payments and Costs

Duraclean does not assess a royalty per se, but does require monthly payments under a Duraclean Cooperative Assistance Program. The amount of these payments varies according to your gross biweekly income. The biweekly payment schedule is as follows:

- $67.00 minimum on gross receipts of up to $520;
- Plus 8 percent more of your gross receipts from $520 to $1,410 ($41.80 to $71.20 more);
- Plus 6 percent of receipts from $1,410 to $3,450 ($84.80 to $122.40 more);
- Plus 2 percent of anything over $3,450.

The initial payment percentage is fairly steep (12.9 percent), but you get to keep more of what you earn as you grow, which is an incentive to encourage rapid growth.

Additional required payments include the following: workers' compensation insurance, employer's liability and comprehensive liability, as well as commercial automotive insurances.

Be careful about your van. Some towns and counties do not allow you to park a commercial van in front of your house, so you may need to consider paying for alternative parking.

You will also face the usual start-up expenses for a business telephone, supplies, office equipment, and the like, but you can keep your overhead to a minimum by working out of your home.

Duraclean also requires you to buy at least five machines and 12 types of chemicals, for which there are no alternate sources of supply. You can buy the equipment new from Duraclean, but you may be able to buy some used Duraclean equipment from other franchises. The prices for the new equipment that you may add to your franchise as you grow are listed below:

Duravan Cleaning System	$8,995
Fabricrafter	4,878
Automatic Extractovator	3,988
Duralizer II	522
Spraymaster II	209

All in all, Duraclean's up-front payments are higher than some other cleaning franchises, but the reputation, history, and support Duraclean provides makes the franchise well worth the cost.

What You Get

You receive extensive training, including six days of classroom training and at least two days of on-the-job training with an existing franchisee. Duraclean saves you a substantial amount of money by paying room and board expenses for you, your spouse, and any partners. It also pays for one round-trip airline ticket to Chicago or a car mileage allowance of up to 21 cents per mile up to the value of the air fare. You have to pay only for your spouse's and any employee's tickets.

You also get the usual range of operations manuals, business management manuals, sales and advertising literature, business builders, and the like. As part of its marketing plan, Duraclean emphasizes a 'fast start' mailing of 2,000 letters, and it pays for the bulk mail postage.

The company also maintains field support staff, regional managers, group insurance programs for dealers, and an advisory committee of dealers, which is made up of dealers elected by franchisees and dealers appointed by Duraclean. The committee meets twice a year to discuss trends and new initiatives.

Duraclean's support package is one of the most extensive and well-managed in the cleaning business.

How Much Can You Make?

Although it does not provide specific earnings projections, Duraclean is far more open about how much you can make than most franchises. The exhibit printed at the end of this section shows the average price charged and gross profits realized as has been reported to Duraclean by it own dealers. The gross profit margins range from a high of 92.0 percent for rental of an air mover to help dry out water-damaged areas to a low of 46.4 percent for cleaning residential draperies. Most services produce gross profits in the 62 percent to 78 percent range. These are very high profit margins. The gross profits already include the cost of labor at $7 per hour, the cost of the Cooperative Assistance Program, and materials costs. You need only to subtract your overhead costs—usually 20 to 30 percent—to determine your net pre-tax profit of 37 to 55 percent on each job.

Duraclean's dealers say that they usually earn their revenues from the following mix of services: 55 percent from carpet cleaning; 30 percent from upholstery cleaning; 10 percent from on-location drapery cleaning; and 5 percent from water-damage restoration. Note that the water-damage restoration services appear to be the most profitable of the 22 services that you can offer through the franchise.

Dealers also report that they usually charge 15 to 18 cents per square foot for residential carpet cleaning, and slightly less for large commercial jobs on which they must submit bids. One dealer reported that, on a 4,093 square foot job, he won the bid for 14.5 cents per foot, with a total bid of $593.49 plus an extra charge for soil retarding service. His total costs were $184.25 and included costs for chemicals, labor, fuel, and meals. He made a 69 percent gross profit of $409.24. The total time involved was about five

Duraclean Franchises' Reported Actual Gross Profits by Service[a]

Service/Conditions	Price Charged	Gross Profit Amount	Gross Profit Percentage (%)
Fabricrafter			
500 sq. ft. carpet	$ 85.00	$63.71	74.9
Extractovator			
500 sq. ft. carpet	100.00	73.43	73.4
Duravan Service			
500 sq. ft. carpet	85.00	66.61	78.4
Water Damage			
Emergency call (1 hr.)	31.15	21.66	69.5
Water extraction	40.68	30.43	74.8
Air mover rental	16.06	14.78	92.0

a. These figures show the average price and gross profits for six services that Duraclean franchisees perform, as the franchisees themselves have reported the results.

hours, slightly longer than average for an hourly gross profit of about $77 per hour. And Duraclean says that there are numerous additional services you can offer that take little or no extra time, but which add significant profits.

Duraclean dealers also report that their advertising tends to be very effective, bringing in an average of $18 to $19 in business for every dollar spent on advertising.

It's clear that if you work steadily in this business, you can easily recoup your investment during the first year. If you lease equipment and your van and also finance your franchise payment, your monthly debt service will be steep. Under these conditions, your ROI will not be in the hundreds of percent for the first year or two, but your return on your actual cash expenditure should be that high.

The cleaning franchise business is very, very competitive, so you do best to go with the leaders. Duraclean has long been one of them and promises to remain a leader for years to come.

SUBWAY SANDWICHES & SALADS

Subway World Headquarters
Doctor's Associates Inc.
325 Bic Drive
Milford, CT 06460
(800) 888-4848, toll-free USA and Canada
0-800-89-1183, toll-free United Kingdom
(203) 877-4281, Offices
(203) 878-7493, FAX

Subway® Sandwiches & Salads is the fastest growing fast-food franchise in the country, increasing its number of shops by more than 1,000 units during 1988. It exceeded 3,800 franchises in October, 1989, and the parent company, Doctor's Associates, has a very ambitious goal of reaching 8,000 franchises by 1995. It plans to do in less than 10 years what it took McDonald's almost 20 years to accomplish. Perhaps most important to potential investors, Subway's existing stores steadily increased their sales 9 percent during 1989; total store volume was an astounding $600 million, more than quadruple the total during 1987.

Subway has several distinct advantages over competing fast-food franchises and is backed by a very aggressive regional development marketing concept:

Very low franchise fee. It costs just $7,500 for a store and only $1,000 more for each additional store. This means that you can add stores and buy larger territories at minimal up-front cost. Of course, with this high growth rate, Subway emphasizes the sale and start-up of multiple unit operations.

Single-unit availability. Only half of all Subway franchisees buy multiple units, so it remains a good way for the "little guy" to get into a very promising cash business.

Low start-up costs. The total initial investment equals about $65,000, but Subway will lease $22,000 worth of equipment with a minimum $2,500 down payment. Therefore, your actual cash payments amount, at most, to about $38,000, or they can be as low as you make them, depending on your credit and borrowing power. You could acquire a similar-type sandwich shop without the Subway name for a much smaller down payment, but your ROI may not be as great.

Good product mix. As people tire of burgers, they turn back to sandwiches, and Subway offers a product line of sandwiches, salads, and combinations that appeals to many demographic groups.

Subway currently has franchises in all 50 states, and in Canada, Puerto Rico, the Bahamas, Bahrain, and Australia. Its products are billed as "The Fresh Alternative" to burger and fried-food franchises because each Subway shop bakes its own (frozen) bread. Each store is about 1,000 square feet and seats 24 or fewer people. Between 85 and 95 percent of the business is take-out. Most stores are located in strip shopping centers, at which the rent is cheaper than at large malls and the take-out parking is ample. Subway keeps its operating overhead low. It takes, at most, two employees to run any given store at peak times. Moreover, there is no cooking or frying on the premises, with the exception of bread-baking. And Subway's decor is no-frills, designed to encourage people to come in quickly and leave just as quickly. Its menu includes 18 items, although just two—the Subway Club and the BMT (everything combo)—make up its sales leaders. Customers usually are from the 18- to 35-year-old, blue collar, or student groups.

How It Works

Subway has just one franchise program: an individually owned shop. You buy one franchise for one relatively small area; and you have the option of buying another Subway within a few miles of your location.

Subway franchise sales, however, are a different matter. Most are handled by *development agents,* the company's term for franchise brokers. These regional agents, usually existing franchisees with some years of experience, sell the franchises, help find sites, give on-site and grand opening assistance and training, and act as Subway's technical or operational area representatives. The agents, in turn, are paid very well, *one-half* of the franchise fee, or $3,750 minimum for each new shop they sell. They also collect one-third of Subway's fairly high 8 percent royalty. Development agents can easily become very rich selling franchises and collecting royalties, but they also must make sure you succeed since so much of their continuing income depends on the royalties that you and other franchisees pay. The incentive system is very powerful.

On the one hand, the system encourages the selling of large numbers of franchises very quickly; on the other, it discourages poor-quality franchises by linking the agents' long-term successes to your own. It is a very smart and very lucrative system, if played right. In late 1989, Subway had development agents in forty-two states, Puerto Rico, Canada, and Australia.

Another strong Subway advantage is that the initial term for the agreement is a very long 20 years, with another 20-year renewal period offered at no additional fee. This creates a good resale value for a Subway franchise. If you had only two years left in a five-year agreement for a franchise, you would be hard pressed to find a buyer who would pay you a high price without demanding a new agreement with the franchisor. If you had 15 years left in your agreement, however, a buyer would quickly realize that this period of time is far longer than most franchises offer and would therefore see your shop as having that much more value.

Litigation and Court Action

Subway has had a few run-ins with franchisees in the courts and through arbitration hearings. None of the court actions have involved any criminal allegations. One such proceeding concerned over-eager development agents. Subway has won judgments and awards against recalcitrant franchisees in several cases, and it has bought back several franchises from failing franchisees. Subway has also paid settlements ranging from about $10,000 to as high as $31,500. All in all, however, you need not consider any of these cases as arguments against buying a Subway franchise, for most involved relatively petty problems.

Nonetheless, be aware that Subway's development agents are independent contractors and therefore are in no way directly responsible to the parent company. Also be careful of overzealous agents who even hint at promises of large incomes or sums of money. Most states with franchise laws prohibit the making of such promises and discussions.

How Much It Costs

The costs should in no way discourage you from looking into a Subway franchise, for they are low and the returns can be very high. As noted previously, the franchise costs $7,500 for one unit and $1,000 for each additional unit, if you are the operating franchisee.

Territory Determinations

Subway uses the Arbitron Rating Company's market breakdown to determine its territories. Arbitron is the company that provides most of the market ratings for local radio stations. Subway intends to set up one store for every 30,000 population within a specific Arbitron market.

Here's another key that is indicative of Subway's grand plan. To compete with the hamburger chain giants, Subway plans to adjust the number of stores that can be opened in each target market so that the total *equals* the number of units operated by the largest fast-food chain in that Arbitron market. For example, suppose McDonald's had five shops in one market with 29,500 population; Subway will eventually want to open five stores in the same area. This is a very aggressive position. Fortunately, however, Subway has much lower operating expenses than a hamburger franchise so that you can make a profit with far fewer customers.

Royalties and Fees

Subway franchisees pay 8 percent royalties *each week* on gross sales of everything sold in the shop. You pay an additional 2.5 percent advertising fee, which is also payable weekly. The ad fee is managed by an advertising fund board of directors that is made up of ten current store owners. The board sets all advertising policies and procedures. Between 70 and 80 percent of the fees you must pay are spent in your market area, while the rest goes for national advertising and development.

Other Start-Up Expenses

In addition to the franchise fees, you must be concerned with the following expenses:

Location rent. This expense is estimated between $500 and $3,000 per month, depending on location.

Insurance. You are required to have $1 million in comprehensive liability insurance and any additional insurance required in your commercial lease. Subway has a group policy that it offers to franchisees, but you do not have to buy it. Subway also makes available group medical coverage for you and your employees, but this, too, is optional. Subway receives a 2 percent rebate for the medical insurance premiums as a sales commission.

Equipment leasing. Subway may execute, for qualified franchisees, equipment leases worth between $17,000 and $22,000. On this basis, your payments would be between $450 and $600 per month plus additional state sales tax (a notable hidden expense) for a term of 60 months. For all franchisees, the lease downpayment is $2,500, half of what it was in 1987. Of course, you need an equipment package for each store, so the lowered down payment significantly reduces your up-front cash outlays for second and subsequent stores.

Subway estimates that the average unit now costs $65,000 for all start-up expenses, with a range between $37,900 for a very small unit to $79,000 for a larger one.

Required Purchases and Approvals

In addition to these costs, the franchise agreement requires you to make several approved purchases, the most important of which includes the Subway mural from Gordon Micunis Interiors. Subway does not make any money from this purchase.

You must also lease your location from the parent company. This is very different from most franchises. Subway values its locations highly—as it should. Subway officials or agents will arrange a lease in the company's name, and the company then subleases the location to you at cost and with no profit. These purchases represent between 4 and 8 percent of the start-up costs and between 5 and 12 percent of your operating expenses.

You must buy your bread-baking equipment and frozen bread dough from only the approved suppliers of each. Other supplies and materials must bear the Subway trademark, and the vendors must meet Subway's quality-control standards if you choose a source other than those the company recommends on its vendor lists.

How Much Can You Make

It is difficult to figure out how much you can make with a Subway shop. The company says that, typically, a unit pays back its original investment in one to two years—a very good payback. In 1988, Subway was ranked as the most profitable of *Venture's* Top 100 most profitable franchises.

Subway also notes that net profits tend to be typical for the restaurant industry and are in the 20 percent range. This is probably very conservative for a successful restaurant, especially one like Subway that operates on an all-cash basis.

You can roughly figure out what you can expect your expenses to be from the following guidelines:

Franchise and ad fees	10.5%
Labor and payroll	20.0% (one-third lower than the average)
Food and supplies	33.0%
Rent and utilities	7.0%
Overhead	5.0%
Pre-tax profit	24.5%

For example, if your rent and utilities total $1,000 per month, you should gross $14,250 per month and take home a pre-tax profit of about $3,200 per month to make it worthwhile. Your costs for second and subsequent units will be lower, so your profits should be several percentage points higher. You could easily net $100,000 or more a year with just three Subway shops. And it's all cash, an important incentive in any food-related business.

It is true that Subway has a very aggressive growth plan, but so far its franchisees appear to be very pleased with their success. Be wary of fast-talking development agents, but consider Subway's spectacular success when you go franchise-shopping.

U-SAVE AUTO RENTAL

U-Save Auto Rental
7525 Connelley Drive
Suite A
Hanover, MD 21076
(800) 272-U-SAV (8728)
(301) 760-4390

U-Save Auto Rental has been listed as one of the most 100 profitable franchises by *Venture* magazine and, for several years, as one of the fastest growing privately held companies by *Inc.* magazine. This auto rental franchise has aimed its appeal directly at, and only to, existing independent automobile dealerships. By and large, these are used car dealerships. U-Save has positioned itself as a new profit center for a used car dealer who is able to use some of his idle inventory as rental cars. In addition, the franchisor is also encouraged to rent both new and used cars for a customer's one-stop shopping approach. U-Save also emphasizes a professional approach in a market that is known for other franchises with cute names, i.e., Ugly Duckling and Rent-A-Wreck.

By late 1989, U-Save had almost 500 franchises in 44 states, with a heavy concentration of these franchises in small cities. U-Save is built on the concept of the utilization of regional and state managers, usually current or former used car dealers or insurance salespeople who are able to communicate easily with their prospects.

U-Save's most important advantage for its franchisees is the following: inexpensive insurance coverage for rental cars, which is an increasingly expensive and difficult chore for any independent rental agency. U-Save arranges the insurance coverage and profits from the administration of the insurance program. It is very up-front about this interest. It has also added a complete support program: a national toll-free reservation system, special car financing programs, new car fleet discounts, car maintenance discounts, and risk reduction procedures that help prevent rental car theft and fraud.

How It Works and How Much It Costs

The maximum initial franchise fee is $17,500, but this amount varies according to population in the area, potential market, marketing demographics, the variety of industrial and commercial travel, seasonality of the operation, number of cars, and the like. The franchisor also charges a minimum flat *monthly* royalty fee of $160 per vehicle for up to 10 cars, $12.50 per month for the 11th through 20th cars, and $10 per month for the 21st and additional vehicles. There are no percentage of gross sales to pay, just the per car fees.

According to company estimates, your total initial investment for a 10-car fleet should range from $40,000 to $80,000, although U-Save adds the caveat—the same one this author would add—that these ranges do not necessarily represent your total investment.

Although it does not do so at this time, U-Save reserves the right to start an advertising fund and charge a 2 percent monthly fee. It does require franchisees to buy an alphabetic listing in a Yellow Pages directory and encourages them to buy display ads in these Yellow Pages as well.

You have a six-month option after you buy your first U-Save franchise to reserve a second franchise territory next to your first one. The option costs $500. If you buy the second territory, the option payment is applied to the total fee.

Although U-Save has never done so, its contract reserves the right to increase franchise fees once a year on the basis of the national Consumer Price Index for All Urban Consumers (CPI-U).

U-Save does not get involved in lease negotiations, remodeling, and rent or leases of fixtures and equipment, with the exception of signage.

U-Save also charges an $8 per reservation fee for each reservation it makes on behalf of your franchise. Any reservation made through a travel agency and/or the U-Save toll-free number is charged at the 10 to 12.5 percent travel agency commission's rates. The $8 fee is waived if the customer does not appear or is unqualified to rent the car.

Total Initial Investment

The table on the following page lists a range of anticipated start-up costs. Table statistics combine U-Save's estimates and the author's additional estimated costs for those categories for which U-Save does not give specific estimates.

	Minimum	Maximum
Franchise fee	$ 5,000	$17,500
Inventory[a]	15,000	50,000
Insurance[b]	690	690
Signage[c]	500	1,000
Real estate leases[d]	400	1,800
Equipment[e]	2,000	3,000
Telephone deposits	50	350
Working capital[f]	5,000	8,000
Miscellaneous	1,000	2,000
Total Estimate	$29,640	$84,340

a. Based on five-car minimum, with passenger cars 3- to 6-years-old.
b. Insurance deposit as described in U-Save's own franchise insurance program.
c. Franchise company provides required signage as part of the franchise fee, but you must pay for shipment and for any additional signs you want. The figures are the author's estimates.
d. Deposits for 200 to 400 square feet of office space for non-dealer franchises. If you are an existing auto dealer, you may have enough space and so may avoid this costs.
e. $2,000 is U-Save's estimate.
f. Initial payroll, your salary, business supplies, and additional costs for one to two months. $5,000 is U-Save's estimate.

You can easily see why an existing auto dealer is attracted to this franchise as compared to an individual. Still, for all prospective buyers, the costs are relatively low as compared to any new car rental franchise.

In the past, U-Save required franchisees to manage their franchise, but in late 1989, U-Save's executives said they were "taking a different look towards investors today and were in the process of changing its participation requirements." By early to mid-1990, therefore, U-Save will begin to encourage investor-owners and, perhaps, master franchisees.

One problem with U-Save is the short term of the initial agreement. It lasts just three years, and the renewal terms can be stiff; you must abide by any changes in royalty fees, changes in territory size, increases or actual imposition of advertising fees, and all other new terms and conditions in the then-current agreement. However, there is no renewal fee, and you can terminate the franchise very easily with just 90-days' notice.

U-Save does take your obligations seriously. Although it had sold almost 500 franchises by the end of 1989, it had terminated a large number of them (219) for failure to pay monies owed to the company: 69 during 1986, 72 during 1987, and 78 during 1988. On the plus side, no franchisees in good standing have been refused renewal, and the franchisor has not bought any franchises from its owners. This means that the franchisor is not interested in taking over your successful operation or in running its own agencies, unlike many major companies, including Hertz and Avis.

How Much Can You Make?

Auto dealers find car rentals a good profit center for several reasons:

- Start-up with little or no added operating expense. Your existing staff can be trained as rental agents, and you need not add much, if anything, to your facilities, except signage and a counter.
- Knowledge of buying, maintaining, and selling cars help you reduce costs and build profits.

Non-dealer franchisees can find good business and commercial markets in rentals through the following:

- Replacement rentals for insurance clients
- Replacement rentals for families whose cars are in the shop
- Individuals or businesspeople taking trips
- Families needing an occasional second car
- Service stations, body shops, repair garages, specialty shops, and other automotive service-related facilities
- Military personnel on leave
- Travel agencies and bureaus

The key to any auto rental franchise is this—strong cash flow, but high expenses for insurance and maintenance, with the latter offset by short (usually three-year) depreciation periods. It would appear that you can easily earn a 25 to 35 percent net pre-tax profit with a U-Save franchise. Based on an admittedly conservative average of 13 cars per agency rented 70% of the time at $25 per day, you can gross about $67,500 and net between $20,250 and $30,000. This figure does not include any income from insurance coverage fees and ancillary sales.

Your high depreciation rates on your rental cars will help you offset your tax obligations in your dealership. This is why used car and independent auto dealers find this franchise so attractive. For a relatively low investment, most of which they can probably borrow, they can easily double their money in two years, plus put to use their idle assets—cars sitting in their lots and underutilized employees.

Note, however, that U-Save's President Joseph Eikenberg insists that the company makes no earnings claims. Even so, U-Save Auto Rental appears to offer a very profitable sideline business for existing used car and independent auto dealers.

MR. ROOTER

Mr. Rooter Corporation
P.O. Box 3146
Waco, TX 76707
(800) 950-8003
(817) 755-0055

Until May, 1989, Mr. Rooter was a small franchise that was struggling along and growing very slowly. Faced with some financial difficulties at this time, the founders sold a large percentage of their stock to one of the most dynamic individuals in franchising—Don Dwyer, founder of Rainbow International, Inc. Since then, Mr. Rooter has become the centerpiece in Dwyer's plan to have seven companies with 10,000 franchisees worldwide in the service industry by 1996. Dwyer heads two other franchises, both of which are discussed in this book: Rainbow International, with some 2,000 franchisees in late 1989, and Worldwide Refinishing Systems.

Mr. Rooter is a plumbing, sewer, drain, pipe, and septic tank cleaning service for homes and commercial buildings. You buy the cleaning equipment from Mr. Rooter, learn its marketing procedures and operations, and provide the service. You have three ways of charging for your service: hourly rate; per call charge; or with annual contracts for businesses such as restaurants that need your services often.

Dwyer bought approximately 32 percent of Mr. Rooter's stock, with an option to buy another 38 percent of the stock at set prices. He now heads franchise marketing and support, while Mr. Rooter's current management team handles the technical, equipment, and distribution aspects of the drain cleaning business.

Dwyer's plan is to create a vertically integrated cleaning franchise empire that covers the world. And he seems to be making strong headway towards this goal as he searches for new service franchises to purchase. Mr. Rooter executives say that in late 1989 they were opening six new Mr. Rooter franchises per month. Management plans to accelerate this pace up to 15 per month during 1990. Its goal is to have between 750 and 1,000 Mr. Rooter franchises within five years.

Although a franchisee faces very tough competition from Roto-Rooter® household name and decades-long reputation, Mr. Rooter offers an inexpensive and very profitable opportunity for people who don't mind getting their hands dirty.

If you consider becoming a Mr. Rooter franchisee, remember to be careful and to make the necessary checks; Dwyer's rapid growth plans and earlier successes with Rainbow International shows that he knows how to sell and market franchises, but still you run the risk, however small, of getting caught up in Dwyer's marketing hyperbole. It appears that Dwyer's executives understand the importance of franchisee training and support, but every rapidly growing company faces stress and strain as it grows. It is therefore likely that Mr. Rooter will face them, too. This does not mean that you should look elsewhere in considering a franchise to buy; it does mean, however, that you should investigate with care any signs which indicate that Mr. Rooter cannot provide you with the support you need to succeed.

How Much It Costs

The franchise fee is a $10,000 minimum for 100,000 population. Check to ensure that your territory includes mostly affluent or middle-class house-holds who can afford your services and many restaurants and commercial establishments as well, for they usually have a relatively high frequency of grease and/or sewage backups. Since these establishments will make up the bulk of your business, it's important that you analyze your territory and its boundaries before you buy.

You can add 1,000 population for $100, or Mr. Rooter will charge you $100 for each additional 1,000 population group in the territory it offers you.

Mr. Rooter may finance up to half the franchise fee if you have good credit and under various circumstances. The company charges a low 12 percent per year interest rate, with minimum weekly payments of $60.

You pay a reasonable 6 percent royalty on *weekly* gross sales, or a minimum royalty of 30 cents for each 1,000 of population, or a minimum of $30 per week ($1,560 per year). You must also pay a 2 percent advertising fee, and you must buy at least a one-quarter-page Yellow Pages ad. As Mr. Rooter franchises grow in your region, the company reserves the right to establish a regional cooperative advertising program to which you may be required to contribute up to 2 percent of your gross sales as well. By late 1989, however, Mr. Rooter had not established any regional co-op programs.

Total Start-Up Costs

Mr. Rooter gives an estimated start-up cost of about $18,422, which in-cludes enough equipment for one truck or van. However, the company ac-knowledges in its UFOC (Uniform Franchising Offering Circulars) that the stated amount does not make up all of your initial investment.

If you don't already own a plumbing or drain cleaning service, Mr. Rooter recommends that you start your business from your home and work with your spouse. Under these conditions, you will not have to rent warehouse or office space, and you will not need to hire an assistant.

Category	Low End	High End
Franchise fee[a]	$10,000	$15,000
Cable Jet® equipment[b]	4,800	10,000
Motor vehicle[c]	0	16,000
Inventory[d]	500	1,000
Security deposits[e]	0	500
Miscellaneous	400	1,000
Travel training[f]	1,000	1,500
Working capital[g]	5,000	15,000
Total	$21,700	$60,000

a. Author's estimate at high end is for 150,000 population.

b. $6,422 to equip one truck seems a reasonable figure.

c. If you own a truck or van, you will not spend anything. If you need to buy a vehicle, a truck will cost you between $10,000 to $15,000, and a van from $12,000 to $16,000. Your actual cash outlay could be as low as a $1,000 down payment on a van or truck. Moreover, you might opt to lease a vehicle and reduce your up-front cash expenditures. With the latter plans, you would finance your vehicle from your cash flow and weekly sales.

d. Mr. Rooter notes that many franchises already own plumbing firms or home repair companies, and so they may not incur these costs.

e. Business telephone line deposits.

f. Travel expenses for training are not included in the fee.

g. Low end for those with existing business who must pay additional workers; the high end is for those who must have living expenses met for the first three to six months.

Note: If you finance half of your franchise fee and make a down payment on or lease your truck and if your spouse works with you, you may reduce your up-front cash expenses to as low as $12,500. This is possible if you start small, or if you already own an existing plumbing service.

What You Get

The term of the agreement is for 10 years, with one option to renew for an additional 10-year term *without* your paying another franchise fee. For a renewal, you do have to sign a new agreement and follow the terms and conditions currently in effect, but you save at least $10,000.

For your franchise fee, you receive an exclusive territory of at least 100,000 people. You also receive an option to acquire one or more additional territories within your area at negotiable franchise fees. And you receive the right to use Mr. Rooter trademarks, systems, logos, and also the right to buy and use Mr. Rooter's exclusive equipment package.

The basic equipment includes the Cable Jet™ high-pressure pipe cleaner and various add-ons for grease removal and other tough jobs. Mr. Rooter also offers—and makes profits from—a product line of six models of drain cleaning equipment that it sells both to its franchisees and outside buyers through its National Power Equipment subsidiary.

You receive a five- to seven-day training program at Mr. Rooter's technical headquarters in Oklahoma City or at another franchisee's location. In addition to the training, you are also required to attend Mr. Rooter's annual convention. As noted, you must pay for your expenses to the training, as well as for the convention. You may bring two additional people to attend the training sessions for free, but you must pay for their travel and lodging expenses. If you bring employees, you must also pay their salaries while they receive training.

Mr. Rooter also provides a grand opening promotional and marketing package of advertising and direct mail materials. After start-up, however, Mr. Rooter's agreement only obligates the company to provide you with support in a general, vague way. Still, Dwyer and Rainbow International have good reputations, so one can assume that Mr. Rooter will follow their lead. Nonetheless, be sure to investigate Mr. Rooter's support programs thoroughly.

How Much Can You Make?

Mr. Rooter's executives state that the amount you can earn depends on you, your self-image, and your desires. Vice President Robert Tunmire states, "I've sold more than 500 franchises. For 95 percent of the time, people earn what they earned in their last job during the first year. If they were making $20,000 a year before they bought the franchise, that is how much they tend to make during their first year. That's the honest way for me to put it."

However, Tunmire follows with good news: "After that, their incomes tend to increase 25 to 50 percent per year until they reach the level they want to reach and at which they are comfortable. Their income level is tied to their self-image."

From a business viewpoint, you can charge from $35 to $100 for each service call, depending on whether it is an easy or difficult one and whether it is a house, an apartment, a business, or a restaurant service call. If $60 per call is a reasonable average, then you must make two calls per day to earn a gross income of $31,200 (52 weeks per year, five days per week). Four calls a day, a reasonable first-year goal, would gross $62,400.

Your net profit margin varies with how much of your start-up cost you finance. If you pay cash for everything, your net margins would exceed 60 percent—perhaps even reach to as high as 80 percent. If you finance your van, your franchise fee, and your equipment, however, you can expect your annual payments to equal $3,120 for your franchise fee, $5,000 for your van (including insurance payments), and $2,500 for your equipment, giving you annual payments in excess of $10,620. If your gross income equalled $62,400, these payments would reduce your net margin by at least 17 percent and your net profit to the $25,000 per year range. These figures do not include the salary or wages you would pay a helper or your own salary.

If you control your expenses and payments, however, you can net $40 or more per job and earn about $40,000 per year, a substantial salary, and cash ROI within the first two years.

COUSTIC-GLO INTERNATIONAL INC.

Coustic-Glo International Inc.
7111 Ohms Lane
Minneapolis, MN 55435
(800) 333-8523
(612) 835-1338

Coustic-Glo is the leading franchise for the cleaning, care, and maintenance of acoustical and similar ceiling materials. The patented Coustic-Glo system offers a strong business advantage: it costs 50 to 70 percent less than the cost of replacing old acoustical ceiling tiles or installing a new ceiling. This advantage is your opportunity.

Acoustical ceilings were first installed in commercial buildings during the 1950s. They offered significant advantages to builders: they were relatively inexpensive; could be installed rapidly; and offered easy access to plumbing pipes and electrical wiring when repairs were necessary. Yet, no one thought what would happen when these ceilings aged, became dirty, or were damaged. A chemical process for cleaning acoustical ceilings was not developed until the late 1970s. Coustic-Glo has patented its cleaning process and has developed a large market for its application.

Coustic-Glo's typical customer is any business, institution, organization, hospital, office, restaurant, etc., with acoustical tile ceilings. In addition, the process works equally well on textured, blown "popcorn," vinyl, and metal ceilings, so your customers can be found in any building locations with these types of ceilings as well.

By late 1989, Coustic-Glo had about 200 franchises, with operations in almost all states and with franchise agreements covering 17 foreign countries. Coustic-Glo's UFOC indicates that the company has experienced a very high rate of franchise closings, although this failure rate has declined since 1986. During 1988, 21 units closed, and 37 new units opened; during 1987, 36 closed, and 40 new ones opened; and during 1986, 40 closed, and 45 opened.

How Much It Costs

Territory and Fees

Coustic-Glo is a turnkey operation. Unlike many cleaning franchises, it does offer an exclusive territory, but you pay for it. The franchise fee ranges from a low of $9,750 to a maximum of $25,000. The fee depends strictly on the population of the territory you license. Your territory depends strictly on how much you are willing or able to pay. The following table gives the costs:

Population	Franchise Fee
Less than 250,000	$ 9,750
250,000 to 499,000	16,750
500,000 to 1 million	25,000
Each additional 500,000	Additional 25,000

The territory is usually a metropolitan area or county, or several counties. By late 1989, all franchisees had territories of at least 100,000 population and, perhaps, as much as 1 million. Using only population statistics to consider whether or not you are liable to succeed, however, can put you at a disadvantage if you are not careful. Fortunately, your territory rights do not depend on any minimum sales volume or market penetration.

Clearly, Coustic-Glo services, for all practical purposes, apply only to commercial or public establishments and, perhaps, apartment buildings, but not to homes or to residential consumers. Therefore, your designated area must have many buildings with acoustical ceiling tiles, preferably older buildings with ceilings that need cleaning. When you consider a territory, look into the "overhead" instead of counting heads; that is, look into the type and quality of the ceilings in the commercial establishments in your territorial area.

You might possibly also save thousands of dollars on franchise fees by selecting the right area with a smaller population, but with more business establishments.

Other Fees and Required Payments

You must also pay a continuing fee (same as a royalty) of 6 percent of gross sales per month.

You are required to buy from Coustic-Glo at least $1,000 worth of Coustic-Glo chemicals per 250,000 population per year. Not doing so can lead to the loss of your franchise.

The franchisor may also charge you the cost of accountants' fees if it audits your books and finds that you have understated your gross revenues by 2 percent or more.

You must buy general liability, product liability, personal property, automobile liability, and other insurance coverages. Coustic-Glo estimates that the cost—not including the auto coverage—will range between $800 and $1,500 per year. This is a conservative estimate. You may decide to use your personal auto insurance for auto coverage. However, if you have an accident while using your vehicle for business purposes, your insurance may not cover it. Check with your insurance agent before you decide to omit the costs for additional auto coverage.

If you sell or transfer your franchise, Coustic-Glo charges you a $2,000 administrative fee.

Additional Costs

Coustic-Glo encourages you to work out of your home, at least at first, to keep your overhead costs down. And you should be able to use your car or van; the Coustic-Glo chemicals are not dangerous or messy.

The company does estimate that you may need incidental equipment, such as ladders, cartop carriers and additional tarps, sponges and rags, at a cost of about $750. This author suggests that you double this amount to be on the safe side. And you should expect to have between $750 to $2,000 or more for working capital, which would include any living expenses you may need until you start generating a salary.

On this basis, Coustic-Glo estimates that your total start-up costs will range from $11,250 to $27,500. A more reasonable estimate would range from $12,500 to $31,250. The table below lists the cost items for these estimates:

	Range	
Cost Item	**Low**	**High**
Franchise fee	$ 9,750	$25,000
Equipment/supplies	750	750
Working capital	750	2,000
Subtotal	$11,250	$27,750
Insurance	800	1,500
Training travel	0	1,000
Miscellaneous	450	1,000
Total	$12,500	$31,250

Unlike some cleaning franchises, you are required to buy a certain amount of the company's chemicals. Expect about 7 percent of your monthly operating expenses to come from the purchase of these chemicals.

Coustic-Glo does not offer a formal training session at its headquarters. It relies instead in on-the-job instruction for a two- or three-day period with an existing franchisee/trainer in your region. You must pay your expenses, including room and board, travel, and any salaries, but your costs should not be as high for local or regional travel as they would be for any interstate travel required.

Coustic-Glo's Advantages

This franchise offers several benefits that many similar cleaning franchises do not.

- Coustic-Glo applies 15 percent of "continuing fees" for advertising, but does not charge you a fee. It also gives its franchisees an annual accounting of these efforts.
- Your territory does not depend on your achieving any sales volume, market penetration, or meeting other required goals. Some franchises will shut you down if you do not meet volume quotas. Since you must buy $1,000 or more worth of chemicals each year, however, it behooves you to work at the business. The $1,000 is a minimum and easily reached figure inasmuch as you need to gross only about $15,000 per year to use the chemicals you must purchase.
- You do not have to manage or operate the franchise personally, and you can hire manages to do so. However, they must pass the training course. Note that Coustic-Glo strongly recommends that the operator have an ownership interest.
- The initial term of the agreement is 10 years, a fairly good time period in which to build a business. You can renew for continuing five-year terms, but you must pay new franchise fees in the amounts other franchisees are paying at the time.
- Your heirs can inherit and operate the business with very little difficulty if they so choose. To do so, they are required to pay a $2,000 fee and attend a training course.
- The "no-compete" clause that prevents you from competing with Coustic-Glo in a similar business is only for one year; most are for two or more years. And it is restricted to just 25 miles from your old or existing Coustic-Glo franchise. This is not bad at all.
- You can sell your franchise under the terms of your original agreement; this provision differs significantly from most franchise contracts. Most require your buyer to pay the then-current franchise fee, or the difference between the fee you paid and the current fee, and also to fulfill all the

terms and conditions of the current agreement. Coustic-Glo simply requires a buyer to pay the $2,000 administrative/transfer fee and pass the required training program.

- Of franchises that have been terminated, Coustic-Glo states that almost all were closed for non-payment of royalties or failure to meet minimum purchase requirements. Coustic-Glo has not reacquired any franchises since 1985. The high turnover rate indicates that Coustic-Glo enforces its minimum purchase requirements very strictly.

How Much Can You Make?

Most Coustic-Glo franchisees do much of the work themselves, certainly at first. They work out of their homes and their vans or trucks, and they keep their overhead very low. Coustic-Glo estimates that most franchisees earn a 70 percent gross profit *after* labor costs, material costs (7 percent), and the 6 percent royalty. This is a very healthy profit margin.

You charge either by the hour, the job, or by the square foot. Your square foot charge averages about 55 cents, with a minimum charge for one small room. Of course, these figures are discounted sharply if you get a contract to do an entire office building or factory. Frankly, you should be able to net $25,000 to $30,000 per year from a population area of 250,000 with an average number of business establishments. With the high net profit margins, you could pay back your investment in less than a year and begin to earn a 50% ROI by the end of the second year.

You may need to hire a salesperson and crews with managers to cover the territory adequately of larger franchises. It would be difficult for you to earn a quick and good ROI if you spent $25,000 for a million-population region, but tried to service it with just one van by yourself. If you choose to buy a major territory, you should assemble the resources to put together three or four crews during the first two years of operation.

Of course, building crews and leasing vans will sharply increase your start-up costs up to around $30,000 and also reduce your net margins to the 30 percent range. However, you should expect to make gross sales of $250,000 to $500,000 within two or three years, with net incomes in the $100,000 to $150,000 range.

All in all, Coustic-Glo offers many advantages compared to some other cleaning franchises, and it offers much lower *total* start-up costs. Unlike most cleaning franchises, however, its disadvantage is that you have little repeat business—that is, you do not get to clean the same ceiling over and over again each week. You must constantly search for new customers and new applications for your products and services. Thus, Coustic-Glo, more so than others, is a sales opportunity for the person who likes to make cold calls.

MINI MAID

Mini Maid Franchising
1855 Piedmont Road
Suite 100
Marietta, GA 30066
(404) 973-3271

Mini Maid's founder, president, and CEO, Leone Ackerly, pioneered the team-cleaning concept in 1973 and began the team-cleaning service franchise business in 1976. Although some maid-service franchises have now surpassed Mini Maid in the number of franchises they have, Mini Maid remains a quality and service leader. First, its $12,500 franchise fee remains the lowest in the industry. Second, it continues to offer its unique and relatively low flat monthly royalty fee payment; no other cleaning franchise offers a flat fee. This means you get to keep a great deal more of your income as you grow. Third, it does not charge an advertising fee. Fourth, it gives its franchisees the largest territory (50,000 to 100,000 population) of any cleaning service. And fifth, it sells only to individuals, for it does not have master franchise or area development agreements.

Mini Maid had more than 150 active franchise operations in 28 states by late 1989—with a relatively slow, but controlled and well-managed growth rate. Its franchises are concentrated in the Eastern Seaboard states and in the South and Midwest. To date, no state has reached its peak number of franchises. Across the country, many excellent opportunities remain open to the individual owner. Mini Maid is not strictly oriented to management professionals who want to get out of Corporate America, like some of its competitors. And it relies on its 15-year reputation for quality and service.

Mini Maid is designed so that your business can grow fairly rapidly. Within this framework, you will need to develop one effective four-person team within the first four to six weeks of your operation, and your business will need to grow to three full teams within the first 9 to 12 months. And you should plan to add one new team each year thereafter.

Mini Maid gives licenses with only a fairly short five-year term; and you can renew for additional five-year terms. Still, you should consider that it may be more difficult to build equity in a franchise with this initial short term. Mini Maid territories generally include between 50,000 and 100,000 population, depending on the demographics. Remember that it is not the quantity, but the quality, of the population that matters. Aim for cities, counties, or suburbs with a very high percentage of affluent middle-aged working couples with or without children; it is this population group that uses a preponderant percentage of the maid services in the U.S.

How Much It Costs

As noted, the fee equals $12,500. The total up-front investment ranges from $18,000 to $25,000, also among the lowest in the industry. This amount does include a down payment on a required station wagon or mini-van, which must be painted in Mini Maid's pale blue color. If you have a station wagon or van, you may be able to use Mini Maid's decals and signage. You will also need auto insurance, a business phone line, and an answering service or someone to answer the phone during business hours—*not* an answering machine.

Mini Maid originated the flat monthly royalty payments. It begins at $350 per month and increases a small amount each year. Moreover, the franchisor does *not* charge the royalty until your third month of business. Even better, it does not charge an advertising fee, but you must spend at least 2 percent of your gross sales revenues on local advertising in the Yellow Pages, weekly newspapers, shopper flyers, or in direct mail pieces. A very effective advertising medium is the local newspaper's society or life-style section. Ackerly notes that Mini Maid now has a very cost-effective national Yellow Pages purchasing program that could save you hundreds of dollars per year. She adds that Mini Maid gives its complete and standardized "hassle free" marketing program to all franchisees.

What You Get

For the franchise fee, you receive the following:

> Start-up supplies and equipment for one four-person cleaning team, which includes uniforms.
>
> The largest exclusive territory per dollar offered in the industry.
>
> Help in your purchase of employee "honesty" bonds—all operations must bond and insure themselves and their employees.
>
> Supervisor's and VCR-based team-training programs.
>
> Field consultations.
>
> Auto leasing assistance, if desired.
>
> Management help, which includes assistance in how to find and how much to pay your employees.

Mini Maid has also expanded its national purchasing programs to reduce your costs for insurance, printing, supplies, and other key expenses. It even manages your employee payroll for you if you choose. Ackerly calls Mini Maid's support system second to none in the industry.

How Much Can You Make?

Mini Maid franchises grossed more than $12 million during 1988, the company states, or an average of between $75,000 and $100,000 per franchise. One published report from 1982 states that a franchisee who had been in business for four years had enough crews to do 450 cleanings per month, and he netted about $42,000 that year. Those figures were based on the time when the average charge per visit was between $16.50 and $20. Today, the national average charge per home is $49.

Mini Maid's crews clean a house in about 55 minutes, and the charge is between $39.50 and $59.50 per house, the average being $49. You also could provide additional services at extra cost and more profit. Your profit margin largely depends upon how well you control your labor costs. They usually account for about one-third of your total costs.

Ackerly says the figures make up a low-estimate average because a typical Mini Maid franchisee has three or four cleaning crews, each of which cleans eight houses a day. This means that each crew brings in $392 per day, five to six days per week. If one remains conservative, this figure equals— based on three crews working five days a week—annual gross revenues of $101,920 per year. Clearly, an average Mini Maid franchisee can gross $100,000 to $150,000 during the first year. But the company makes no earnings claims and asked this author to include such a disclaimer in this book. Nonetheless, you can expect to earn a net pre-tax income of $30,000 to $50,000 or more each year during the first two years, and you can expect to have your income grow rapidly each year thereafter.

Note that the flat $350 per month royalty rate equals a percentage fee of just 4 percent, the lowest in the industry. This flat royalty arrangement will probably save you at least $1,000 to $3,000 per year during your first two years in business.

These totals give you a very significant ROI in excess of 100 percent per year on a total cash investment of less than $30,000 (including vehicle costs). Mini Maid offers the distinct advantage of having given birth to the team-cleaning concept and to charging a flat rate royalty. Another benefit of Mini Maid is the fact that it does not employ franchise brokers or use "master" or regional franchisees. This policy means that the company is left with more of your fee to spend and to support your efforts.

And as you grow, you can expect to expand with Mini Maid during the 1990s. Mini Maid plans to offer allied services, including commercial cleaning, party help services, and a "Tuff-Task" division to do heavy cleaning.

Although not the largest, Mini Maid appears to be one of the best maid-cleaning-service franchises available, especially for individuals who want to work directly with the parent company.

JANI-KING

Jani-King
4950 Keller Springs
Suite 190
Dallas, TX 75248
(800) 552-5264
(214) 991-0900

Jani-King is the leading office and commercial cleaning franchise, with more than 1,000 franchises in the U.S. and Canada. It functions through the regional sales and support-center concept, with 28 such centers around North America. Each regional center is owned and operated by a master franchisor who sells to new owners, trains them, and helps them start up their own operations.

One of the more attractive aspects of a Jani-King franchise is that you can keep your current daytime job while you build a Jani-King business during the evenings. Many Jani-King franchisees start by working part-time in the evenings, cleaning office buildings or supervising crews that clean them. Note that Jani-King requires you to participate directly in the management and operation of the franchise because it builds its reputation on quality owner-management and participation.

Jani-King has almost tripled in size since 1984, spurred by the regional franchise concept and its willingness to provide much of the financing that a franchise needs to begin. Many Jani-King franchisees do not have direct experience working with banks, or they may not have enough assets to obtain a loan, so Jani-King finances several essential costs: part of the franchise fee; equipment purchase; and new office cleaning contract fees. Yet, be forewarned—as Jani-King will warn you—that too much financing can be dangerous.

On the other hand, Jani-King sees its financing program as creating an opportunity for its franchisees to grow more rapidly. Jani-King executives say that many franchisees borrow so that they can build their business quickly. The franchisee and/or his/her spouse continue to work at full-time jobs. They pay back their living expenses from their full-time jobs and plow back their Jani-King income into the franchise growth. Note, too, that company executives advise that Jani-King is not a get-rich-quick business. You must work hard and continuously increase your high contract volume and your crew numbers, and you must provide high-quality, on-time service to your clients, Jani-King executives advise.

With this caveat out of the way, it is important to say that Jani-King is a very good and profitable franchise. It rates very high in *Venture, Entrepreneur,* and other magazine ratings. Moreover, it is relatively inexpensive compared to many of its competitors.

How Much It Costs

Jani-King offers five franchise packages and fees:

Plan	Fee
A	$ 6,500
B	9,500
C	12,000
D	14,000
E	(maximum) 50,000

But your total start-up costs should not exceed $22,000 with any of the first four plans. The new Plan E can go as high as $50,000, depending on the amount of territory you purchase. This is a fairly reasonable structure compared to similar franchises.

Jani-King's financing program works like this: Under Plan A, you pay $1,950 down and finance the remaining $4,500 at 16 percent for three years. Under Plan B, you make a $2,850 down payment and finance $6,650 at 16 percent interest over five years. Under Plan C, you pay $6,000 down and finance $6,000 at 16 percent interest for four years. Under Plan D, you pay $9,800 down and finance $4,200 at 16 percent for two years. Jani-King advises that you may be able to get better terms at lower interest rates from your bank.

Note that the lowest priced Plan A franchise is only available in regions where fewer than 50 Jani-King operations already exist. Plans B, C, D, and E are available in regions with more than 50 existing franchises. You would save thousands of dollars if you are among the first franchisees in a region.

Remaining start-up costs range between $1,000 to $6,000, with the higher figure more likely than the lower.

The royalty fee equals 10 percent per month. But you must pay a monthly minimum of $100 for all gross sales after the first $1,000 per month offered to the franchisee by Jani-King's office under Plan B. Under Plan C, you must pay a minimum fee of $250 a month after the first $2,500 in contracts offered by Jani-King. Plan D requires a minimum fee of $300 per month after the first $3,000 in contracts Jani-King offers.

A Unique Guarantee

For your investment, Jani-King provides a unique guarantee: contracts worth $1,000, $2,000, or $3,000 or more in business *per month*. Jani-King's regional offices have direct salespeople whose jobs are simply to find cleaning contracts for its franchisees. This eases the very heavy pressure on you to sell contracts; to do so might require you to take time away from your full-time career. They sell, and you clean.

Working under standard industry practice, Jani-King charges a finder's fee for selling your clients. The company charges about three times the actual contract amount; however, this is less than half the industry standard, which is five to seven times the contract amount. So, Jani-King's finder fees, the equivalent of a 25 percent commission, are among the lowest in the industry. You can pay the finder's fees up-front, or Jani-King will finance those payments, too. You pay about three times the monthly gross for new business that Jani-King offers you each month.

For example, if Jani-King offers you $1,000 in new monthly business, you would pay a $3,000 finder's fee. You should consider this expense seriously when you forecast your profits. In this business, your growth will be expensive, and Jani-King also advises you to consider this fact carefully. If you finance the new contracts with Jani-King, you must make a 20 percent down payment and pay the balance at 16 percent interest in 13 to 52 equal monthly installments.

A finder's fee for a one-time contract is charged at a flat 28 percent and with no installment payment plan offered.

Of course, you are not obligated to accept any new contracts Jani-King offers. You can sell on your own. Fortunately, you do not pay royalties in addition to the finder's fee; you pay the royalty only on any new business you or your staff acquires.

Although you can see how easily you could get into debt, Jani-King executives say few franchisees actually take advantage of all the financing methods. Because most also work full-time jobs, they fund their growth with their work. Jani-King executives explain that with the company's financing plans, you can expand in a controlled manner. And Jani-King's sales contracts are well worth the finder's fees; they are guaranteed business as compared to the generally poor results one receives from dollars spent on advertising and public relations. Of course, you are not obligated to accept any new contracts Jani-King offers.

Jani-King does not charge an advertising fee, but reserves the right to implement it.

It does charge a $50 complaint fee anytime an account complaint is handled by its regional office. The complaint fee is increased by $50 per *hour* if any crew from the regional office must satisfy the client. Jani-King instituted this complaint fee when high-quality franchisees argued that poor franchisees who did not fulfill their contracts were harming the company's reputation. Jani-King executives say the complaint fee has reduced the problem very effectively. Only one of 1,400 franchisees has ever paid the complaint fee twice, and only a few have had to pay it even once.

Other Start-Up Costs

Under all five plans, you must purchase, lease, or have access to commercial cleaning equipment: a vacuum cleaner, a floor polisher, and a wet-dry vacuum. Jani-King estimates that this equipment will cost between $2,000 and $2,500.

You can lease the equipment from Jani-King Leasing Corporation, a company subsidiary, at a total cost of $1,990. Here again would there be a monthly payment that you owed the parent company. The initial payment would be $265 for the first and last month's payments, and $135 per month for 10 months. You can buy out the equipment at the end of the one-year lease for 20 percent of its purchase price, or for an additional $400.

You will also need business licenses and permits, security deposits, telephone deposits, and working capital. Jani-King estimates these additional costs will range from $415 to $2,500. You must also buy a comprehensive liability insurance plan—blanket fidelity bond, broad form liability, worker's compensation, property, bodily injury, automotive, and product liability. Jani-King estimates adequate coverage will cost between $800 and $1600.

A low estimate for the total start-up investment for a Plan A Jani-King franchise would equal $18,650, but your actual cash expenditure could be as low as $3,580: the low amount would include a $1,950 franchise fee down payment; $800 for insurance coverage; $100 for expenses; $265 for equipment lease; $150 for supplies; and $315 for working capital.

A high estimate of the total start-up investment would equal $21,600: $16,500 cash for the franchise fee; $1,000 working capital expenses; $1,600 for insurance coverages; and $2,500 for equipment package.

What You Get

In return for these fees, you receive the following:

Designated territory and contracts for business, depending on the plan and area you purchase. Although the territories are *not* exclusive, Jani-King promises to restrict the number of franchises in any region to the number that can be serviced adequately by its regional office. Generally, new Jani-King territory boundaries are drawn along county lines; older territory boundaries were based on a number of miles from a downtown area. The latter proved difficult to manage, so Jani-King changed its policy several years ago.

Jani-King executives say they will not sell a new franchise in an area where its sales force cannot find any business to give a franchisee. They say that the franchise territory aspect controls itself as the number of franchises increases. They also note that the franchise contract requires them to provide new monthly contracts, or they will be in violation of its terms.

Two-week training program. The training program is conducted at the regional office or on the premises of businesses that are already being serviced by a nearby Jani-King franchise. Thus, it is unlikely you will incur any training travel expenses. This should save you several hundred to several thousand dollars.

Regional office sales, training, and service support in any area where there are more than 25 existing franchises.

Responsibility for handling billing and accounting services for the franchisees. Jani-King bills and collects all bills for each franchisee, subtracts the amount of money the franchisee owes Jani-King for royalties, installment loan payments, finder's fee payments, and the like, and sends the difference to the franchisee.

Jani-King offers a program through which, for a 3 percent administrative fee, Jani-King will send you a check based on your monthly *billings* minus your payments to the company. In the past, you were paid only after your bills were actually collected. Most franchisees use this program, so they get their money each month instead of waiting for collection efforts.

The company offers this accounting and bookkeeping service because many of its franchisees have little or no experience in billing, bookkeeping, accounting, or collections.

A very good 20-year term for the initial agreement, and an option to renew for up to four more 20-year periods. Best of all, you do not have to pay an additional franchisee or a renewal fee at this time. This lengthy term adds a great deal of value to the Jani-King name and allows you to build more equity. As explained before, a franchise with a longer life span can be sold for more money than one with a three- or five-year term.

How Much Can You Make?

Your average pre-tax net income should equal between 30 and 40 percent of your gross income. You can gross between $1,000 and $10,000 per month managing a crew of two working at night between 6 and 11 P.M.

Published reports show that Jani-King was among the most profitable franchises in the country, with second-year gross sales averaging more than $70,000, and net profits averaging more than $30,000. Note, however, that this net profit would be considered the owner/manager's salary or net income. Even so, this is still a significant ROI on a low up-front cash investment. However, it is likely that if you finance your fee, lease the equipment, and finance finder's fees, your first year's net income will be fairly low. You could even show a paper loss.

The best Jani-King franchisees, working full-time with several crews, earn up to $30,000 per month on contracts with corporations and building management companies. A typical franchisee—a husband-and-wife team with one helper—can gross about $2,500 per month working about four hours a night, five days a week. You work long days if you and your spouse work full-time, but most franchisees build their businesses rapidly so they can leave their jobs. Depending on your situation, you could go full-time when your billings exceed $5,000 per month, perhaps in about two years.

WORLDWIDE REFINISHING SYSTEMS, INC.

Worldwide Refinishing Systems, Inc.
1010 North University Parks
P.O. Box 3146
Waco, TX 76707
(817) 776-4701

Worldwide Refinishing Systems, Inc., was originally Gnu Tub, a successful franchise during the 1970s that fell on hard times during the late 1980s. In late 1988, Don Dwyer, Rainbow International Inc.'s dynamic president, bought Gnu Tub as part of his drive to establish a home services empire of 10,000 franchises worldwide by 1995. (In early 1988, Dwyer had bought Mr. Rooter.)

Backed by Dwyer's marketing expertise, Worldwide Refinishing began to grow very rapidly by late 1989, with more than 130 franchises in operation. This was triple the number of franchises a year earlier.

Worldwide Refinishing offers a very simple, inexpensive, low-overhead service business; it provides the service of refinishing everything from bathtubs and sinks to practically any surface made of porcelain, vinyl, ceramic tile, fiberglass, wood, steel, and cultured marble. The simple process involves heating the old surface to a high temperature and coating it with Worldwide's special materials. The company claims that its new finish has the highest quality on the market. As a franchisee, you must offer a one-year warranty for the new finish, and Worldwide suggests that you offer an extended 10-year warranty.

Although you sell the service primarily as an inexpensive home remodeling alternative—replacing a tub costs about $1,500 to $2,000 and refinishing one costs about $275—you also establish commercial accounts. Worldwide suggests that you emphasize fiberglass surfaces and chairs in fast-food restaurants, and the like, to gain repeat business or long-term contracts. Worldwide suggests that you start your business from your home and build it up during the first six months to a year. Then, you should hire independent contractor route managers who do the work while you manage the operation and sell your services. You make far more profit by growing as rapidly as you can to a four-route manager or greater operation.

Worldwide does face some stiff competition in the market. Perma Ceram, Bathcrest—both of which are described in this book—and at least one other franchise offer similar services. Each company makes its own product, service, and franchise support claims, so you do best to investigate all four before you act.

How Much It Costs

Worldwide Refinishing's franchise fee is a low $7,500, with total estimated start-up costs ranging between $13,350 and $20,000. The following table includes estimates from both Worldwide's UFOC and the author.

Category	Low End	High End
Franchise fee[a]	$ 7,500	$ 7,500
Equipment and supplies[b]	3,616	3,616
Van down payment[c]	1,000	2,000
Training travel[d]	450	1,000
Van decal package[e]	285	285
Working capital[f]	500	5,000
Total	$13,351	$19,401

a. For a 100,000 minimum population territory; $75 for each additional 1,000 population.
b. Required equipment package purchase. Can be leased through Ames Financial.
c. If you have a van, you will not need another one. You can also lease a van through Ames Financial, and this figure includes lease deposits if you choose that route.
d. A week in Waco, Texas, at headquarters.
e. Required for vans; can also be leased through Ames Financial.
f. The company allows a very low $500. This amount is obviously not enough for living expenses, legal fees, business licenses, required insurance deposits, and the like.

Royalties, Fees, and Purchases

You must pay a 5 percent royalty and a 2 percent advertising fee each week. You are required to buy from Worldwide most of your essential materials, such as etching compounds, solvents, coatings, etc. These purchases should total about 15 percent of your gross annual sales. Although Worldwide sets no firm limits on the amount, you must do local advertising and promotional efforts and also run a Yellow Pages ad. At this time, Worldwide does not offer a cooperative ad program or an ad fund council.

What You Get

For your fees and royalties, you receive the following privileges and services:

Exclusive territory. Your territory includes at least 100,000 people, but be sure that your area encompasses middle-class and affluent households and many fast-food or similar-type restaurants—probably your primary customers.

Ten-year term. The original agreement term is a respectable 10 years, and it can be renewed for additional 10-year terms. You do not have to pay any additional franchise fee to qualify for the first renewal. However, unlike many franchise companies, Worldwide does not allow the franchisee to terminate the contract. This is a disadvantage, and you should determine what happens if you do not do well.

Since Dwyer bought Worldwide in 1988, growth has occurred so rapidly that the author cannot evaluate the success rate these new franchisees are experiencing. The mid-1989 UFOC states that only one of its 50 franchisees had been canceled and that one because it was inactive. Apparently, if one does not work at the business or make required product purchases, Worldwide will cancel the contract rather than allow you to leave the system.

Training. You receive one week's training in Waco in all aspects of the business—selling, marketing, hiring and managing technicians and route managers, applying the finishes, etc. You also can get first-hand experience by working with local Waco crews. After you begin, Worldwide offers training seminars that you or your technicians can attend.

Technician training. The company provides a weekly training package to help you teach your technicians and route manager how to improve their performance and productivity.

Advertising and promotional campaigns. The company provides advice and materials to help you get started and also continuous advertising support.

Telephone hot line. You can call the company through a toll-free number for help during business hours.

On-going research and support services. Worldwide also has a research program through which it tests new products, equipment, and surfaces that you can refinish, thereby expanding your market. Worldwide also has field representatives who visit franchisees to offer guidance.

How Much Can You Make?

Worldwide is very forthcoming about estimated earnings, but the company emphasizes that its estimates do not reflect any actual results and will not necessarily accurately predict how well you will do. Note the disclaimer within the potential return pro forma statements given at the end of this section.

Worldwide executives stress that your potential profits depend directly on your management style, whether and how you follow the company's guidelines, and "how you watch your nickels and dimes." They note that during 1988 the leading franchisee—in business for 17 years as a Gnu Tub franchisee—grossed more than $850,000, managed an 8,000-foot showroom, and ran a full-fledged home remodeling business.

More realistically, a late 1989 company newsletter sent to its franchisees reported that some relatively new franchisees—in business for about a year—were grossing about $2,000 per week or an annual rate of $104,000 per year. One franchisee reportedly made a $100,000 agreement with a hospital to refinish 405 tubs at $250 each. A technician can do about two tubs per day, so the project would require about 200 work days. Several crews could complete the work within two to three months.

The company reports in its literature that "the good people in this business" earn between $35 and $80 per hour, with a typical bathtub refinishing billed at $275; materials cost about $40 per tub for a gross profit of $235 per tub, not including labor and overhead. The company estimates that if you do the work yourself, you may gross between $1,200 and $2,000 per week, or about five to eight tubs per week. At the low end, you should have net pre-tax profits of about $29,000 per year; in the middle, those profits should increase to about $40,000 per year.

The pro forma statements also show how much profit you should expect from an independent technician or route manager's work. You should net between 23 and 39 percent from each technician's work, depending upon how high your weekly sales reach. The company's estimates reach only $1,500 per week sales levels; $2,000 and higher weekly sales will bring net profit margins greater than 40 percent.

In short, you can expect to recoup your investment within the first year easily, and within six months if you lease your van and equipment, and you should make 200 percent net ROIs by the end of your second year.

Potential Return, First Pro Forma
Based on Sales of $1,500 per Week per Truck

	1 Truck O/O[a]	2 Trucks O/O; 1 RM[b]	3 Trucks O/O; 2 RM	4 Trucks 4 RM	5 Trucks 5 RM
Sales:	$ 6,000	$12,000	$18,000	$24,000	$30,000
Expenses:					
Sales promotion	480	980	1,440	1,920	2,400
Chemicals	800	800	800	—	—
Royalty fees	300	600	900	1,200	1,500
Truck payment	275	275	275	275	275
Gas	120	130	140	140	140
Repair	40	50	60	80	100
Insurance	100	120	140	160	180
Telephone	40	60	80	100	120
Answering service	200	250	600	800	800
Rent	—	—	500	500	500
Route manager	—	2,400	4,800	9,600	12,000
Meeting/travel	75	75	125	150	200
Total Expenses	$ 2,430	$ 5,740	$ 9,860	$14,925	$18,215
Profit monthly	3,570	6,260	8,140	9,075	11,785
Annually	$42,840	$75,120	$97,680	$108,900	$141,420

Second Pro Forma
Based on Sales of $1,200 per Truck

Profit monthly	2,430	3,980	4,720	4,515	6,085
Annually	29,160	47,760	56,640	54,180	73,020

Caution: *These figures are only estimates of what Worldwide thinks you may earn. There is no assurance you'll do as well. If you rely on these figures, you must accept the risk of not doing as well.*

Table Footnotes:
a. O/O stands for owner/operator
b. RM stands for Route Manager.

Notes: The following information will help you understand the pro forma:
1. All figures are based on a four-week month.
2. Route managers are independent contractors. They pay for their own trucks, expenses, chemicals, and insurance.
3. In a four-truck operation, we assume that the owner will not run a truck. Therefore, the table shows a slight decrease in income until the next truck is added or the franchisee increases the gross of the existing trucks.
4. In the first pro forma, we are assuming that each truck will meet a minimum standard of $1,500 per week, which can only be achieved by following the World-

wide system exactly as it is taught. The second pro forma assumes average performance.

5. We assume that you will rent a small office shop/showroom when you add the third truck.

Technician Pro Forma Based on a $1,000 Week

Plan II

Weekly income of 40% of $1,000, or $400. One-half is for expenses; the other half for salary.

$200 for Expenses:

Less expenses:	
Van payment	$ 45.00
Gas	20.00
Maintenance	10.00
Van insurance	10.00
Total Expenses:	$ 85.00
Excess:	$115.00

$200 Taxable:

Salary	$200
W.H. and S.S.	40
Net:	$160

Summary of Income:

Salary	$200
Excess expenses	115
Total	$315
Less taxes	−40
Take home	$275

Franchisee Pro Forma Based on a $1,000 Week

Plan II

Technician (40%)	$400
F.F. (5%)	50
Advertising (10%)	100
Liability insurance	15
Telephone	25
Miscellaneous	10
Taxes on technician	15
Total expenses:	$615
Net profit:	$385 or 38.5%

Technician Pro Forma Based on a $1,500 Week
Plan II

Technician weekly income of 40% of $1,500 is $600. One-half is for expenses; one-half for salary.

$300 for expenses:

Less expenses:	
Van payment	$ 45
Gas	35
Maintenance	10
Van insurance	10
Total Expenses:	$100
Excess:	200

$300 Taxable:

Salary	$300
W.H. and S.S.	60
Net:	$240

Summary of Income:

Salary	$300
Excess expenses	200
Total income	$500
Less taxes	−60
Take home	$440

Franchisee Pro Forma Based on a $1,500 Week

Plan II

Technician (40%)	$600
F.F. (5%)	75
Advertising (10%)	150
Liability insurance	30
Telephone	25
Miscellaneous	10
Taxes on technicians	30
Chemical cost (15%)	225
Total:	$1,145
Net profit:	$335 or 29.5%

Technician Potential Income

Plan I

Assumptions:

1. Drive a 1986 van at a cost of $6,000, with payment of $200 per month for 36 months.

2. The technician will spend $20 to $35 per week for gas, depending on volume.

3. The technician's insurance will run $520 per year, or $10 per week.

4. Maintenance won't cost more than $520 per year, or $10 per week.

5. The technician will earn 55% of the gross.

6. One-half of the technician's income will be allocated to the cost of chemicals and van expenses.

7. The technician will pay for his or her own chemicals at a cost of 15%.

Technician Pro Forma Based on a $1,000 Week

Plan I

Weekly income of 55% of $1,000 is $550. One-half is used for expenses; the other half for salary.

$275 for Expenses:

Less expenses:	
Gas	$ 20.00
Van payment	45.00
Maintenance	10.00
Chemicals (15%)	150.00
Van insurance	10.00
Total Expenses:	$235.00
Excess:	$ 40.00

$275 Taxable:

Salary	$275
W.H.	45
Net:	$230

Summary of Income	
Salary	$275
Excess expenses	40
Total	$315
Less taxes	−45
Take home	$270

Franchisee Pro Forma Based on a $1,000 Week

Plan I

Technician (55%)	$550
F.F. (5%)	50
Advertising (10%)	100
Liability insurance	15
Telephone	25
Miscellaneous	10
Taxes on technician	17
Total	$767
Profit	$233 or 23.3%

Technician Pro Forma Based on a $1,500 Weekly Average

Plan I

Technician weekly income 55% of $1,500 equals $825. One-half applies to expenses, and one-half goes to salary.

$412.50 for Expenses:

Less expenses:	
Gas	$ 35.00
Van payment	46.50
Maintenance	10.00
Chemicals	225.00
Total expenses:	$316.50
Excess:	$96.00

$412.50 Taxable:

Salary	$412.50
S.S.	30.94
W.H.	52.00
Net:	$329.56

Summary of Income

Salary	$412.50
Excess expenses	96.00
Total	$508.50
Less taxes	−82.94
Take home	$425.56

Technician Potential Income

Plan II

Assumptions:

1. Drive a 1986 van at a cost of $6,000, with payment of $200 per month for 36 months.

2. The technician will spend $20 to $35 per week for gas, depending on volume.

3. The technician's insurance will run $520 per year, or $10 per week.

4. Maintenance won't cost more than $520 per year, or $10 per week.

5. The technician will earn 40% of the gross.

6. One-half of the technician's income will be allocated to the cost of chemicals and van expenses.

6

Franchises with Fees from $10,001 to $15,000

Rainbow International
The Maids International
AAA Employment Franchise, Inc.
Molly Maid, Inc.
Homes & Land Publishing

SERVPRO Industries, Inc.
RE/MAX International, Inc.
Video Data Services
Century 21 Real Estate
 Corporation

RAINBOW INTERNATIONAL

Carpet Dyeing and Cleaning Company
1010 North University Parks Drive
P.O. Box 3146
Waco, TX 76707
(800) 433-3322
(817) 756-2122

In contrast to many similar cleaning service franchises, Rainbow International Carpet Dyeing and Cleaning emphasizes dyeing, tinting, and coloring carpets with steam cleaning, carpet shampooing, carpet repair, flood and water damage restoration, odor control, drapery cleaning, and furniture cleaning and dyeing as auxiliary services.

It was listed 16th on the *Venture* magazine Franchise 100 list, with an average two-year return on investment of more than 124 percent. *Entrepreneur* magazine rated it the fifth fastest growing franchise during 1989, and it usually ranks in the top five among the best franchises in the magazine's Carpet, Upholstery, and Drapery Cleaning category. By the end of 1989, there were more than 2,000 Rainbow franchises sold and more than 1,150 in operation. With President Don Dwyer's very ambitious plans to own a franchise conglomerate with 10,000 franchises by 1995, Rainbow expects to reach 4,000 franchises by that date.

Rainbow executives believe that your business will grow if you grow personally, so they stress personal growth and working with a person who believes in the "American Dream" and wants to be successful. It relies heavily on motivational, personal development, and incentive programs for its own staff and its franchisees.

How Much Does It Cost?

Rainbow charges a fairly high franchise fee for a cleaning service—$15,000 minimum. The fee is based on a charge of $300 for every 1,000 population in an exclusive territory with a minimum population of 50,000 people. However, unlike most franchise companies, Rainbow will finance 76 percent of the fee; it charges a weekly payment of $50 per week at 12 percent interest. The first payment does not start until two months after you have opened your business.

As the author has noted several times in this book, be careful about how much financing and debt you take on as you get started. Although financing significantly lowers your up-front costs, it may raise your monthly operating expense for several years. You may pay Rainbow $200 to $250 per month for about five years to cover your franchise fee, much less a required minimum royalty of 7 percent of your gross sales volume.

Total Start-Up Cash Expenses

Rainbow estimates your total up-front cash expenditure will equal the following:

Category	Amount
Franchise down payment	$ 4,000.00
Supplies and equipment[a]	5,497.85
Van down payment	1,000.00
Truck signs[a]	350.00
Training, travel, expenses	450.00
Miscellaneous	500.00
Total	$11,797.85

a. These must be purchased from Rainbow International.

The author's estimate of your total start-up costs would include the total franchise fee and miscellaneous expenses:

Category	Amount
Franchise fee[a]	$13,500
Supplies and equipment	6,000
Van down payment[b]	2,000
Truck signs	350
Training travel[c]	1,000
Utility deposits	1,000
Insurance	750
Initial advertising	1,000
Working capital[d]	2,500
Total	$28,100

a. Rainbow gives a 10 percent discount for up-front payment.
b. For a new van that meets Rainbow's specifications and includes a required color.
c. For a week's training in Waco, Texas.
d. Includes basic living expenses for two or three months.

The $28,100 figure is definitely at the high end of the range, but you can safely estimate a total up-front cost of about $20,000 before you start earning an appreciable income.

The only other fee is a 7 percent weekly royalty on gross sales of all of the varied services you can offer. Rainbow could charge an advertising fee, but never has and has no plans to do so.

What You Get

As noted, Rainbow gives you a minimum 50,000-population territory. With 2,000 territories already sold, it may be that many of the most lucrative areas have been sold. You can always try to buy an existing Rainbow franchise, but if it is successful, you can expect to pay more for it than you would to start your own. Therefore, be very careful and investigate your proposed territory for a market with the right demographics—middle-class two-income households and commercial and business offices—before you go with Rainbow.

Rainbow also emphasizes a wide variety of services that differ from the many carpet cleaning competitors, but it competes head to head with the formidable ServPro, ServiceMaster, and Duraclean. But Rainbow itself is a very strong company with excellent marketing programs, and it could not have grown as large and successful as it has without knowing its markets and effective strategies to deal with the competition.

You also receive a variety of on-going training and support programs:

- One week of start-up in Waco at its headquarters. You not only take classroom training but you also get your hands dirty at the company's actual working franchise in Waco.
- Ten former and successful franchisees who do nothing from 7:30 A.M. to 9:30 P.M., six days a week, but answer toll-free phone calls from franchisees and provide support.
- Thirty-four regional meeting for training and marketing updates.
- Monthly updates in newsletters and mailing.
- National accounts sales department that generates national contracts and referrals from major corporations and chains. For example, notes Dwyer, Rainbow has a nation-wide contract with a major insurance repair and restoration firm, Ultra-Care, through which local Rainbow franchisees provide maintenance services on insurance claims.
- Research and development department that perfects new products and marketing ideas, most recently a "Designer Dyeing" concept. With this new method, you can dye any pattern into an existing carpet and offer a new service to your customers.

All of this adds up to an effective support program backed by dozens of regional support staff members.

How Much Can You Make?

No typical Rainbow franchisee exists any longer; Dwyer says that, today, many new franchisees are professional businesspeople with management skills, and they start up with four-, five-, or even ten-truck operations. Many others represent the traditional one-person franchisee, who wants to leave a mundane job and start his or her own business.

In any case, Rainbow is very forthcoming on prospective gross and net earnings and provides a detailed estimate of how much potential return one can earn with five differently sized operations. Dwyer adds, too, that one can look at the actual results of the Waco company-owned franchise. He said that, during 1989, it grossed more than $400,000, with a likely net profit in the $100,000 range or about 25 percent. One can expect to earn the same or a somewhat higher net profit margin, especially if, at first, you do the work yourself. Given below is an explanation of potential returns based on weekly sales of $1,200 per truck. The estimate shows five operations: from one truck in which you do the work yourself to five trucks with individual route managers.

Realistically, if you run a one-truck operation, you should plan to earn a reasonable salary in the $25,000 per year range and double your investment in two to three years. Of course, if you have a large territory with numerous route managers, you can make far greater profits much faster, as the following table shows.

The virtue of the route manager system is that route managers work as independent contractors, so you do not have to pay for their trucks,

Potential Return Based on Sales of $1,200 per Week per Truck

	1 Truck (O/O[a])	2 Trucks (O/O, 1 RM[b])	3 Trucks (O/O, 2 RM)	4 Trucks (4 RM)	5 Trucks (5 RM)
Sales					
Sales promotion	4,800	9,600	14,400	19,200	24,000
Expenses					
Sales promotion	480	960	1,440	1,920	2,400
Chemicals	288	288	288	—	—
Royalty fee	336	672	1,008	1,344	1,680
Truck payment	200	200	200	200	200
Gas	120	120	120	120	120
Repair	40	40	40	40	40
Insurance	100	100	100	100	100
Telephone	40	40	60	80	100
Answering service	200	200	250	300	400
Rent	—	—	—	—	150
Route manager	—	2,400	4,800	9,600	12,000
Meeting travel	75	75	75	75	75
Total expenses	1,879	5,095	8,381	13,779	17,265
Profit monthly	2,921	4,505	6,019	5,421	6,735
Annually	$35,052	$54,060	$72,228	$65,052	$80,820

a. O/O—Owner/Operator
b. RM—Route Manager

expenses, chemicals, insurance, withholding taxes, or expenses. You pay them an agreed-upon fee for each job and make sure they follow your and Rainbow's quality standards. You would then devote most of your time to managing their work and selling your franchise's services. If you don't, you will need to hire a salesperson and do a lot of direct mail solicitations and direct sales to commercial accounts.

Rainbow International is a dynamic franchise with excellent growth potential into other areas, but you should plan to expand into a multi-van operation as soon as possible to maximize your investment return.

THE MAIDS INTERNATIONAL

The Maids International
4820 Dodge St.
Omaha, NE 68132
(402) 558-5555
(800) THE-MAID (843-6243)

The Maids International is a very professionally managed and potentially lucrative residential cleaning franchise. The company aims to attract buyers with management experience who are eager and can afford to expand their franchises rapidly. Yet, its low initial investment makes it very attractive for the individual owner-operator as well.

The Maids asserts it is the largest franchised maid-service company founded by cleaning industry experts. And it claims that its four-person cleaning system—based on professional time-and-motion studies—makes it the fastest, yet most thorough, service.

For the buyer or investor, The Maids offers one significant advantage over its competitors: as you make more money, you pay a lower royalty percentage. Its royalty structure, based on gross weekly sales, now looks like this:

Gross (Weekly Sales)	Royalty Rate (%)
$ 0 to $ 8,000	7
$ 8,001 to $16,000	6
$16,001 to $24,000	5
$24,001 and up	4.5

By late 1989, The Maids had more than 200 active franchises. It plans to add as many as 50 more each year during 1990 and 1991. The franchises are scattered around 38 states and several Canadian provinces, but only a few states and a handful of metropolitan areas, which include San Diego, Dallas, and Pittsburgh, have any significant franchise concentration. So, the opportunity remains fairly open across the country.

The Maids is a leader in an industry that is predicted to grow rapidly through the early 1990s. A recent update of a franchising study by futurist John Naisbett anticipates that the home services category will grow between 10 and 15 percent per year through the early 1990s. Naisbett estimates the residential cleaning industry to increase to a potential *$9 billion market*. This author predicts that intense competition and a sluggish economy will reduce the rate of growth somewhat, but that the demand for quality maid services will grow rapidly. If The Maids maintains its quality standards and reasonable prices, its franchisees should continue to do well.

How Much It Costs

Franchise Fees

The Maids' franchise fee for your first territory totals $15,900; additional units or territories can be purchased for $12,900 each. Clearly, The Maids encourages investor/managers to take advantage of this discount and the reduced royalty percentage for high volume operations.

The Maids' fee includes an initial equipment and materials package worth more than $3,500. This package is large enough to equip two four-person teams easily. Second and subsequent equipment packages are included in the fees for additional territories.

The company provides fairly complete estimates of total start-up costs and initial investment. The Maids' estimated budget is shown opposite.

Of course, opening additional units should cost about half this amount, and yet you could quickly double your sales volume. More important is the fact that when you open two or more additional units, The Maids will help finance that expansion with promissory notes for between one and three years at or near current market interest rates. This would be a far cheaper rate than most franchisees could obtain from a bank.

What You Get

Exclusive Territory

The company places a great emphasis on how it bases its territories on customer demographics, not population. This distinction is crucial. If you buy a franchise based solely on population, you could end up with few people who need your service. For example, where would you think a maid service would do better, Beverly Hills or Harlem? This is an exaggeration,

The Maids Budget Table

Item	Amount	
	Low Range	**High Range**
Paid to The Maids		
Initial franchise fee	$15,900	$15,900
Subtotal	$15,900	$15,900
Paid before Opening		
Initial labor, training	$ 700	$ 1,200
Advertising	3,000	5,000
Auto leases (2 cars required)	1,400	1,800[a]
Phone deposits	100	200
Legal/accounting fees	200	600
Travel expenses	600	1,500[b]
Computer hardware buy	1,500	3,000[c]
Insurance	500	2,000
Office supplies	50	200
Signage	100	800
Local supplies & misc.	100	250
Subtotal	$ 8,250	$16,550
Possible Additional Costs[d]		
Rent, first month	$ 350	$ 1,000
Security deposit	350	1,000
Furniture	1,500	2,500
Fixtures	100	250
Decorating	500	1,000
Manager/supervisor salary	800	1,400[e]
Working capital	750	2,500
Subtotal	$ 4,350	$ 9,650
Total Estimated Investment	$28,500	$42,100

Notes:
a. The Maids has an excellent long-term lease arrangement, with the required yellow and green "The Maids" logo and colors already painted on the car.
b. For a six-day training session, this should be a per-person figure. If you take a manager, a supervisor, or an employee, this amount will be higher.
c. The Maids has an easy-to-use computer system that you may lease from a third party; you use it to fulfill your weekly reporting requirements. You can also do it manually and save this expense, at least at first. If you grow rapidly, however, the system will help simplify complex bookkeeping tasks. This franchise is very

part-time labor intensive, and its success depends on quick, accurate, and thorough recordkeeping.

d. Directly related to costs of renting an office. Eliminate these costs if you plan to run your first operation from your home or an existing office.

e. First month's salary of full-time manager/supervisor if you do not manage the business by yourself.

---

but the principle is true. The Maids makes a point of making sure your territory includes a goodly number of homes with potential customers.

The Importance of Demographics

The Maids' market research shows that its customers overwhelmingly display the following characteristics: a married working woman between the ages of 35 and 54 whose husband also works. The primary wage earner—either one or both—is employed as a professional or a manager. Most live in a house they have owned for more than four years, and many have lived in the same house or the same area for more than 10 years. More than two-thirds have done their own housecleaning. Look for affluent suburban or urban areas, and that is where you will find the typical and best The Maids' customers. They are also more likely to be customers for additional services, such as window washing, oven cleaning, floor waxing and polishing, and so forth.

Very Detailed Training

The Maids training program is one of the most detailed of any franchise. It offers a "unique constellation of pre- and post-training" service, according to company executives. It is an eight-week course, six days of which are spent at the company headquarters in Omaha, Nebraska. For between three and four weeks before the course, you study training materials and videos at your home. For three to four weeks after the training, you talk with a post-training service person each day to monitor your progress.

Computerized System Management

Although you can buy the computer hardware or lease it through a recommended third-party leasing company, The Maids provides, as part of the franchise package, an advanced service management package that streamlines your bookkeeping, payroll, and tax payment procedures. If you run two or three crews, you could easily have 8 to 20 part-time employees, and their tax records could take several hours a week if you completed them manually. The time savings may make the system worthwhile.

Access to Insurance Services

The Maids has also put together the most comprehensive package of insurance protection available among home cleaning service franchises, including the following: premises, product, and completed operations liability; theft and vandalism from autos; third-party legal liability and crime for you and your clients; care, custody, and control to protect you if an employee damages a client's property; extended property damage; lost key liability protection; commercial umbrella; business automobile; and other coverages. These are essential to protect you and your business.

Advertising and Marketing Package

The Maids' executives take pride in their marketing and promotion efforts, saying that "our precisely targeted marketing program is one of our special strengths." The Maids specializes in direct-response ad packages for its franchisees. More than one-quarter of all customers are generated by these targeted and very cost effective mailings.

In addition to the 2 percent national ad fee you pay, you must spend at least 3 percent of your gross income per year on local advertising, including a national Yellow Pages campaign—the second best ad medium; newspapers—the third most effective draw; radio and, in large multiple-unit territories, television, as well as for brochures, and the like.

The Maids offers a broad and deep cooperative ad program through which the company helps franchisees reduce their marketing costs. These include billboards, newspaper inserts, etc.

The company's ad fund is administered by an advisory council made up of leading franchisees appointed by the company's managers. This is not an "independent" board, but it does have the power to set advertising policy for the entire company.

How Much Can You Make?

Clearly, you can make a great deal of money with The Maids franchises. A recent issue of *Inc.* magazine reported that Harry Aker, The Maids' largest Pittsburgh franchisee, surpassed the $1 million in annual sales and earned a net *after tax* profit of 18 percent, or about $180,000. Aker has four offices and dozens of crews. By the same token and with just one office, Tom Herr, a franchisee of The Maids in Hawaii, surpassed $1 million in gross revenues. Other very successful franchisees, run by experienced managers and with at least two offices and four crews per office, report gross revenues between $600,000 and $900,000 with consistent 15 to 20 percent net after-tax profit margins.

Here's how you make these hefty profits cleaning one house at a time.

How can you make high gross volume? It may not be as hard as it sounds. The Maids advises that you charge between $40 and $80 per house. The company reports that the average charge during 1989 equalled $57. The team cleaning system is organized so that a crew can clean an average three-bedroom, two-bath house in less than an hour. One crew should be able to clean between five and eight houses a day, allowing time for driving and lunch. This one crew should be able to gross between $200 and $640 per day, or at least $1,000 to $3,840 per week.

On average, your crew should gross $285 per day, or $1,425 per week (five-day work week), or $74,100 per year. If you manage the crew yourself, you should have a net pre-tax income between $22,500 and $37,000 during the first year and build beyond the high end of that range during the second year. Your ROI on an average investment of $30,000 (the amount the company cites) should exceed 100 percent per year by the end of the second year. You can expect to earn net pre-tax margins between 30 and 40 percent, or between $12 and $32 per job.

It's clear that it would pay to push your additional, more expensive services that add profits at little additional labor cost.

The multiple-territory franchisees could have net incomes in the $150,000 to $300,000 or more per year range. The ROIs on these operations would be in the 175 percent to 350 percent range after the first several years of operation.

In short, The Maids is an excellent growth opportunity, and the company provides among the most sophisticated support available. But to whom much is given, much is required, so be prepared to follow The Maids' tough requirements. Company executives say they have learned to be very selective in their franchisees. They ask applicants very tough questions about their experience and financial assets to ensure that new franchisees can expand as rapidly as both The Maids and the buyers would like.

AAA EMPLOYMENT FRANCHISE, INC.

AAA Employment Franchise, Inc.
5533 Central Ave.
St. Petersburg, FL 33710
(813) 573-0202

AAA Employment Franchise is one of the most reasonably priced employment service franchises available. It has been in business since 1957 and began offering franchises in 1978. The company is relatively straightforward about its earnings potential. Executives stress that their franchisees tend to follow one of two paths: (a) high volume, that is, the franchisees do numerous low-fee placements in states such as Florida and Mississippi, where the wage rates are low; or (b) low volume in states or metropolitan areas where professionals or academics with high salaries are concentrated, such as in Boston or Wilmington, North Carolina. With either method, you may be able to earn a ROI of several hundred percent on your actual cash investment during your first two years in business.

Like your profit from other service franchises, much of your AAA Employment profit will derive from your active participation and your willingness or ability to take relatively low salaries during the first year or two.

You should be aware of one caveat concerning AAA Employment. Of its more than 140 operations, some two-thirds are company-owned units in four Southern states: Florida, Georgia, Alabama, and Mississippi. AAA offers franchises in all the 46 other states, but by late 1989 there were only about 50 of these individual franchises. AAA added 10 franchises in the last two years—a slow, but steady, growth rate. The company restricts its own operations to those four states, so you should find that it will be eager to help you grow in your own region.

The company appears to be financially strong with consistently profitable results. AAA Employment reported total franchise and operations sales volume of more than $6 million for the 1988 fiscal year, and the franchise operation alone showed a substantial profit.

AAA Employment offers a full-service employment agency franchise that has as its marketing advantage a low fee—just three weeks' salary. Although AAA works both ways, the job seekers and not the employers usually pay the fee. This makes the AAA service more attractive to employers than those employment agencies that charge the employer fees often two or three times greater than AAA's low fee. AAA also offers a payment plan for applicants, and it accepts credit cards. The payment plan is one-half of the fee upon acceptance of the job, with the other half paid in two weekly installments.

Company executives emphasize that AAA offers you several advantages over other employment service franchises:

- Low-cost financing with low-interest rates (see below);
- A low 10 percent royalty fee and *no* additional fees or charges;
- Exclusive territory and a cooperative national network;
- Stable and continuing support programs
- A financially strong, experienced parent company
- Low-fee permanent placement service without the hassles of temporary employment services.

How Much It Costs

The franchise fee varies with the population of the territory. The schedule is given on page 148.

Population	Franchise Fee
0 to 50,000	$10,000
50,001 to 100,000	15,000
100,001 to 150,000	20,000
150,001 to 200,000	25,000
200,001 and more	30,000

However, you need make only a 40 percent down payment, except for the largest franchises. For these, the down payment totals $15,000 or 50 percent.

AAA also charges a very favorable interest rate on the balance, just a one-time interest charge of 10 percent added to the unpaid franchise fee. You then pay the balance with weekly payments of $50 until the fee is paid in full. If you buy the smallest franchise, this means that you would pay a total of $6,600 over 132 weeks or for two and one-half years. Of course, if you buy the largest franchise, you would make total payments on $16,500 over 330 weeks or for about six and one-half years.

You also pay a 10 percent weekly royalty on your gross receipts; this rate is very low in the personnel placement and employment agency industry. Other than for some minor required office stationery and supplies purchases, you do not have to buy anything or make any other required payments—no ad fees—to the franchisor.

AAA estimates that your additional start-up costs will equal about $4,000 for rent of about 400 square feet of office space, supplies, licenses, and rented office furnishings. These estimates seem a little low. Perhaps a total of $5,000 to $6,000 would be more reasonable. This higher estimate includes costs for business telephone deposits and installation, advertising, insurance coverages, and working capital.

In any case, you can probably open your doors for a total cash investment ranging from between $7,000 to $30,000, a very reasonable amount for this kind of franchise.

What You Get

In return, you receive an exclusive territory, depending on the size of the territory you license. AAA emphasizes that city and county boundary franchises are available across the country. The company also helps you select the best location for your service, but does not help negotiate the lease. You remain responsible for the final decisions on the lease and the location. The territory size and boundaries follow city and county lines, but you could press for an area with lots of major businesses and those with frequent turnover of employees. Your success depends on choosing a good area in which you can follow either AAA Employment path: high or low volume. Look for a territory in a growing, dynamic area where businesses hire often, or a more stable community with numerous professionals and academics.

The franchise term is very good: 10 years, with automatic one-year renewals with no additional franchise fees.

You receive an extensive two-week training program. It combines classroom instruction with on-the-job training in one of AAA's company-owned locations near its St. Petersburg, Florida, headquarters. However, you must pay for room and board and travel. This should add between $600 and $2,000 to your start-up costs.

As important, AAA sends an experienced trainer to work with you during your first week of operation. This person or the company also helps you obtain any required employment agency licenses from your state or local government, establish an advertising schedule, set up a financial budget, hire office personnel (usually an assistant at first), and so forth.

In short, AAA offers a solid support program to help you get started on the right track.

How Much Can You Make?

AAA executives emphasize that high-volume franchisees tend to succeed in very transient, low-wage areas, while low-volume franchisees do equally well or better in stable communities with colleges and professionals. AAA franchises appear to have earned net incomes as high as $175,000 per year. Information about AAA company-owned locations in two Southeastern states published in 1981 shows that franchise buyers tend to take salaries out of the franchise ranging between $25,000 and $30,000 per year, and they add net profits to that salary. AAA executives say that they will provide franchisees with specific earnings information if and when they apply for a bank loan. The earnings figures will be based on the results from franchisees close to their location. Giving specific information from high-volume company-owned businesses may mislead, they say, for they do not accurately reflect what may happen in various regions of the country.

Even so, on a total start-up cost ranging from $27,000 to $60,000, you can breakeven after just one year—including your salary—and turn a 50 to 100 percent ROI by the end of the second year. Your cash investment ROI could easily exceed 100 percent during your first year.

It appears that you may do best in a smaller city where you face less competition and reduce your overhead expenses. It is clear, too, that your profits are directly reduced by the salary amount you choose to take during the year. How you choose to treat your profits and pay taxes depends on your situation. By following the AAA method, however, you can earn a substantial return on your cash investment very quickly.

MOLLY MAID, INC.

Molly Maid, Inc.
707 Wolverine Tower
3001 South State St.
Ann Arbor, MI 48108
(800) 331-4600
(313) 996-1555

Molly Maid is the most straightforward and open franchise of any company in this book—and perhaps in all of franchising—about how much money its franchisees earn per year. In its UFOC, the company publishes a complete list of the average weekly earnings for all of its franchisees. And the list is divided by region and shows how many weeks each franchise has been in business. The list is given at the end of this section.

The gross income results show quite excellent ROI potential. ROIs for a total initial cash investment of between $25,000 and $30,000, or less, often exceed 200 to 300 percent per year. More than 43 percent of all of Molly Maid's some 160 U.S. franchisees earned an average gross income of $143,000 per year; that includes new franchisees whose first-year incomes tend to average only $25,000 to $30,000 per year.

More important, the average gross incomes of franchisees in business more than two years exceeded $200,000 per year. The highest reported annual gross income for a franchise two-years-old or older equalled more than $385,900, while the lowest was more than $54,000. Net profits before taxes range between 25 and 35 percent, for an average net income of $35,750 and $61,250 after two years, with the higher figure more likely.

This section begins with the potential gross income and return on investment results because Molly Maid's above-board approach should encourage potential franchisees to consider the company.

The Molly Maid Difference

Molly Maid is distinctive among the six other major household cleaning franchises in that it seriously promotes an up-scale professional image for its franchisees and their employees. Company executives say they have made a fetish of their professional image. The franchisees wear designer clothes, their employees wear English maid uniforms, and all drive distinctively marked dark blue cars with the company's pink logo. The executives say that this approach gives to its affluent two-income family customers a psychological value that other maid services cannot offer.

The executives also maintain that they have elevated the occupation from "maid" or housekeeper to professional cleaning person. Franchisees must recruit the best available people and pay them more than the average. Employing the best employees reduces costly turnover, saves training costs, provides continuity for customers, and reduces labor costs in the long run. And the company structures its payroll so that it rewards performance. The best cleaning people may earn $15,000 to $18,000 a year and drive a company car. This income is between 50 and 80 percent more than an average maid makes.

With more than 160 U.S. franchises and more than 170 Canadian franchises by the end of 1989, Molly Maid is the second largest household cleaning franchise. It was rated among the Top 500 franchises both in *Entrepreneur* and *Inc.* magazines during 1989. It plans to expand to about 750 franchises worldwide by 1993, the executives say.

More than 85 percent of its customers are affluent, two-income families, with the rest being largely the elderly, the ill, busy families, or single people with little time or desire to clean.

Molly Maid also acquired a very significant corporate investor during 1988. The S.C. Johnson Wax Family of Home Care Services bought a one-third interest in Molly Maid, bailing the company out of short-term financial difficulties and giving Molly Maid the right to advertise itself as a member of that prestigious family of companies.

How Much It Costs

Although not the least expensive maid service franchise, Molly Maid is reasonably priced. The following table shows the total costs; this author has added certain categories which the company does not include in its initial investment table:

Category	Low End	High End
Franchise fee	$14,500	$14,500
Equipment package[a]	2,400	2,400
Auto leases[b]	800	1,200
Phone deposit	200	400
Insurance[c]	2,000	12,000
Start-up ads	2,000	4,000
Training travel[d]	200	400
Working capital	2,000	4,000
Rental deposit[e]	0	1,500
Total	$23,380	$40,400

a. Required package of equipment and supplies for two cleaning crew start-ups.
b. Initial deposits to lease two Molly Maid-style Toyota Tercels or similar car models.

c. The high figure includes an upper estimate of annual costs for worker's compensation and similar employee insurance benefits. Your insurance costs run high for cleaning services because you must pay for your employees' protection.

d. Molly Maid offers a generous travel allowance for your training in Michigan. The company gives you $400 if you live east of the Mississippi; $600 if you live west. You pay all costs beyond that allowance, but Molly Maid is one of only two franchises in this book that helps pay your travel expenses.

e. Most franchisees start from their homes, but you must carefully check parking ordinances, zoning codes, and community association covenants before you do so. If you can't work from home, you will need to rent inexpensive space, perhaps a small executive office.

The average total investment equals between $25,000 and $30,000, making this a very inexpensive franchise which can bring you a potential two- to three-year net ROI exceeding 200 percent per year.

Other Fees and Required Purchases

You pay a weekly royalty fee based on a declining percentage scale that allows you to keep more money as your gross income increases. But you also must make minimum royalty payments if you do not do well. Here are both required payment schedules:

Declining Percentage Scale	
Annual Gross Income	**Royalty (%)**
Up to $250,000	8
$250,001 and $500,000	6
Above $500,000	4

Minimum Royalty Requirement	
Minimum Royalty	**Weeks in Business**
Stated percentage	0–10
$40 per week	11–26
$80 per week	27–52 (first year)
$160 per week	53 and beyond

You also pay a 2 percent national advertising fee each week and spend at least 3 percent of your gross revenues or $5,000, whichever is less, on local advertising. And you must participate in the company's National Cooperative

Trademark Yellow Pages listing program, which can save you a substantial amount because the national ad fund pays half of the costs. If two or more Molly Maid franchisees share the same Yellow Pages directory, they can share the costs of the same ad and reduce their expenses even more.

You must also buy required uniforms and clothing from Molly Maid, but the company does not profit from these sales. And as you expand, you must lease a new vehicle for every new two-person cleaning team that you field.

What You Get

You obtain all of the benefits that Molly Maid's professional image brings. In this competitive business, perhaps the most encouraging information about Molly Maid is that only 11 of its franchisees—about 3 percent per year—went out of business between 1985 and 1988, the latest year for which statistics were available. Three of them did not pay royalties; five voluntarily dropped out; and Molly Maid repurchased three. This is a very high success rate among cleaning and maid service franchises. With about 160 U.S. franchises, Molly Maid offers plenty of opportunity in the U.S. and foreign countries other than Canada, where Molly Maid began and has successfully saturated the market.

For your franchise fee, you receive the following:

Exclusive territory. You receive a territory based on a population of about 50,000. Of course, as for any other maid service, you want your territory to be one where 85 percent of your potential customers are affluent, two-income families. Look for these customers in your region and be among the first to choose your boundaries.

Agreement term. Your initial agreement lasts 10 years—plenty of time to build equity. And you can renew the agreement for repeated five-year periods with only a $1,000 additional fee. You also have a generous 60-day contract cancellation clause through which you can drop out of the system. And you can easily sell your franchise to a third party.

Corporate strength. Although Molly Maid faced financial difficulty in 1987, now that Johnson Wax owns one-third of it, it will have the financial strength to grow rapidly and yet provide quality support services.

Training program. You receive five days of training at corporate headquarters in Ann Arbor, Michigan; the training covers marketing, operations management, employee relations, recruiting, and accounting systems.

On-going support. Molly Maid offers region representatives and a toll-free hot line for technical support.

The company also holds seminars, workshops, conferences, and an annual convention, which teach marketing, sales, merchandising, quality performance, and personnel training.

Access to low-cost leasing. Its leasing program does save money over the price you can obtain leasing cars on your own.

Overall, Molly Maid's program enjoys a strong reputation, and company executives are very dedicated to promoting its professional image. They know that it makes them a cut above their competition, and they expect their franchisees to be equal to that task. So, franchisees tend to be teachers, nurses, and other professionals who suffer occupational "burnout" or relatively young retired couples, such as those from the military, looking for a challenge. The franchise does not encourage bored housewives.

How Much Can You Make?

As the beginning of this section shows, you can make an ROI in the hundreds of percent by your third year in business. The excellent statistics Molly Maid provides are duplicated below, so you can determine for yourself how well you may do.

You earn income by charging between $50 and $85 per house cleaning. This means that you need to rapidly increase both your marketing efforts and the numbers of crews you have. An average crew can clean six to eight houses per day. To gross $300,000 a year, your crews must clean 5,000 houses per year, at an average charge of $60 per house; that's slightly more than 16 houses per day with a six-day work week, or the amount two crews can do if they work at maximum efficiency. You probably will need to field three crews.

Note from the statistics that Molly Maid franchises tend to hit their stride by the middle of their second year, and most third-year franchises exceed $200,000 in gross revenues. So, patience and persistence will pay off in this business.

Note, as well, the company's disclaimer at the end of the listings. These are actual results; do not use them to predict your own success because that depends on many factors, including territory quality, your own effort, local competition, and more.

Regardless, Molly Maid's professional image, attitude, and its forthright publication of its franchisees' actual results show that the company deserves your close attention.

MOLLY MAID FRANCHISEES' ACTUAL RESULTS FOR 1988

The tabulation set forth below is based upon the actual operations of Molly Maid franchise owners in each respective geographical area. The figures appearing in the tabulation are extracted from the data contained in the weekly reports submitted by Molly Maid franchise owners as required by the standard Molly Maid franchise agreement.

The franchisor has not undertaken to specifically substantiate the accuracy of the data reported by each individual franchise owner. The tabulation is divided into six geographic regions in order to permit the prospective franchisee an opportunity to make meaningful comparisons.

Northeast Region

Franchise Owner	Number of Weeks in Business	Average Weekly Gross Sales
1	75	$3,255
2	118	3,357
3	122	3,212
4	50	597
5	122	4,892
6	133	3,882
7	50	2,764
8	19	310
9	98	2,267
10	11	164
11	27	1,540
12	118	5,002

The Northeast Region is composed of the following states: Connecticut, Massachusetts, New Hampshire, New Jersey, and Pennsylvania.

Mid-Atlantic Region

1	96	$ 606
2	108	2,345
3	75	1,586
4	79	1,928
5	129	3,911
6	145	3,794
7	127	7,404
8	66	1,338
9	159	3,708
10	15	493
11	94	5,555
12	155	2,635
13	83	4,038
14	191	4,553

The Mid-Atlantic Region is composed of the following states: Maryland, North Carolina, South Carolina, and Virginia.

Midwest Region

1	59	$ 482
2	237	12,730
3	45	2,385
4	17	233
5	64	1,578
6	54	1,130
7	22	553
8	41	2,019
9	120	6,156
10	172	2,861
11	83	1,288
12	120	2,007
13	96	2,240
14	70	776
15	127	7,044
16	116	2,230
17	111	5,322
18	54	1,046
19	120	2,740
20	124	2,798
21	93	1,382
22	15	191
23	15	127
24	17	403
25	72	1,207
26	104	3,017
27	17	74
28	28	567
29	31	1,175
30	104	2,889
31	124	4,850
32	124	3,886
33	160	4,630
34	106	4,862
35	44	706
36	75	2,411
37	54	1,056
38	183	4,450
39	75	2,091
40	183	3,288
41	72	1,703
42	183	5,312
43	31	1,195
44	200	1,140
45	106	1,428
46	129	4,127

The Midwest Region is composed of the following states: Illinois, Indiana, Michigan, Minnesota, Missouri, Nebraska, Ohio, and Wisconsin.

Southeast Region

1	141	$6,015
2	104	2,195
3	172	1,958
4	166	3,848
5	163	3,373
6	153	3,322
7	106	3,011
8	184	2,707
9	135	5,265
10	163	7,422
11	111	2,682
12	52	587
13	96	2,031
14	141	1,040
15	163	2,446
16	41	993
17	124	6,132
18	124	6,168
19	98	2,210

The Southeast Region is composed of the following states: Florida, Georgia, Kentucky, and Tennessee.

Southwest Region

1	176	$4,898
2	85	864
3	135	3,889
4	106	3,668
5	172	3,698
6	88	1,908
7	75	1,788
8	181	2,181
9	166	4,744
10	85	1,551
11	127	3,810
12	124	4,117
13	53	395

The Southwest Region is composed of the following states: Arizona, Colorado, New Mexico, and Texas.

West Region

1	120	$5,333
2	75	1,912
3	102	2,583
4	104	1,478
5	66	2,626
6	102	1,252
7	72	1,116
8	94	1,410
9	70	2,001
10	52	2,176
11	90	3,593
12	52	1,823
13	59	981
14	141	2,267
15	114	4,077
16	124	3,233
17	15	441
18	94	2,547
19	172	3,236
20	102	1,499
21	59	1,764
22	153	5,930
23	54	999

The West Region is composed of the following states: California, Oregon, and Washington.

43 percent of Molly Maid franchisees in operation as of December 31, 1988, attained or surpassed the annual average gross sales level of $140,000. 54 percent of Molly Maid franchisees have been in operation two years or less.

> *The gross sales listed in the tabulation set forth above are of specific franchises and should not be considered as the actual or potential gross sales that will be realized by any other franchise. The franchisor does not represent that any franchisee can expect to attain these gross sales.*

Substantiation of the data used in preparing the tabulation will be made available to the prospective franchisee upon reasonable request. However, the franchisor shall not disclose the identity of any specific franchise owner.

Except for the foregoing, the franchisor does not furnish or authorize its salesperson to furnish any oral or written information concerning the actual or potential sales, costs, income or profits of a Molly Maid franchise. Actual results may vary from unit to unit, and the Franchisor cannot estimate the results of any particular franchise.

HOMES & LAND PUBLISHING

Homes & Land Publishing
1600 Capitol Circle SW
Tallahassee, FL 32310
(904) 574-2111

Homes & Land Publishing Corporation is the largest real estate advertising publication franchise in the U.S., with more than 400 franchises operating by the end of 1989. Homes & Land achieved this remarkable growth in less than six years of offering franchises, although it has been in business since 1973.

Homes & Land is essentially an advertising sales and magazine distribution service franchise. It requires very low start-up costs and operating overhead—you can easily run your business from your home—but it does require hard work. You not only sell advertising space to local Realtors and real estate agencies but also you must take the photograph of each home or property that appears in your publication. That means you must constantly drive around your territory not only selling ads and servicing customers but also taking pictures of houses, buildings, and lots. To succeed with this business, it appears you must like to be constantly on the go and have, or be able to learn quickly, excellent personal selling skills. In short, this is a very difficult, time-consuming business, but you can also make very large profits.

Homes & Land now has about 410 franchises in 43 states and several Caribbean countries, but it has franchises available in all 50 states. Only California, Florida, Oregon, South Carolina, and Washington State have few available territories, according to company literature. The states with the most available territories include Connecticut, Iowa, Louisiana, Minnesota, Montana, North Dakota, Rhode Island, South Dakota, Utah, Vermont, Wisconsin, and Wyoming. Major markets are available in Arkansas, Idaho, Kansas, New Jersey, Oklahoma, Pennsylvania, Tennessee, Texas, and Virginia. And the company adds that the available markets change frequently, implying frequent ownership turnover.

The company states that, by the end of 1989, its "associate publishers" or franchisees distributed more than 3 million magazines per month free through various distribution points, usually racks within or in front of real estate offices, but also in or in front of grocery stores, convenience stores and shopping center anchor stores, or directly by real estate salespeople.

How Much It Costs

Homes & Land Publishing gives very low start-up cost estimates, including a fee of $15,000 for its flagship *Homes & Land* magazine franchise, and lower fees for additional rights in the following publications: *Homes & Land Digest,* $10,000; *Home Guide,* $1,500; and *Rental Guide,* $5,000. The company states that it estimates you need only $1,000 in additional start-up costs and several months' living expenses. Its estimate appears to be very low. A more reasonable estimate is given in the table below:

Category	Low End	High End
Franchise fee	$15,000	$15,000
Automobile[a]	0	1,500
Business phone deposit	200	500
Photography equipment	100	1,000
Office supplies, stationery	100	250
Insurance[b]	100	250
Travel training costs[c]	500	2,000
Living expenses[d]	1,500	6,000
Total	$18,000	$26,500

a. Nothing if you already own a car, but the high end covers the cost of a down payment, taxes, and tags for a new car or a lease. The range covers the cost of maintaining your car for three to six months because you will put hundreds of miles per week driving to your sales and photography calls.

b. Office contents rider to your homeowner's or rentor's insurance policy.

c. Costs of air fare, lodging, and board for a week in Tallahassee, Florida.

d. From a $500 per month base if your spouse supports your efforts to an estimated three months' living expenses (mortgage, car payment, food, utilities, basic bills).

What You Get

Homes & Land's best advantage—the magazine *Homes & Land*— is that it is the largest, best known, and most reputable of the numerous real estate advertising publications. It does offer a higher quality product than most of its competition, and it seems to enjoy more support among Realtors and real estate salespeople as well.

For your fee, you receive the following:

Training. You receive six days of training in sales, business, management, marketing, printer selection, layout, and photography at corporate headquarters.

Start-up field support. You receive on-site field support from a company representative as you start selling and putting together your first issue.

Start-up advertising and promotional materials. You receive 10 floor racks, 40 counter top racks, 10 outdoor racks, a direct mail solicitation brochure, advertising copy and materials, business cards, rate sheets, and a sales manual.

Homeline Service. Homeline Service is a toll-free hot line which gives to any caller two free copies of any Homes & Land magazine published anywhere in the country. The company says it receives 9,000 inquiries per month through this service. And the company inserts more than one million mail-in reply cards in Homes & Land magazines every three months; these cards also generate requests for free magazine copies.

This service allows you to act as a referral service for your customers—the local real estate agencies and Realtors who buy your ads. This value-added service proves to them you are a valuable source of leads for prospects.

On-going support. The company also provides promotional materials and ideas, telephone or on-site technical assistance, magazine layout and preparation supplies, a broker's newsletter for your clients, and regional and national meetings.

Printing service. The company will print and send you your copies each month. Of course, it charges you for this service and makes most of its revenues from printing charges and royalty fees incorporated into its advertising rate sheets. You can arrange for your own printing, but your printer must meet the company's quality standards. Most franchisees use the company's printing service for its uniform quality and relatively low cost.

Miscellaneous. You also receive a bulk mailing postal permit and a year's local Chamber of Commerce membership fee.

Royalty Fees

The royalty rate you pay varies from 6 percent to 16 percent, depending on how many copies you print each month and how many pages your magazine has each month. The company did not make available for this book copies of its printing costs or advertising and royalty rate sheets.

How Much Can You Make?

Homes & Land does not publish or make available any estimated earnings figures. The company advises you to contact current franchisees and discuss their earnings. It does claim that its franchisees' success rate is high; the dropout rate is about 10 percent per year. Although this 10 percent may be low in the real estate magazine franchise industry, it is three times higher than the national average failure rate for all franchises. This failure rate strongly indicates that this business requires strong selling skills and intense effort.

Homes & Land also reports in its literature that, as the company advises, most of its franchisees work full-time; their franchise provides their only or main source of income, the company adds.

Comparing Homes & Land to similar publication franchises, this author estimates that, with a 16-page monthly publication, you should earn net pre-tax profit margins of about 40 to 50 percent, depending on how well you control your expenses. And you should net $2,000 per month or about $25,000 per year by the end of the first year. By the end of the second year, you should net more than $40,000 per year. Many Homes & Land magazines are 48, 56, 64—or even more—pages thick, with dozens of real estate agencies represented by full pages of house and property pictures.

Clearly, two factors will determine how well you succeed: (1) whether or not you have previous *successful* sales experience, as the company emphasizes, but also (2) the health of the local real estate market. You will have a more difficult time in areas with weak real estate markets, where few people buy and sell relatively few properties each month. You can expect this business to follow the trends in your local real estate market. But, if you live in an average or active real estate market and have successful selling skills, you can achieve and maintain a very affluent annual income working from your home since this business has a very low overhead.

SERVPRO INDUSTRIES, INC.

SERVPRO Industries, Inc.
575 Airport Blvd.
Gallatin, TN 37066
(800) 826-9586 (franchise sales only)
(615) 451-0200

SERVPRO is one of the largest and most established cleaning franchises, with more than 730 franchises in operation during 1989. It has been consistently rated among the Top 5 Carpet Cleaning Services in the annual *Entrepreneur* magazine survey and, on occasion, has been rated the best. It was rated eighteenth in the 1985 *Venture* magazine list of the most profitable 100 franchises, with a stated average return on investment of more than 118 percent. It has been offering franchises since 1969 and now has franchises in every state, with a heavy concentration in California and other similar populous states.

SERVPRO emphasizes marketing your services to insurance companies for water and fire damage restoration, retail stores, real estate and property management firms, commercial and institutional buildings, and home owners.

How Much It Costs

SERVPRO offers *two types of franchises,* but they are sold and administered through a complex master distributor organization.

B.S.M. Deluxe Package I

The least expensive opportunity is the relatively new Building Service Maintenance (B.S.M.) operation. Its total non-cash cost is $19,500; if you pay cash, the price is reduced 10 percent to $17,500. If you finance the franchise fee, your standard (though negotiable) down payment is $12,000, with $6,500 financed at 13.5 percent over 48 months.

This franchise includes an equipment package valued at $7,500, leaving a franchise fee of $11,585 to cover all the training and other features you receive.

Both franchise packages offer similar training and support services, but with the B.S.M. you receive only enough equipment and supplies to offer retail store and office building maintenance services. Of course, your additional costs for this "starter" package will be less as well.

SERVPRO Cleaning Franchise

The regular SERVPRO franchise includes one more complete equipment and supplies package. It costs $32,500 if you finance it, and $22,100 if you pay cash. You can finance about half of the total with $15,000 down for 60 months, with an estimated 13.5 percent interest rate. The total payment to SERVPRO includes a $14,700 equipment and products package, so the franchise fee portion, including training costs, would equal $17,800.

If you buy an additional equipment package, you can finance up to 50 percent of that amount for between one and five years at an interest rate of between 12 and 15 percent.

Be very careful about all of this financing. It does reduce your cash up-front costs, but it puts very heavy pressure on you to succeed quickly just so you can pay off your debt to SERVPRO.

General and Director Distributors

SERVPRO also licenses experienced franchisees to sell franchises and act as trainers and support people for new and existing franchisees. General distribution rights cost $36,000, while director distribution rights are offered at $150,000. When one distributor buys another, the price is reduced by a maximum of $5,000 to eliminate redundant training and commission fees. However, if you buy a distributorship with existing franchises, you may have to pay 5 to 15 times the projected annual commissions associated with the territory and training rights. You can get a 20 percent discount on each for cash payments.

You can finance the purchase of these distribution rights: two-thirds of the general distributorship price ($24,000) at between 12 and 15 percent interest for up to seven years (84 months). You can finance up to 80 percent of the $150,000 ($120,000 after a $30,000 down payment) director distributorship price under the same terms. And you can finance 80 percent of any additional fees charged for existing goodwill from existing franchises in your territory under the same terms as well.

General and director distributors are also expected to purchase and maintain a 45-day supply of the chemicals, supplies, and parts normally used by the franchisees in their territories.

To become a franchise salesperson, a distributor must sign a contract, but SERVPRO does not charge a fee to engage in sales. Obviously, it would be unwise just to train new franchisees and not engage in making sales and earning hefty commissions.

Trainers and directors for SERVPRO generate income in three chief ways after they invest:

1. They share the royalties which franchisees pay. They receive 60 percent of all royalties paid to SERVPRO.
2. They receive directors' and trainers' commissions on product and equipment sales to their franchisees.
3. They are paid for selling and training new franchisees.

As a franchisee, you are also required to buy chemicals, supplies, and business forms from SERVPRO; those purchases will equal between 5 and 6 percent of your total operating costs per year. SERVPRO cannot force you to buy the chemicals from the company, and it has developed, over the past 20 years, an extensive list of *approved* suppliers.

Total Start-Up Costs

Your total start-up costs for a regular SERVPRO franchise will fall into a very broad range, primarily determined by how much you finance. If you finance everything you can, including the sales commission, your cash investment will be approximately the following:

Down payment	$13,000
Minus commission	− 3,800
Net down	$ 9,200
Added costs	1,330
Total Cash	$10,530

If you do not finance anything, pay all cash, and incur the maximum additional costs, your cash investment approximates—

Cash payment	$22,100
Added costs	12,550
Total	$34,650

Buying additional equipment options, working capital, start-up delays, etc., could raise that total to $42,150.

Royalty Structure

Regular franchisees also pay royalties (a $100 per month minimum) on gross monthly volume through a staggered, declining scale. These figures are shown in the following table:

Amount	Percentage (%)
Regular Franchisee	
$0 to $5,999	$ 45 + 10.0
$6,000 to $9,999	65 + 9.0
$10,000 to $14,999	85 + 8.0
$15,000 to $19,999	95 + 7.5
$20,000 and up	115 + 7.0
Subcontracted services	5.0
General Distributor	
Cleaning, deodorizing, etc.	$ 45 + 10.0
Subcontracted services	5.0
Director Distributor	
Cleaning, deodorizing, etc.	4.0
Subcontracted services	3.0

Advertising and Other Fees

You may also have to pay a monthly advertising fee of 3 percent, although SERVPRO did not charge this fee during 1989. The company reserves the right to impose service charges for automated bookkeeping systems.

Additional Costs

You can anticipate the following additional costs as part of your initial investment. Add in your own expectations of greater or lesser expense, depending on your circumstances.

	Low Range	High Range
Van lease or purchase[a]	$ 500	$10,000
Van painting	200	400
Liability insurances	500	1,000
Business licenses	0	200
Telephone deposit	30	250
Office supplies/equipment[b]	100	700
Total[c]	$1,330	$12,550

a. Depending on lease deposits or down payments, or on cash purchase prices, SERVPRO encourages the purchase of a used van or a lease to reduce up-front costs.
b. The office supplies cost includes a desk and typewriter, so go with the higher figure here unless you already own these items.
c. Note that SERVPRO does not include any figures for working capital, employee wages, etc., so add your own expectations (at least $1,000 to $3,000) for these costs.

What You Get

In return for these fees and payments, you receive the following:

Non-exclusive territory. A territory usually consists of an area with a population of between 25,000 and 80,000, or an area large enough to support a prosperous franchise. A general distributor's area will encompass at least 6 franchise areas, with a minimum population of 150,000. A director distributor's area will encompass at least 30 operating franchises and a population of at least 750,000. Although the territories are not exclusive, in only 10 cases out of more than 700 have the territories actually overlapped. Because SERVPRO emphasizes the retail store and insurance company markets, it has a special territory policy that limits how widely you can solicit this business outside of your territory boundaries. You may have to pay a commission to a different franchisee if you do this special work in his or her territory.

Four-step training. One of the best features of SERVPRO is its training program. It includes the following: a formal home-study course; on-the-job production training of about 13 days (10 days for applications, two days for sales, and one day for management); set-up training for two days at your new location (most often your home); and classroom training for a total of seven days, usually at SERVPRO headquarters. Area general and director distributors also give training seminars.

Paid transportation. SERVPRO also pays for the round-trip transportation costs for both a franchisee and a spouse for the classroom training.

Continuous support. SERVPRO is old enough and large enough to understand the need to provide quality-support teams either at the director and general levels or through national headquarters.

How Much Can You Make?

The most profitable SERVPRO franchisee in the country reports that he grosses more than $1.2 *million* a year. His franchise operates 8 trucks and has 15 employees. He has bought about $150,000 worth of equipment. The franchise divides the work about 50-50 between home cleaning (specializing in carpet and upholstery cleaning) and work procured through insurance companies (repairing and restoring water and fire damaged premises). The owner gives seminars to insurance agents interested in post-fire cleanups. He finds that providing this information also helps generate customers and build referrals.

A below average SERVPRO franchisee grosses less than $50,000 a year and earns a relatively low return on his cash investment. Note, however, that the average SERVPRO franchisee, as stated previously, earns an annual return of about 118 percent on his or her total two-year investment on gross revenues of between $60,000 and $100,000 a year. The average SERVPRO franchisee has only one van, one full-time employee and, occasionally, one part-time employee.

SERVPRO is well established and has embarked on a deliberate policy of steady growth. Obviously facing increasingly difficult competition, SERVPRO still remains a very successful company in a recession-proof industry.

RE/MAX INTERNATIONAL, INC.

RE/MAX International, Inc.
P.O. Box 3907
Englewood, CO 80155-3907
(800) 525-7452
(303) 770-5531

RE/MAX International is a rapidly growing real estate franchise driven by one simple concept: keep more of what you sell. Usually, typical real estate sales agents pay 55 percent of their gross commissions to the brokers who employ them. But top sales producers become very frustrated with paying this high percentage, and many leap at the opportunity to move to a company that gives them the chance to keep *100 percent* of their commissions.

RE/MAX's simple principle—100 percent commissions—is unique in real estate. As self-employed sales associates, however, RE/MAX sales associates must share the cost of office overhead. They must also pay for their own advertising, telephone, and other expenses. Nonetheless, they keep, as net profit, 70 to 80 percent of their commissions compared to much less than 45 percent for a typical real estate salesperson. This acts as a powerful incentive for aggressive, productive sales agents who average *28* transactions per year, as compared to 7 for the typical real estate agent.

Brokers like the franchise, too. They make more money because the total sales volume from the office is so much higher than a normal one, and they do not have to train novices or waste time with poor performers.

During 1988 and 1989, RE/MAX continued its phenomenal annual growth rate. During 1988, total system sales volume equalled $45.8 billion and increased to more than $58 billion during 1989; executives expect to exceed $70 billion during 1990. During 1988, the system had 1,466 franchised offices, with more than 22,000 sales associates earning gross commissions totalling almost $1.5 *billion.* During 1989, they earned almost $1.9 *billion* in commissions. By late 1989, the numbers had increased to 1,619 offices with more than 25,430 agents. During 1988, these agents closed more than 481,449 transactions.

The figures show that during 1989 an average RE/MAX sales associate earned almost *$75,000* in gross commissions, six to seven times more than the average real estate salesperson.

Clearly, RE/MAX is the best franchise for the most successful and ambitious brokers and sales associates. The company and its sales associates spent more than $90 million on advertising during 1988, a combined amount almost three times greater than Century 21's corporate ad budget. Moreover, like Century 21, RE/MAX is also rapidly becoming a household name.

RE/MAX relies on a very extensive subfranchisor system to encourage this rapid growth. By late 1989, there were state or regional subfranchisors in 49 U.S. states and all Canadian provinces. These subfranchisors receive the franchise fee payments and send a portion of these amounts to international headquarters. Since RE/MAX franchisees should be licensed brokers, the subfranchisors seek out the best existing small brokerages or the best brokers with large firms as the best prospects.

How Much It Costs

A RE/MAX franchise costs between $15,000 and $25,000 for an exclusive territory. The fee varies by region. The "territory" is limited, however; RE/MAX promises not to open another franchise within a one *mile* radius of yours. Moreover, for "low density franchises," those in areas with fewer than 10,000 people, the fee is reduced to $10,000; in an area between 10,000 and 15,000 people, the fee is $12,500.

Beyond the fee and the cost of attending RE/MAX's training, existing brokers with offices probably will face few additional start-up expenses. If you plan to open an office, however, you must anticipate some fairly large office expenses. RE/MAX estimates that your start-up costs will range from $10,000 to $50,000. First, you must rent (or own) 1,200 square feet of office space from the start. Second, to meet RE/MAX's minimum expansion requirements, you will have to lease substantial amounts of office furniture, arrange for telephone installation, purchase signage, and incur the other usual office expenses. However, you will recoup your up-front expenses from your sales associates who pay your overhead costs. RE/MAX estimates you need between $10,000—for an existing space—to $50,000 or more for a substantial new office.

With the company's recruiting requirements, the higher figure is more likely to occur. RE/MAX requires that you have a *minimum* of 7 sales associates at work within the first 12 months and expand to a minimum of 15 by the end of the second year—at least, in most cases. This means that you may have to search aggressively for the best producers in existing brokerages and "raid" these brokerages for their best talent.

Complex Fee Schedule

RE/MAX charges a complex fee schedule based on a 15 percent commission or royalty from the amount that the franchisee receives from his or her sales agents. RE/MAX also charges a variety of complex fees, most of which the franchisee/broker collects from his or her sales associates.

Management fee. You must pay a minimum of $80 per month for each sales agent, or one-fifth of the management fee that the sales agent pays you each month. During 1987, RE/MAX suggested that this monthly fee should equal $400.

Annual dues. You must pay $270 per year for each salesperson registered in your office. You must collect the first-year dues from each sales agent. In second or subsequent years, your agents should pay their own dues directly to the franchisor.

Advertising fee. Each associate must pay, through you to the franchisor, a monthly advertising fee that varies from $50 to $100 per month depending upon the region. You collect these funds from all your brokers and associates. This amount is used exclusively for regional advertising on your behalf.

Institutional advertising development fund. This is equal to $5 per person per month for national advertising and promotion.

Renewal fee. Each franchise runs for a rather short five-year term. To renew the franchise, you must pay a fee equal to 50 percent of the then-current franchise fee. For example, suppose that you paid $15,000 for your initial fee in 1987. In 1992, you want to renew the agreement. The then-current franchise fee has increased to $25,000, so you will have to pay $12,500 to renew the franchise.

What You Get

Primarily, you get the benefit of the RE/MAX concept of encouraging the best sales agents and brokers to break loose from the bondage of the 45/55 commission split. This alone should encourage aggressive brokers to rapidly build staff while they continue to sell on their own.

You also receive five days of training, which is not necessarily in selling but in applying the unusual RE/MAX approach to agents and the marketplace. The broker/owner does not have to be actively involved in the business. If not, his or her responsible broker or office manager must take the training course.

Most importantly, you get the benefit of the enormous RE/MAX marketing machine, with its thrust to push the company ahead of Century 21 during the 1990s. This push brings tremendous benefits in name recognition, training and educational services, client referrals, and the like.

How Much Can You Make?

Your income is derived by charging your sales associates monthly fees and making each associate pay a proportional share of your overhead costs, including the cost of secretaries or office managers. Look at some easily discerned results. First, you charge the sales associate between $400 and $500 per month as a management fee. This amount does not include the apportioned office expenses. You must send $80 of this amount to the company, so you keep between $320 and $420 per associate per month, for a minimum monthly income ranging between $2,240 and $5,040, depending on whether you have 7 or 12 agents working out of the office. Therefore, the larger your office and the more aggressively you recruit top selling agents, the more money you make.

During 1989, RE/MAX salespeople earned almost $1.9 billion in commissions. This means that the company's 1,619 franchisees probably averaged between at least $27,000 and $60,500 in payments from their agents. Not bad for arranging office space and managing an office! Of course, any broker in an agency like a RE/MAX one will be selling on his or her own, too, and earning even more money.

A license broker may recoup his initial investment in a RE/MAX franchise within a year and start earning a ROI in the 50 to 100 percent per year range within two years, thereafter. But RE/MAX executives caution that how much you earn depends directly on how aggressively and successfully you recruit new agents. Your profit is based on the number of successful agents you field and how smart you are in managing your office well. RE/MAX is truly an exciting opportunity for the hottest real estate brokers in small firms around the country.

VIDEO DATA SERVICES

**Video Data Services
24 Grove St.
Pittsford, NY 14534
(716) 385-4773**

With more than 230 franchises, Video Data Services (VDS) is the largest and most successful videotaping service franchise. Between 1984 and 1989, *Entrepreneur* magazine rated it the best video service franchise each year; *Venture* rated it the 47th best business opportunity out of a Top 100.

VDS is a very simple, inexpensive service business in which you can easily quadruple, quintuple, even sextuple your investment during your first two years in business. In this business, working with "state-of-the-art," professional video equipment, you tape all events—from a wedding to a trial to a legal deposition to a local sports event to a business convention to a speech, and to many more. You may do insurance inventories for businesses and homeowners, and you can provide very high-profit ancillary services, such as film-to-tape transfers. In a VDS newsletter, for example, one franchisee noted that he charges $65 per film-to-tape transfer, yet his costs equal just $5. He thus make a $60 or 1,200 percent profit, or a 95 percent profit margin.

Best of all, you can begin the service part-time from your home and thus keep your overhead costs very low. You can use your own car or mini-van as well. VDS is also an excellent franchise for women, and many of VDS's leading franchisees are women who work full time. Certainly, it is one of the few businesses in which women can earn as much as men and reach six-figure incomes as quickly.

If videotaping services are so lucrative, why can't you do it on your own instead of buying a VDS franchise? You can if you want to do all of the leg work, spend a year or two learning how to sell your services, and pay retail prices for professional video equipment—in short, do things the hard way. VDS executives make the excellent point that you can also open your own hamburger stand, but most people would rather own a McDonald's franchise. The author doesn't claim that VDS is the "McDonald's" of videotaping; still if you avoid reinventing the wheel, you do better in the long run.

Money-Back Guarantee

Perhaps best of all, VDS is the only franchise the author knows that offers a 100 percent money-back guarantee. If you are dissatisfied *after* your training session and want to drop out, VDS will refund all of your money. A few other franchises will give most of your money back, and most will refund your money if they flunk you out of their training course, but only VDS gives you the choice. That undoubtedly explains why *no* VDS franchisee was terminated or left the system between 1984 and 1989. This is a phenomenally high success rate compared to any other franchise's record, even the other companies in this book.

How Much It Costs

VDS is inexpensive compared to the very high short-term potential income. The total payment to VDS equals $15,950, of which about $10,000 is considered the franchise fee. The rest pays for a panoply of professional video equipment. The following table estimates your total start-up costs:

Category	Low End	High End
Franchise payment	$15,950	$15,950
Lease deposits[a]	0	1,200
Fixtures, improvements	500	1,500
Initial advertising	1,000	2,000
Vehicle	0	2,000
Insurance[b]	600	600
Amiga computer[c]	0	2,500
Working capital[d]	2,000	5,000
Total	$20,050	$30,750

a. Nothing if your start at home, the recommended course; about $400 per month for 400 square feet in warehouse-type space. VDS recommends a minimum of 400 square feet if you have an office.
b. VDS has arranged a very inexpensive liability policy; you can buy it from any source, but VDS's rate is excellent.
c. You don't have to buy this graphics system at first, but its low cost and high-profit potential make it an attractive option as a first-year purchase.
d. Includes one to three months' living expenses.

Other Fees and Payments

You also pay a 3 percent royalty on gross sales, or a minimum of $500 per year. VDS reserves the right to charge a 1 percent per month advertising fee, but by early 1990, it had not chosen to do so. That's it; as a wholesaler of video equipment, VDS sells a lot of equipment and encourages you to buy the equipment from the company, but it does not *require* you to do so.

What You Get

Obviously, the two most important aspects of this business concern marketing and the equipment package. The equipment package includes a professional video camera, VHS editor with special effects, color monitor, film-to-tape transfer equipment, electronic editor, and many accessories.

The marketing program teaches you how to identify and sell to five important targets, all of which VDS teaches you at its three-day training program. The targeted markets include the following:

1. Conventions, exhibits, seminars, and speaking engagements
2. Home, school, and industry movie conversions to tape
3. Weddings, birthdays, receptions, retiree parties, etc.
4. Legal depositions and trials
5. Tour of homes for local real estate agencies

The training program begins with two weeks of study at home. It is followed by a three-day classroom training, and then by six weeks of post-classroom, at-home study, with training tapes and materials, as you begin your service. VDS's intense schedule for the three-day session emphasizes marketing and using the equipment.

You also receive an exclusive territory. The population of that territory includes about 200,000 people in two or more contiguous zip codes, according to the company's most recent UFOC. Be sure that your territory includes numerous affluent households, hotels where conventions and business meetings are held, lawyers' offices and—at least—one courthouse, insurance agencies, real estate agencies, and other similar high-potential customers.

The initial franchise agreement's term is 10 years, with the right to renew for additional 10-year terms. The UFOC does not specify whether you must pay additional fees, but VDS reserves the right to set those terms and conditions and apply them equally to all franchisees.

In addition to these elements, VDS provides strong support through newsletters, telephone consultation, advice about sources of supply, and—at a price equal to VDS's cost—advertising and promotional brochures and materials. It does charge an hourly fee for telephone consultation that exceeds two hours per month per franchisee; but that appears reasonable since VDS is a small company and the president provides most of these services.

How Much Can You Make

With VDS, you create multiple opportunities to earn income. *Home Office Computing* magazine reported the story of VDS franchisee Virgil Miller who began his business full-time in 1987 after recovering from an injury as a deputy sheriff. By the end of 1989, and after less than two years, Miller reported that his annual income had exceeded the $100,000 level. Six-figure incomes are apparently quite common among established VDS franchisees.

You earn income in many ways. VDS reports that its franchisees charge $500 for an average taping session. One female franchisee began in 1985 charging $200 for a wedding, yet she found she was not charging enough; in late 1988, she was charging $850 per wedding. Reportedly, she had more business than she could handle.

The 95 percent profit margins on film-to-tape transfers has been noted. In the future, offering the services of computer graphics, adding graphics to video presentations, and other similar high-technology services will prove very lucrative for VDS franchisees. With a $2,000 Amiga computer system, VDS franchisees can produce graphics similar to those created by professional systems that cost $20,000 or more. And you can charge $200 to $300 or more for each graphics job.

VDS provides these examples of gross income potential, which do not include any ancillary service income:

	Per Day	Per Year
One taping per week[a]	200	$ 10,400
One taping per day	200	52,000
Two tapings per day	400	104,000

a. The $200 per job figure is certainly a low average among franchisees. One can easily tape one wedding per week for $500 or more.

Apparently, the average VDS franchisee earns a moderate net income during the first year, but builds her or his volume very rapidly during the second year. Net pre-tax profits average 60 to 80 percent because your overhead and capital expenditures are very low compared to your gross income. Videotaping is a very lucrative opportunity, and VDS is the best franchise to teach you the business.

CENTURY 21
REAL ESTATE CORPORATION

Century 21 Real Estate Corporation
International Headquarters
Century Centre
2601 S.E. Main St.
P.O. Box 19564
Irvine, CA 92713-9564
(714) 553-2100

Century 21 is the dominant real estate franchise company in the world. It has more than 7,000 franchisees in the U.S., Canada, Japan, Australia, New Zealand, France, Mexico, and the United Kingdom. During 1988, these franchisees earned more than $2 billion in commissions from sales, representing more than $60 billion worth of real estate. Franchisee commissions increased an average of 23 percent during 1988, although sales only increased 13 percent. And Century 21 has an approximately 11 percent share of the market for brokerage residential home sales in the U.S. *Entrepreneur* ranked Century 21 as one of the best 15 franchises in the country in its 1989 survey.

Century 21 offers several advantages compared to other real estate franchises, company executives say:

Incredibly high name recognition: Its name is recognized by 98 percent among the middle-income group and by 87 percent of all people. Century 21 encourages this name recognition with more than $40 million per year in national and local advertising expenditures. It does have an effective network television campaign that promotes its corporate image.

Regional franchise owners and brokers. In the early days, Century 21 grew rapidly because it helped pioneer the concept of regional franchise owners. The regional offices continue to sell the franchises, provide training and support services, and collect royalty fees. Today, Century 21 has acquired most of the regional offices and would like to acquire the remaining 11. This turn comes from a new corporate direction set in 1986 by its then-new owner, Metropolitan Life Insurance.

Training and support. Century 21 does offer a very deep and broad level of training for both franchise buyers, who are usually experienced real estate brokers or service owners, and their staffs.

Range of services. In recent years, the franchise has expanded its service offices, moving more into investment property brokering, real estate syndications, property management, national account selling, and mortgage brokering through 15 offices. Now, Century 21 wants its franchises to move towards the one-stop financial services concept. Corporate headquarters wants its franchisees to expand their offices and include insurance and similar services, as well as real estate.

National network. This has been established for client referral/relocation and investment property brokering services.

Protection in hard times. During the last real estate bust in 1982, 16 percent of Century 21's franchises failed. That number was just half of the number of brokerages that closed nationwide, a figure in excess of 31 percent. Real estate is a very cyclical business, and it may pay to work with a well-known franchisor to protect yourself when hard times arrive.

How Much It Costs

In addition to the normal start-up costs for a real estate broker's office, Century 21 charges a franchise fee that ranges from $10,500 to $25,500. The actual amount varies according to office size, geographic and demographic area serviced, etc. Century 21 does *not* offer exclusive territories; in fact, some franchisees complain that Century 21 is so well known that most clients do not know that each office is independently owned.

In addition, you pay a monthly 6 percent royalty on gross *commissions* that your firm earns and a 2 percent advertising fee. These royalties and fees go to the regional offices. In turn, the regions send 15 percent of their service fees and 10 percent of their advertising fees to corporate headquarters, which had an income of more than $117 million during 1988, a 31.6 percent increase in just two years.

The 6 percent royalty is more attractive to small offices and new brokers, but less so to larger, established brokers, so Century 21 offices tend to be small. This means that there will be many small offices in any market area, but their collective presence will create a dominant impact. Nonetheless, the offices range in size from one or two people to one in southern California with 500 agents, who sell $45 to $50 million worth of houses per *month.* The largest office pays royalties in excess of $500,000 per month, and the owner maintains that the benefits—on-going training for all levels, cooperative advertising program, image-building ads, and print media advertising programs—outweigh the cost of the royalty payments.

Additional costs to open a real estate broker's office depend entirely on how many salespeople you have, and local circumstances. The costs should range from $10,000 to $50,000.

If you already own an existing brokerage, converting to a Century 21 franchise should cost $5,000 to $10,000 for signage, advertising, office supplies, changes in telephone directory listings, travel for training, and the like.

What You Get

Essentially, what you receive is the dominant Century 21 name recognition and visibility and its wide range of services that are provided mostly through its regional offices. The company outspends its nearest franchise competitor five times to one in total advertising dollars.

Century 21 also stays very close to its brokers through a series of national, regional, and local meetings. City or state brokers' councils meet at least *six* times a year with their regional directors. In turn, the regional director meets with corporate officers three times a year. And regional directors and corporate management meet twice a year with the National Brokers' Communication Congress, a group of local franchisees selected from each region. One broker represents every 100 brokers, meaning a group of more than 65 people. And thousands of people attend a national convention each year.

These meetings tend to bring market trends and franchisee needs to the attention of corporate executives very quickly, so they can react to situations, a crucial marketing advantage in any business as competitive as real estate.

How Much Can You Make?

As in any real estate business, you make commissions on what you sell. Those commissions normally range from 2 to 3 percent for sales made through multiple listing services to 6 to 10 percent for exclusive sales. The national average for Century 21 salespeople is 4 percent of gross sales. In real estate, gross sales equal the total amount of the value of real estate sold; gross sales of $20 million means that the broker sold $20 million worth of property—*not* that he or she earned $20 million in commissions.

According to a real estate magazine, two leading Century 21 sales-people earned gross commissions totalling more than $850,00 and $650,000 during 1988. They worked in the franchise owner's offices. As a franchise owner, you may earn 40 to 65 percent of gross commissions, depending on your pay structure. From those two salespeople alone, the franchise owner received gross income of about $750,000.

You should reap a net profit of 30 to 40 percent of your share of gross commissions after subtracting royalties and fees, commissions paid to salespeople, and overhead. Thus, if your office sold $1 million worth of real estate each month (just 10 houses valued at $100,000 each), your firm's average gross commissions would equal $40,000 (4 percent). Your brokers would receive an average of 50 percent, leaving you a gross profit of $20,000. After royalties and overhead, your net would range from

$6,000 to $8,000 per month. You could recoup your investment in the franchise in six months to a year and earn substantial ROIs above 100 percent during the first two years. Century 21 is one of the two best available real estate franchises, and it is likely to grow steadily and become stronger during the coming years.

7

Franchises with Fees from $15,001 to $20,000

Decorating Den Systems, Inc.
Management Recruiters
   International, Inc.
Merry Maids, Inc.
Pak Mail™ Centers of America, Inc.
Adia Personnel Services
Bio-Care, Inc.

Mail Boxes Etc. USA
Haircrafters and Great
   Expectations Hair Salons
Cost Cutters Family Hair
   Care Shops
Four Seasons Greenhouses Design
   & Remodeling Centers

DECORATING DEN SYSTEMS, INC.

Decorating Den Systems, Inc.
4630 Montgomery Ave.
Bethesda, MD 20814
(301) 652-6393

Decorating Den Systems, Inc., offers an interior design franchise on wheels; that is, its franchisees—some 98 percent of whom are women—offer in-home comprehensive interior decorating services to middle-class and afflu-ent homeowners. Rather than their customers visiting a showroom, the franchisees bring with them in a special Colorvan more than 5,000 samples of window treatments, wall coverings, furniture, floor coverings, carpets, and accessories. This mobile franchise has been shown to have tremendous appeal both to busy working singles and two-income couples who do not have time to coordinate their own interior decorating and to consumers who dislike going to big showrooms or stores.

Franchisees offer products from 30 leading suppliers and name-brand companies, including Waverly and Kirsch. The company challenges these vendors to provide quality products on a very timely basis because, too often, customers must wait 8 to 12 weeks or more for their new window treatments and furniture. But Decorating Den franchisees try to make sure its vendors deliver within 4 to 6 weeks. They also arrange for professional installation and receive commissions from the installers; they rarely do any heavy or complex installation work themselves.

Franchisees make their money on the retail mark-ups on their customers' purchases; they do not charge fees for their services. These retail gross mark-ups range from as low as 20 percent to as high as 70 percent, with 40 to 50 percent as the average. The company reports an average sale is about $1,500.

By the end of 1989, Decorating Den had more than 1,000 franchisees around the U.S. and in Canada. During 1988, Decorating Den franchisees had more than $39 million in system-wide sales, and the company estimates that 1989 sales exceeded $50 million.

Decorating Den began in 1969 in the Midwest under a different name when a fabric dealer decided to try to make interior decorating and design services affordable. It began franchising in 1978; the current president and CEO, James S. Bugg, bought into the business that same year. Since 1985, system-wide sales have almost quadrupled.

To better serve the local franchisees and sell more franchises more rapidly, the company has divided the country into 50 regions, some 42 of which have been set up. In most regions, Decorating Den has licensed a regional director to provide training and support services to franchisees, sell more franchises, and collect royalty payments. In other cases, Decorating Den employees manage the regions.

The typical franchisee is a woman who would like to own an interior decorating business, but who does not have the know-how or the money to open an interior design showroom or business. In any case, the high end of the market, in which interior designers (with American Society of Interior Design credentials) compete vigorously for a small market of wealthy patrons and corporations, is already very crowded. The Decorating Den approach brings interior decorating services to a growing number of middle-class and affluent Baby Boomers and Yuppies.

How Much It Costs

Decorating Den offers two types of franchises:

Senior franchise. For an exclusive territory based on zip codes, you pay a franchise fee between $15,900 and $18,900, depending upon a complex retail market formula. The formula, which results in a whole number between 1 and 4, gauges what Decorating Den calls the "relative retail sales potential" of the zip code area. The number corresponds to the number of Colorvans that Decorating Den assigns to that zip code.

The basic fee is $15,900 for a retail market number of 1—with 1 Colorvan®. You add $1,000 for each additional whole number up to 4—with 4 Colorvans®. A Number 4 (four-van) territory's fee equals $18,900. The company may divide any zip code with a higher sales potential into two territories, and it may combine two or more zip codes with retail sales potential equal to less than one van. Decorating Den applies this formula in the same manner to every zip code in the U.S.

The formula is based on three factors:

1. Number of households, according to the latest Census Bureau data
2. Median income, according to the same data
3. Gross retail sales for the zip code

Associate franchise. Since 1987, the company has also offered what it calls an "associate franchise" for a small fee of $6,900. The major difference between associate and senior franchisees is the amount of royalties they pay. The following tables show the sliding scale fees each pays:

Decorating Den Royalty Rates

Senior Franchise

Annual Total Paid ($)	Percentage (%)
0–11,000	11
11,001–15,500	9
15,501–19,500	8
19,501–23,000	7
More than $23,000	6

The fee drops from 11 percent to 9 percent after you pay the first $11,000 in royalties (make your first $121,000 in gross income) and so forth.

Associate Franchise

Annual Total Paid ($)	Percentage (%)
0–15,000	15
15,001–21,500	13
21,501–27,500	12
27,501–33,000	11
More than $33,000	10

> Note that Decorating Den reserves the right to raise or lower the
> royalty rates once a year according to the U.S. Consumer Price
> Index for Urban Wage Earners and Clerical Workers, U.S. City
> Average.

Clearly, if you want an associate franchise, you trade a lower franchise fee for a much higher royalty during the life of your franchise. You must make remarkably high sales as an associate franchisee to reduce your franchise fees to the senior franchisee's highest level. The $9,000 difference in the franchise fee is a relatively small amount compared to the ten years of high royalty payments you must make as an associate. You would do best to raise the capital or borrow the $9,000 difference to take advantage of the lower royalty payment percentages.

Another major difference between a senior and associate franchisee is that Decorating Den can assign an associate franchisee to a senior's territory if that senior franchisee is not generating a large sales volume. Decorating Den's UFOC does not cite the specific circumstances under which this would occur, but it does state that senior franchisees have the right to refuse to allow an associate to compete in his or her territory.

And associate franchisees assigned to a one-van territory must fulfill a minimum annual sales quota of $30,000; senior franchisees with larger territories must fulfill higher minimum quotas during their second and subsequent years in business.

Start-Up Costs

Your total start-up costs, especially if you lease your Colorvan®, will be relatively low. Note that usually this is a home-based business, and these estimates do not reflect any start-up costs for office space. The following table shows the company's and the author's estimates:

Category	Low End	High End
Franchise fee^a	$ 6,900	$18,900
Colorvan®^{b}	1,000	18,000
Insurance^c	800	2,000
Working capital^d	5,000	9,000
Living expenses^e	5,000	15,000
Total^f	$18,700	$62,900

a. From the associate fee to the highest senior fee.
b. Low end reflects one van lease down payment; high end shows one van's purchase price, if you pay cash.

c. For comprehensive business and Colorvan® insurances; from down payments to total annual costs. Vehicle insurance varies widely from place to place.

d. Decorating Den lists initial advertising, telephone answering service or business telephone deposits, travel training expenses, and living expenses before you begin work.

e. The author adds estimates for three to six months' living expenses you will need as you get started, unless a spouse supports your efforts. Either way, you will require this much for operating capital and personal expenses during your first six months.

f. This shows a very wide range; more than likely, your start-up costs will fall in the $30,000 to $35,000 range.

Fees, Quotas, and Requirements

Besides the royalty sliding scale payments described above, you must pay a 2 percent or $83 per month minimum contribution to a National Marketing Fund. This, too, can be adjusted once a year according to increases in the Consumer Price Index.

If you have a one-van territory, you must also fulfill an annual gross sales quota of at least $30,000 to retain your franchise rights. After the first year, that minimum increases with your territory's sales potential, that is, the number of Colorvans the company believes the territory will support. The following tables show these requirements:

Potential	Year 1	Year 2	Year 3	Years 4–10
1 van	$30,000	$30,000	$30,000	$ 30,000
2 vans	30,000	60,000	60,000	60,000
3 vans	30,000	60,000	90,000	90,000
4 vans	30,000	60,000	90,000	120,000

Note: For territories with 5 or more vans, add $30,000 per year minimums for each additional year.

Clearly, Decorating Den gives you time to grow, but does insist that you work hard to develop your territory. "Use it or lose it" is the company's appropriate philosophy.

Other than transfer fees if you sell your franchise and fees for advanced training courses, Decorating Den requires no other fees or payments. You must, however, buy your supplies and products from approved suppliers; Decorating Den receives incentives and commissions from some vendors. Since the company only works with well-known and high-quality vendors, this requirement works overall to your advantage.

What You Get

In exchange for your fees, you receive a very successful and potentially lucrative franchise program:

Territory. In most cases, as a senior franchisee, you receive an exclusive territory based on the one- to four-van formula described above. According to the company's UFOC, Decorating Den gives senior franchisees very specific promotional rights within a territory, as well as the right to approve the assignment of any associate franchise in his or her territory.

Decorating Den has a 10-point statement in its contract that defines how regional directors should apply these promotional and territory rights to avoid conflicts, such as media advertising that crosses zip code boundaries, i.e., radio, television, major newspaper, and Yellow Pages advertising.

If you receive a two- to four-van territory, you must develop that territory and add those vans according to a schedule you work out with Decorating Den executives; or you can allow associate franchisees into your territory. An average Number 1 franchise territory includes about 4,000 households, according to the company's UFOC; at least, the company agrees to grant no more than one franchise for every 4,000 households per state.

Associate franchisees do not receive exclusive territories, and they must meet $30,000 annual minimum gross sales quotas.

Term. The initial agreement lasts 10 years, and you may renew for additional terms by signing the then-current contract and paying a small amount equal to 2 percent of the then-current initial franchise fee.

Preferred suppliers. To succeed in this business, you must offer well-known name-brand products, and Decorating Den offers products through 30 major brand names, including Waverly and Kirsch.

Training. You receive five to eight days of training at the company headquarters' Introductory Design and Sales School. The training emphasizes four chief topics: product knowledge, life-style design, sales and marketing, and business management. The company also provides start-up training and on-going seminars and training support through its regional directors. After you begin, you train yourself at home and with the regional director for 12 more weeks.

Advertising. The company provides a start-up package of advertising planning, programs, and promotional pieces, as well as seasonal promotions and ad layouts. A grand opening promotion lasts three weeks and includes direct mail, media advertising, and special discount promotions from approved suppliers.

Services. Decorating Den also provides a buying service to identify and help introduce new products into the system, a merchandising service for special promotions and discounts, advanced training programs, and marketing counseling, as well as the usual newsletters and telephone hot lines. You receive most of your help from your regional director.

Decorating Den's regional directors (who may be existing franchisees or company employees) appear to work well in providing the services you may need at the local level.

How Much Can You Make?

Remember that interior design is a very competitive business. Not only do you compete against professional interior designers at the high end of your market, you compete against major retailers, most notably J. C. Penney and Sears, and thousands of small interior decorators as well. This business requires hard work and personal promotion for you to succeed.

If one assumes a moderate start-up cost of $30,000 and an average sale of $1,500 per customer, you must make 20 sales during your first year to reach the breakeven point.

Many Decorating Den franchisees work part-time and earn relatively little. Those who approach this system as a full-time business average gross annual sales of about $50,000. This total equals the franchisees' 40 to 50 percent gross margins on product sales of about $100,000 to $120,000 per year.

The franchisees who do best work hard to promote their service through home shows, referrals, public relations in local newspapers, workshops of various types, and personal networking through women's and business organizations.

Decorating Den sponsors a growing Century Club for those franchisees whose gross sales exceed $100,000 a year.

It appears that, working from home, you can net between 50 and 80 percent of your gross income. Within two years, you should be able to reach a net income of $25,000 to $40,000 a year after you payback your initial investment during your first year. Thus, you can generate 100 percent ROIs after your second year.

MANAGEMENT RECRUITERS
INTERNATIONAL, INC.

Management Recruiters International, Inc.
Statler Office Tower, Suite 1400
1127 Euclid Ave.
Cleveland, OH 44115-1638
(800) 366-8744
(216) 696-1122, collect
(216) 696-3221, FAX

Management Recruiters is the leading management and employee search and recruitment organization in the U.S., with more than 560 franchised offices around the country. About 10 percent are company-owned. Management Recruiters concentrates on placing personnel in permanent jobs; it does not participate in the temporary employment field. It has two major operating divisions: Management Recruiters for technical, administrative, engineering, data processing, financial, and clerical positions; and Sales Consultants for sales professionals, managers, and marketing talent. Within Management Recruiters, separate divisions exist: one is called OfficeMates/5, which places clerical/administrative support staff; and CompuSearch, which places data processing personnel within Management Recruiters.

Management Recruiters' marketing strategy centers around its "contingency" fees. Unlike most of its competitors, it does not require any upfront retainer from an employer, who does not pay until the office finds a suitable job-hunting prospect who is offered and accepts the position. However, the fees that you receive when you do place a prospect are substantial: 1 percent per thousand of salary and then a flat 30 percent above this amount. The average fee during 1988 was between $9,000 and $10,000, up 12.5 percent since 1986.

By late 1987, Management Recruiters had 510 franchises and 50 company-owned outlets. During 1988, total network sales exceeded $200 million, up one-third since 1985, for average franchisee new revenues of more than $400,000 each. Management Recruiters competes primarily against Dunhill Personnel System.

A typical office includes between two and eight account executives, an owner/manager, and a clerical support person. It is usually located in and around major cities, but many offices are located in rural areas and rely on telemarketing to serve employers and candidates nationwide.

Since it began in 1965, Management Recruiters has developed what is clearly the best franchising program in its market niche. In 1987, it won the prestigious Franchise Relations Award from the International Franchise Association. The award is granted to only one franchisor in the world each year.

How Much It Costs

The company's franchise fee follows an increasing scale that is based entirely on population and demographics:

Population	Franchise Fee
250,000 and under	$20,000
250,000–500,000	25,000
500,000–1,000,000	30,000
1,000,000 and more	Individually priced

When choosing a territory, be careful to find one with excellent demographics for white-collar, professional jobs. Of course, you want the local economy to be doing well, and you hope it encourages a lot of positive job turnover, with employers looking to expand and add new people.

Start-Up Costs

Under the company's system, your initial investment is relatively low, often lower than the franchise fee. Management Recruiters states that the average start-up costs will range from $4,000 to $6,000, with $3,500 a minimum and $7,400 a maximum. The table that follows lists these figures:

Description	Low Estimate	High Estimate
Franchise fee	$20,000	$25,000
Start-up expenses	4,000	7,400
Working capital	16,000	27,600
Total Investment	$40,000	$60,000

Savings and Expenses

The company recommends that you borrow money to buy office furniture. You can also lease it or rent it month-to-month when you get started to keep your costs down.

You can expect average monthly operating expenses of about $5,500, including the following: $1,800 for telephone; $1,000 for an office worker's wages; $800 for rent on an 800-square-foot office; and the rest for advertising, insurance, accounting, and furniture payments. You also have to pay your travel and room and board costs for a three-week training program in Cleveland at an estimated cost of $2,000.

Account Executive Commissions

You must hire account executives to sell your services and place job applicants, but you do not have to pay them a salary. Most franchisees pay only commissions on fees earned from actual job placements. You can expect these commissions to range from a low of 30 percent for the lowest fees to as high as 50 percent, with a first-year average of 35 percent. Commissions, payroll taxes, and unemployment compensation costs will equal about 40 percent of your gross receipts.

The majority of franchisees now follow this commission schedule for their account executives, as shown on the next page.

Commission (%)	Net Cash in Each Quarter
30	of the first $ 5,000
35	of the next 10,000
40	of the next 15,000
45	of the next 20,000
50	of any over 25,000

Royalty and Fees

You also have to pay a straightforward 5 percent royalty on your gross, which declines as your income increases. And you have to pay a very low one-half of 1 percent (0.5%) for a national advertising fee. The company uses these fees for an impressive national campaign in the best business, personnel, and recruiting publications.

The royalty is paid on the sliding scale that is shown below:

Net Cash-In/Month	Royalty (%)
$ 2,521,637 or less	5.0
2,521,637– 5,043,276	4.0
5,043,276– 7,564,914	3.0
7,564,914–10,086,553	2.0
10,086,553 and over	3.5

There are no other fees or required payments to the company—a very simple and straightforward arrangement.

What You Get

Franchise Structure

The company encourages four types of franchises:

1. Individually owned
2. Conversion from an existing personnel agency to a franchise
3. Two-tier, with an expanded territory
4. Three-tier, or master franchise program that allows a distributor to sell individual franchises within his larger territory

The initial term is 60 months, and it can be renewed without an additional fee for successive one-year terms. It also allows the franchisee to name the length of the agreement.

Sophisticated Training

Management Recruiters' training program is one of the most extensive of any franchise's. Owner/managers are strongly urged to run their own offices. You must spend three weeks going through an intense, multimedia, multi-level training program. It includes role playing, actual interviews, and telephone marketing done in the real Cleveland marketplace. But it also focuses on how to hire and train account executives because they form the foundation of your success. Next, a trainer comes to your location and works with you for three weeks while you set up your office. Field staff reps will visit you quarterly for additional training. You can ask for more visits or take refresher courses in Cleveland at no additional charge, a real benefit because more and more companies are adding post-opening training charges as new hidden costs.

You also receive perhaps the best marketing program in the industry and a superb public relations and promotional effort.

How Much Can You Make?

With the high level of support and service, you can earn very high returns on your cash investment, especially if you borrow some of the funds. In its UFOC, Management Recruiters publishes an operating ratio study of its franchisees' operations. This study (printed below) compares the "net cash-in," that is, the actual fees collected during the year, operating expenses and net profit before royalties, and owner's compensations for three types of offices: those with two to four account executives; those with five to seven; and those with eight or more. The results for the year 1988, the latest year for which these figures were available, were very revealing. Even a middle-range, small office can quickly recoup its initial investment. The tables appended to the study below present the study comparisons.

The company anticipates that you reach the breakeven point during your third month and start earning a return on your investment thereafter. The best franchisees net more than $700,000 a year for the owner; and low to average offices net between $50,000 and $100,000 per year. This is a very substantial annual return on your initial investment and an excellent way to make money.

MANAGEMENT RECRUITERS—1988 OPERATING RATIO STUDY

The primary factor that determines the success of your office is volume of placements. However, effective control over expenses can significantly increase an office's profitability at any given level of sales volume. To provide you with a guideline for use in analyzing and controlling your expenses, we have compiled the seventeenth annual Operating Ratio Study from Income Reports submitted by Management Recruiters and Sales Consultants offices.

We have again combined the operating results of Management Recruiters offices with the operating results of Sales Consultants Offices. Prior year studies indicate that expenses generally do not vary significantly among Management Recruiters and Sales Consultants offices of similar size and profitability. Combining the MR's with the SC's creates a larger population and makes it statistically possible to have larger size categories.

The 1988 Operating Ratio Study results are expressed on an annual basis. All dollar amounts are rounded to the nearest hundred dollars.

The study is based on Income Reports for the twelve-month period January 1988 through December 1988. All MR and SC offices which were open the entire 1988 calendar year and averaged two or more filled desks are included in this study, except for ten offices which failed to submit their data as of the date required. Offices opened subsequent to January 1, 1988, are not included in the study because their operating results are not representative of the results of more tenured offices. This year, we have again grouped the offices into three desk-size categories: 2–4, 5–7, and 8 or more desks. The categorization is based on the average number of filled desks during 1988. We are distributing the studies for all three size categories to all offices.

The report format of the Operating Ratio Study conforms very closely to the Form 10 Income Report, which is our source document. In each category, each line item represents the dollar average of the reported results of all offices in the category, which are then also expressed as percentages of the average net cash-in for the category.

As with previous Operating Ratio Studies, we have used "Quartile Analysis" in the presentation of the operating ratio results. The *High Quartile* column reflects the average operating results of offices whose net profit ranks in the upper 25 percent of offices in their size category. The *Middle Range* column reflects the average operating results of offices whose net profit ranks in the middle 50 percent of offices in their size category.

We hope that this study will provide you with some meaningful information to use while evaluating your own operating results and managing your business for increased profitability. Please feel free to call if you have any questions or comments.

MANAGEMENT RECRUITERS—1988 OPERATING RATIO STUDY[a]

Offices with 2 to 4 Desks

	High Quartile		Middle Range	
	Dollars	Percentage[b]	Dollars	Percentage[b]
Net Cash In	383,800	100.0	217,600	100.0
Operating Expenses				
Account executives				
compensation	125,600	32.7	74,900	34.4
Office payroll	13,200	3.4	9,500	4.4
Hospitalization and insurance	8,100	2.1	6,200	2.8
Payroll and other taxes	12,600	3.3	8,800	4.0
Advertising	4,300	1.1	3,100	1.4
Dues and subscriptions	1,300	0.3	1,200	0.6
Equipment: Lease,				
depreciation, etc.	4,800	1.3	5,100	2.3
Office supplies and expenses	7,300	1.9	5,600	2.6
Professional services	3,700	1.0	2,500	1.1
Rent and utilities	13,900	3.6	13,200	6.1
Telephone	25,700	6.7	19,500	9.0
Travel and entertainment	9,400	2.4	6,100	2.8
Miscellaneous and repairs	3,400	0.9	2,600	1.2
Total	233,300	60.7	158,300	72.7
Net Profit before Royalties or				
Owner/Manager Compensation	150,500	39.3	59,300	27.3

a. Based on the 12 months, January through December 1988

b. All percentages are expressed on the basis of *net cash in.*

MANAGEMENT RECRUITERS—1988 OPERATING RATIO STUDY[a]

Offices with 5 to 7 Desks

	High Quartile		Middle Range	
	Dollars	Percentage[b]	Dollars	Percentage[b]
Net Cash In	745,600	100.0	447,500	100.0
Operating Expenses				
Account executives compensation	300,800	40.3	180,300	40.3
Office payroll	21,500	2.9	17,800	4.0
Hospitalization and insurance	18,900	2.5	13,500	3.0
Payroll and other taxes	25,700	3.4	19,300	4.3
Advertising	9,600	1.3	7,200	1.6
Dues and subscriptions	1,900	0.3	2,200	0.5
Equipment: Lease, depreciation, etc.	10,800	1.4	6,600	1.5
Office supplies and expenses	12,000	1.6	11,600	2.6
Professional services	7,200	1.0	5,600	1.3
Rent and utilities	30,900	4.1	23,500	5.3
Telephone	43,000	5.8	35,000	7.8
Travel and entertainment	18,100	2.4	11,300	2.5
Miscellaneous and repairs	5,600	0.8	4,200	0.9
Total	506,000	67.8	338,100	75.6
Net Profit before Royalties or Owner/Manager Compensation	239,600	32.2	109,400	24.4

a. Based on the 12 months, January through December 1988

b. All percentages are expressed on the basis of *net cash in.*

MANAGEMENT RECRUITERS—1988 OPERATING RATIO STUDY[a]

Offices with 8 or more Desks

	High Quartile		Middle Range	
	Dollars	Percentage[b]	Dollars	Percentage[b]
Net Cash In	1,535,800	100.0	878,900	100.0
Operating Expenses				
Account Executives				
compensation	694,400	45.2	392,400	44.6
Office payroll	34,100	2.2	29,300	3.3
Hospitalization and insurance	33,400	2.2	24,200	2.8
Payroll and other taxes	49,600	3.2	35,000	4.0
Advertising	21,300	1.4	12,100	1.4
Dues and subscriptions	2,900	0.2	2,500	0.3
Equipment: Lease,				
depreciation, etc.	14,600	1.0	12,900	1.5
Office supplies and expenses	16,300	1.1	14,800	1.7
Professional services	8,400	0.5	9,900	1.1
Rent and utilities	39,600	2.6	43,200	4.9
Telephone	75,900	4.9	61,200	7.0
Travel and entertainment	34,100	2.2	22,700	2.6
Miscellaneous and repairs	7,300	0.5	6,800	0.8
Total	1,031,900	67.2	667,000	76.0
Net Profit before Royalties or				
Owner/Manager Compensation	503,900	32.8	211,900	24.0

a. Based on the 12 months, January through December 1988

b. All percentages are expressed on the basis of *net cash in*.

MERRY MAIDS, INC.

Merry Maids, Inc.
11117 Mill Valley Road
Omaha, NE 68154
(800) 345-5535
(402) 498-0331

Merry Maids is the highest rated maid service franchise in the country. In the *Venture* survey of December, 1988, it was rated 34th of the Top 100 franchises; and in January, 1989, *Entrepreneur* ranked it 71st in the Top 500 franchises. Its ratings in these two annual surveys have consistently improved since 1986. In the mid-80s, it was rated the best maid service franchise by Dan Dorfman in an article in *New York* magazine. The article was based on information from Sommers Retail Expansion Consultants, Inc.

By the end of 1989, Merry Maids had 475 active franchises in 45 states and four foreign countries. Merry Maids is an excellent, relatively low-cost franchise both for men and women; 39 percent of the franchises are owned by women (down slightly since 1987 at 42 percent). Many more are owned by husband/wife or family teams.

Unlike other services, this franchise is based on a two-person team. This team takes a longer time than a four-person team, for it can clean only two to four houses per day. With this smaller team, however, you can field twice as many teams and cover a broader area than with the larger team operation.

Merry Maids' executives expect to double to 1,000 franchises within five years. Merry Maids may succeed because it offers a relatively low cost ($17,500) franchise fee as compared to most other franchises' high fees and since there is a growing demand for this type of service among Baby Boomers and older people.

How Much It Costs

For the $17,500 franchise fee, you receive an exclusive territory, complete training, and enough equipment and supplies to equip 2 two-person teams. Start-up costs are estimated to equal the amounts shown in the table on page 195.

Other Costs and Fees

You also must pay a weekly 7 percent royalty, or "service fee" as Merry Maids calls it, on your first $500,000 of annual sales, but only 5 percent on anything over $500,001.

You are required to maintain a full-time telephone with a 24-hour answering service (not a machine) and advertise continually in the local Yellow Pages.

Category	Low Estimate	High Estimate
Franchise fee	$17,500	$17,500
Phone, utility deposits	200	500
Training travel	200	500[a]
Insurance deposits	500	1,000
IBM computer system	3,000	3,000[b]
Office rent deposits	250	500[c]
Office furniture, etc.	500	1,000
Total	$22,150	$24,000

Notes:

a. Merry Maids provides the room and board during the week-long training; you pay only for transportation.

b. Unless you already own a compatible PC that will run Merry Maids' exclusive data management software programs.

c. You can run the operation from your home, but Merry Maids advises against it.

Although you are not charged for use of the company's computer software during the first 90 days, you must pay a weekly fee of $14.40 per week thereafter until you reach $3,000 per week in gross sales. At this level, the company considers that the charge is part of the royalty fee.

And you are required to carry liability insurance, which could cost $2,000 to $4,000 per year.

The company will charge you a 10 percent renewal fee of the then-current franchise fee. If your managers need additional training, you will have to pay $300 per day for this training.

All in all, however, Merry Maids' fees are very simple and easy to understand. You have to buy equipment, supplies, and uniforms, which your crews must wear, from Merry Maids. If you add another cleaning crew, you must buy more equipment, supplies, and uniforms, which cost a minimum of several hundred dollars. This investment is small compared to the potential return from another full-time cleaning team.

Considering these other costs, your total out-of-pocket expenses and working capital should range between $25,000 in most cases to $30,000, at worst.

Required Sales Volume

Merry Maids' biggest drawback is a weekly sales quota. If you do not achieve weekly sales volume of $2,000 per week by the end of your first year in business, Merry Maids has the right to terminate the contract. However, as you will read below, very few franchisees fail to achieve this sales level, and the minimum sales is just the beginning of how well you can do. One thing is certain: Merry Maids wants its franchises to be full-time, rapidly growing businesses. The owner is not required to manage the franchise on a daily basis, but is required to hire a full-time manager who spends all of his or her time handling your teams. Of course, hiring a manager sharply reduces your profits unless you are an investor who wants the cash returns from this service.

What You Get

You receive an excellent package of benefits and support from the company:

Five-year term. The original agreement lasts five years, a fairly short period, but you can renew it for two additional five-year terms. This policy gives you a chance to build equity in the business.

Exclusive territory. It will have between 8,000 and 10,000 qualified households, and the company emphasizes franchises in middle- and upper-middle-class areas where its customers can be found. Merry Maids has sharpened its customer demographic profiles and clearly identifies the best areas in which you should sell your services. In the past, the company awarded franchises based on total households; however, the secret to success is owning a precisely targeted territory full of affluent, two-income, professional households.

Training. Initial training lasts five business days at the company's headquarters and emphasizes two aspects: professional cleaning services and team management; and effective marketing and promotion. The company also holds regional and national seminars, and a national convention. It provides you with a video library with which you can train your teams in the proper cleaning techniques.

Data management system. The company's exclusive computer programs make managing your labor costs, schedules, and bookkeeping very easy. Although you have to buy the hardware, the initial software license fee is included in the franchise fee for 90 days. The subsequent weekly charge is described above.

(By the way, Merry Maids has the best written, most logically organized, and easily understood UFOC (Uniform Franchising Offering Circulars) of any of the 50 franchises reviewed in this book. The presentation of its materials is very professional and of high quality. Some other franchises fail to approach this quality in their UFOCs.)

Although Merry Maids is growing very rapidly, its franchise success rate is very high. Of its 400 franchises by the end of 1988, only 10 had been terminated for non-payment of royalties or because they failed to perform up to standards; only 9 had voluntarily terminated their franchises; 5 franchises had been mutually terminated; and 11 had been temporarily re-acquired before they were sold again. These totals show that the franchisees tend to have strength and deliver consistent performance. The numbers also show that Merry Maids genuinely cares about its franchisees' success.

How Much Can You Make?

Merry Maids franchises appear to do very well. *Venture* has reported two-year ROIs of more than 147 percent. Several franchisees consistently achieve gross sales in excess of $500,000 per year, starting in their second or third years. One Boston area franchisee couple quit teaching and spent about $28,000 during their first year to get started. This husband-and-wife team built their business to more than $400,000 gross sales and net profits of $80,000 to $120,000 per year in just four years. This amount is a cumulative ROI in the hundreds of percent.

Your operating costs should remain low. Your chief cost will be labor; you pay housekeepers between $4 and $7 an hour on average, but you charge an average of $52 per cleaning job. If you pay a 7 percent royalty, allow 30 percent for overhead, 5 percent for supplies, and 33 to 40 percent for labor; on this basis, your net pre-tax profit should equal between 18 and 25 percent.

According to Merry Maids' in-house publications, more than 150 of its franchisees reached or exceeded the $2,000 per week sales volume level during 1988. That meant that the typical franchisee was achieving net profits of about $600 per week, or in excess of $30,000 per year. Many franchisees earn $200,000 during their first 12 months, and they net $50,000 to $60,000 per year. The best Merry Maids achieved *$20,000 per week* during late 1986. It is likely that you can begin to net in the middle five figures during your second year in operation, and you can reach the breakeven point within six months to a year.

Merry Maids is undoubtedly among the Top 3 maid service franchises, if not the best, and it deserves serious attention.

PAK MAIL™ CENTERS OF AMERICA, INC.

Pak Mail™ Centers of America, Inc.
10555 East Dartmouth
Suite 360
Aurora, CO 80014
(303) 752-3000

Pak Mail Centers of America, Inc., is the second largest packing, shipping, and small business convenience services franchise in the nation. With about 200 franchises by the end of 1989, Pak Mail plans to add 50 to 75 more per year for the next several years. Pak Mail offers a relatively low start-up cost, averaging about $55,000 per outlet, and the opportunity to average a $60,000 per year return on investment within three to four years.

Pak Mail Centers operate very simply: you set up a retail outlet in a strip shopping center and offer convenience packing, mailing, and small business communications services to the public. Pak Mail sells convenience to the busy consumer and businessperson who does not have time to stand in line at UPS or who does not want to buy a facsimile machine to send only one or two fax messages per week. You charge for packaging everything from business letters to heavy gifts and make shipping arrangements with companies such as United Parcel Service, Federal Express, and the U.S. Postal Service. You also sell packaging supplies, office supplies, and convenience items, such as packing tape, greeting cards, gifts, etc. In fact, your profit margins on the ancillary items are quite substantial.

However, the packaging and shipping franchise business is very competitive. This book describes both a very inexpensive franchise (Packy the Shipper) for existing retail outlets like florists and card shops and Mail Boxes Etc., the largest franchise with more than 1,000 outlets. Other franchises exist, and hundreds of local Mom and Pop packaging stores have opened during the past five years as well.

Note, however, that Pak Mail experienced serious financial difficulties during the 1987–1988 period, but reorganized its board of directors and used the proceeds of a public stock sale to bolster its sagging finances. It seems to have made an excellent financial recovery during late 1988 and 1989, with its most recent profit-and-loss statement showing strong improvement. Its mid-1989 financial reports show that its gross sales increased by almost 46 percent compared to the same 1988 period. The company predicted its 1989 sales would exceed $2.3 million, almost double its 1988 results. But it may be wise to ask your accountant to analyze Pak Mail's long-term financial situation before you buy the franchise.

How Much It Costs

The franchise fee ranges from a low of $1 to a high of $29,500 depending on many factors, but the usual franchise fee is $17,500. Although Pak Mail reserves the right to charge any franchise fee, its offering circular does state that, usually, local packing and shipping stores converting to Pak Mail franchises pay the lowest fees. But everything—especially this fee—is negotiable, so if you have a prime location or want to open an area where Pak Mail does not now have franchises, you, too, may be able to negotiate a lower fee.

Pak Mail's UFOC notes that the franchise fee varies according to the following factors:

Location. A place where you can earn less income should cost less.

Number of franchises purchased. (See explanation below about multiple-franchise purchases.)

Franchisee's situation. Your business experience, education, financial condition, and business capitalization, i.e., how much cash and assets you have.

Prior experience. For packing store conversions, or former managers or owners of similar operations. Conversion store fees vary according to how much income the existing store generates.

The company emphasizes that it does not use a formula to set the fees; this means they will negotiate each fee individually.

Pak Mail offers three types of franchises:

Individual. For one store in one territory of between 35,000 and 50,000 people.

Five-pack. If you want to open five stores in one area within five years.

Area development agreement. If you want to buy the rights to an entire state, region, or major metropolitan area.

Obviously, if you want to buy one of the latter two franchises, you will pay a higher fee for the privilege.

Other Required Fees

You also must pay a reasonably low 5 percent royalty on monthly gross sales and contribute 1 percent more to a separate national advertising fund. You must also buy an unspecified amount of local and regional advertising each year, including Yellow Pages ads, newspaper ads, direct mail, and the like. The operations manual and company executives will help set those limits as you plan your opening.

Start-Up Costs

The table on page 200 shows an estimated range of start-up costs; the figures are adapted from Pak Mail's UFOC, with the author adding his own estimates to include costs the franchise circular does not have. Pak Mail states that the average start-up costs equals $55,000.

Clearly, this wide range means you must make sure your location has the potential to earn enough income to break even within the first 12 to 18 months. The ideal location is an existing retail storefront, with little refurnishing required, in a high traffic strip shopping center that faces a main highway. The worst is a new storefront, having only a dirt floor and no walls,

Category	Low End	High End
Franchise fee[a]	$17,500	$29,500
Salaries[b]	1,000	3,000
Office equipment[c]	6,000	12,000
Business forms/materials[d]	1,000	2,000
Advertising[e]	1,000	4,000
Training travel	1,000	2,500
Lease[f]	1,500	5,500
Leasehold improvements[g]	1,000	10,000
Working capital[h]	5,000	12,500
Miscellaneous[i]	2,500	3,000
Insurance[j]	500	1,000
Total	$38,000	$85,000

a. Conversions or sharp negotiators can save substantially on this low-end estimate.
b. You need at least one employee unless your family helps. This covers the working capital you need to pay them until you generate enough cash flow. You will need additional help during the holiday season.
c. Cash register, copier, fax machine, packing equipment, etc.
d. Part of the required Pak Mail purchases.
e. Start-up and grand opening costs.
f. Lease deposits and first-month rents.
g. Pak Mail does not include this category in its estimates, but you undoubtedly have to refurnish your store, possibly from the ground up.
h. Your cash requirements and living expenses for the first 30 to 60 days.
i. Accountant, attorney, professional fees, business licenses.
j. Another required expense Pak Mail leaves out of its UFOC. A retail outlet must have plate glass insurance.

off a main highway, on which one or two competitors already have franchises. This business does not follow the fast-food restaurant principle: you should *not* cluster convenience packing and mailing franchises as McDonald's, Burger King, Wendy's, and Hardees do. The packaging business does not offer enough sales volume to carry several similar stores in one location.

Note that Pak Mail does not offer financing of franchise fees or any start-up costs, although it will help you with sample business plans and financial statements.

What You Get

You receive all of the usual things a franchise offers: the right to use the name, business system, trademarks, copyrights, operations manual, etc.

The franchise agreement's first term is 5 years. As long as you meet its requirements, Pak Mail automatically renews the agreement for successive one-year terms. This is a double-edged sword that keeps you on your good behavior after the first five years, e.g., paying your royalties on time, etc.

Most important, you receive an exclusive territory of between 35,000 and 50,000 population. However, large numbers do not necessarily make a good territory. Look for one with many small businesses or self-employed people who need small business convenience services, or one that has many retirees who ship packages or goods frequently. Areas with lots of military personnel, who often ship packages frequently to their distant families, also make good choices. A combination of two of these will help you profit during both the busy holiday season and the rest of the year.

You receive a thorough 5- to 10-day training program that teaches you how to manage your store, stock your inventory, market your services, do your required accounting procedures, choose your location, furnish and lay it out, and so forth. After you take classroom instruction at Pak Mail's headquarters, you work in an existing franchise in an on-site management class. Pak Mail also offers area workshops and meetings, and an annual convention, all of which you may have to attend.

Pak Mail also has a separate advertising fund that it is obligated to use for regional and/or national advertising to promote its franchises, not to sell more franchises.

And field representatives make regular visits and offer retraining classes to help you if you run into any problems.

You can also call the company for telephone support. Although it teaches you how to find a location, Pak Mail does not make the choice for you—you find the location and Pak Mail approves it. And you must negotiate your lease yourself, so be sure to have a good commercial real estate attorney review the lease.

How Much Can You Make?

Despite Pak Mail's own 1987–88 financial difficulties, its franchisees seem to have done quite well. Of more than 100 franchises open before 1989 began, only three had closed for not paying royalties, and Pak Mail had reacquired only one. This record indicates a very low failure and a very high success rate and one that should encourage potential buyers.

Pak Mail does not publish any earnings claims to avoid trouble with the FTC. But according to published reports, the average Pak Mail Center breaks even in six to seven months, with a payback of your total initial investment within about 18 months. Centers that are three- to four-years-old average gross sales ranging between $250,000 and $300,000, with net profits before taxes between 30 and 40 percent, or about $75,000 to $120,000 per year. This total includes your salary if you manage the store full time; you will lower your net profits by about half if you hire a full-time manager.

Existing stores' results show that they earn net profits equalling $12,000 to $18,000 during their first 18 months; $30,000 to $40,000 during their second full year; and $40,000 to $120,000 during their third to fourth years. A good average equals $60,000 during the fourth year.

Pak Mail is growing rapidly and is aggressively marketing its franchises. It plans to add 50 to 75 new stores during 1990, with plans to have 2,000 stores within 10 years.

With a good location and a cautious eye on Pak Mail's finances, you can expect to realize cash ROIs in the 100 percent per year range by the end of the third year.

ADIA PERSONNEL SERVICES

Adia Personnel Services
64 Willow Place
Menlo Park, CA 94025
(415) 324-0696

With more than 500 company-owned and franchised offices in more than 40 states, Adia Personnel Services is one of the largest temporary help and permanent employment agencies in the U.S. It is a subsidiary of a Swiss firm, Adia, S.A., the second largest personnel agency in the world. Both groups are publicly traded companies: the parent company is on the Zurich Stock Exchange, and the U.S. subsidiary on the NASDAQ Exchange. Adia U.S.—the corporation, not the franchise subsidiary—totalled more than $421 million in sales during 1988, making it a financially strong company.

The temporary personnel market in the U.S. has increased more than 800 percent during the past 15 years. The temporary help market grew from $1.3 billion in 1975 to more than $10.2 billion during 1986, according to U.S. government payroll data. Office/clerical and light-industrial temporary-help employment accounts for about two-thirds of this market.

Although experts expect this market to continue to grow strongly, one must remember that Adia faces stiff competition in every major metropolitan location. More than 2,500 firms that are operating more than 7,500 offices compete; most firms are small independent operations with one or two branches. Moreover, Adia competes as well against such giants as Kelly and Norrell, its leading competitors.

In the permanent placement field, Adia competes against leading national franchisors, including Snelling & Snelling, Management Recruiters, Dunhill, and more. Both types of businesses are very competitive and require knowledgeable, aggressive salespeople and recruiters. Temporary help agencies' greatest problem today is not finding employers who need employees, but finding *employees* in an increasing tight labor market. To succeed in the future, personnel agencies must recruit good-quality employees to make their clients happy. This task will become more difficult because education standards are falling, yet technology advances demand better-skilled and more highly trained personnel than ever before.

Adia entered the U.S. market in 1972 when it acquired Massey Temporary Services, then operating in Texas and California. Since 1972, Adia has opened several specialized temporary help operations under the following names:

Adia Personnel Services

ATS Temporary Help

Parttime, Inc., Temporary Help

Vencap, Inc., Subsidiary

Accountants on Call

TempWorld (a 1988 acquisition)

The accounting help division was begun in 1986 and offers temporary help for accounting, bookkeeping, and financial firms. The first four listed offer both temporary and permanent placement in clerical, light industrial, and technical service businesses.

TempWorld, a new division established in 1989, offers franchises outside of markets that Adia already serves. By September 1, 1989, Adia had 15 company-owned TempWorld offices, but no franchises. Note that TempWorld, Adia, and Vencap overlap in their markets for clerical and light-industrial temporary help; moreover, Adia, TempWorld, Vencap, and Accountants on Call overlap in that they all offer light-bookkeeping temporary help services. And Adia also owns a number of temporary help services under other names and trademarks as well.

Adia began offering permanent placement services in 1983, and its franchisees can choose whether or not to offer these services. Its UFOC covers both lines of businesses.

Adia separates the territories where it sells franchises from where it establishes company offices as follows:

Company-owned: In major metropolitan areas that can support five to seven offices. This policy gives Adia the benefit of the most efficient marketing through newspapers, radio, and TV.

Franchised: In metropolitan areas that will not support five to seven offices.

Under the Adia name, as of late 1989, the company owned 158 offices, and franchisees owned 122 offices (43.6%). Adia's corporate goal is to maintain a 60%-company to a 40%-franchise ratio. Adia Personnel Services works like this: temporary help recruits become employees of the corporate Adia Personnel Services entity. Adia corporate takes 35 percent of your gross billings as fees to manage payroll, bookkeeping, and accounting through one of its 10 payroll processing offices. Adia also provides advertising and training services for its franchisees.

During 1989, Adia also automated all its company and franchised branches, and franchisees could choose to purchase hardware and license the software to run the Adia Office Automation (AOA) System.

How Much It Costs

Adia charges a reasonable franchise fee of $17,500. Adia will reduce the fee by a negotiable amount for an existing personnel agency which converts to become an Adia franchisee. And Adia will allow a franchisee to open a branch office within their existing territory for a reduced franchise fee of $5,000.

Adia bases its charges on a two-tier royalty structure:

- *Permanent placement royalty:* A simple 7 percent of all receipts from clients.
- *Temporary help continuing fee:* For the first three months, 35 percent of the gross margin per billing period or 6 percent of net billings. After this time period, the continuing fee equals the *greater* of one of three amounts:
    1. $500 per period
    2. A percentage of gross margin based on a declining scale amount
    3. Six percent of the net billings

The table shown below gives Adia's "volume incentive schedule," which encourages franchisees to increase their billings rapidly. Note that conversion franchises pay lower continuing fees, which are set during contract negotiation.

Adia bases the continuing fee percentage for one year on the *total* temporary employee hours for the previous year, so you use the lowest percentage of gross margin in one year as the initial percentage for the next year. If, in any calendar year, your total hours amount to fewer than the total hours during the previous year, your percentage for the next year may be increased. The next year's percentage is based on the lower total.

Adia retains an amount equal to the continuing fee during each accounting period. After Adia deducts the fee and any collection expenses, Adia sends a check for the gross margin's balance to the franchisee.

Volume Incentive Schedule

Total Temporary Employee
Hours Billed for the Year

Greater Than	And Less Than or Equal to (in hours)	Percentage of Gross Margin (%)
0	20,000	35
20,000	40,000	34
40,000	60,000	33
60,000	80,000	32
80,000	100,000	31
100,000	120,000	30
120,000	140,000	29
140,000	160,000	28
160,000	180,000	27
180,000	200,000	26
200,000		25

However, in a complicated formula, you must also pay Adia the equivalent of interest on the franchisee's share of uncollected net billings, even though Adia's UFOC states that "interest is not paid on franchisee's share of the uncollected net billings. Interest is paid by Adia retaining such amount from the franchisee's share of the gross margin before distribution." The effect is the same: you fund Adia's interest payments on its credit line.

Estimated Start-Up Costs

After the fee, you can expect to pay between $20,000 and $22,000 for the required office automation system for an office with four or five employees. Smaller offices spend less; larger ones, more. Franchisees do not have to buy the system, but it is to their competitive advantage to do so. It may help speed up your cash flow, too.

Here are estimated start-up costs from Adia's UFOC, in which the author has increased certain amounts.

Categories	Low End	High End
Franchise fee	$17,500	$ 17,500
AOA system[a]	0	22,000
Furniture/equipment	12,000	18,000
Lease payments	1,000	2,500
Training travel[b]	2,000	2,500
Working capital[c]	40,000	80,000
Total	$72,500	$126,750

a. Optional. Cost given for a 4- to 5-person office.
b. Costs for you and an office manager.
c. Three to six months' office expenses, employee salaries, insurance, advertising, signage, telephone and utility deposits and bills, and legal and accounting services.

Clearly, you can start a moderate-sized office for much less than $100,000.

What You Get

Adia provides everything you need to start your business: signage, equipment, systems, training, site location assistance, start-up assistance, etc.

Training is lengthy—10 to 15 days of intense training in operations, recruitment, sales, and management. Of course, Adia also provides all of the billing, payroll, and bookkeeping services for your temporary help side.

Territory Conditions

Your exclusive territory will consist of one or more counties in a small- to medium-sized metropolitan area or the urban area of a city. The franchise agreement covers only one office within that territory. However, you may not place temporary employees with any business within another franchisee's territory or outside your own territory unless no franchise-owned or company-owned branch is in that territory.

Adia does not restrict you from recruiting from outside your own territory, although you cannot advertise for recruits outside it. However, the sword cuts both ways: other Adia franchisees can accept recruits from your area. This advertising prohibition will create problems in major areas where phone directories, radio stations, and TV stations serve overlapping territories. One possiblity for you to consider is that you may choose to work with other Adia franchisees or Adia corporate to negotiate arrangements when overlapping problems occur.

Satellite Branches

You can open satellite branches within your territory for a fee of $5,000 if you meet the annual temporary hour quotas described in the following table. And Adia gives you the right to buy another temporary or permanent placement agency that the corporation buys within your territory. You also have the right of first refusal to operate any new business activity, such as TempWorld or Accountants on Call, which Adia develops and offers to its franchisees.

Minimum Hours Quota

Year of Franchise	Minimum Hours per Year
1	12,500
2	18,750
3	25,000
4	37,500
5	50,000
6	55,000
7	60,000
8	65,000
9	70,000
10	75,000
Over 10	75,000

Adia's franchisees seem to succeed fairly well. And Adia is very sensitive to failures. During the first seven months of 1988, for example, 10 franchises closed, but Adia repurchased 8 of them, sold one to a neighboring franchisee, and sold the other to a third party. In the previous three years, only 10 more franchises had closed, and eight of these were acquired by Adia, as well. Adia does resell these offices after it buys them. It even closes its own corporate branches when they don't succeed: 14 were closed during the four years before the end of 1989. Adia has franchised an average of 25 new offices per year for the past four years.

How Much Can You Make?

Gauging the return on a temporary employment service is not easy because the billing structures are so complex. Permanent placement profits are much easier to measure. Usually, you charge three months' salary: for example, if you place someone making $24,000 per year, your fee will equal $6,000—that is, $2,000 per month for three months. If you place 50 people per year, about one per week at that level, you can gross $300,000 in sales.

The temporary help business works on percentages of hourly wages. If you charge an employer $18 per hour for a word processor, Adia will receive $6.30 of this amount. You must pay the word processor $9 an hour, at least, so your gross profit margin—before overhead expenses—would equal only $2.70 per hour. You could net $1 an hour or less before taxes. Therefore, you have to place many (50 or more) temporary employees with clients every day to begin to realize $400 per day—$2,000 per week or $100,000 per year. It is

BUSINESS PLAN WORKSHEET

	Month 1	Month 2	Month 3	Month 4	Month 5	Month 6	Month 7	Month 8	Month 9	Month 10	Month 11	Month 12	Yearly Total
Hrs./Day													
Hrs./Week													
Hrs./Month													
Monthly Billings													
Payroll Expenses													
GMS													
Placement Income													
Gross Income													
Continuing Serv. Fee													
Perm. Placement Royal.													
Financing Charge													
Total Fees													
Adjusted Income													
Office Expenses													
Net Income													
Operating Capital													

difficult to do this consistently, and you must either hire or work yourself as an effective recruiter and a dynamic salesperson to reach this level.

Usually, a franchisee performs one function and hires someone to do the other; he hires *either* a good salesperson or recruiter *or* an office manager or assistant. This increases overhead substantially, but it gives each person to chance to build from his or her strengths instead of wasting time compensating for weaknesses.

Adia does provide a comprehensive worksheet, with which you can estimate your capital operating expenses. It is printed on the back of its UFOC and is reproduced with permission on page 208.

BIO-CARE, INC.

Bio-Care, Inc.
2105 South Bascom Ave.
Suite 240
Campbell, CA 95008
(408) 559-7500

Bio-Care, Inc., offers a unique franchise with potentially very lucrative profits. Capitalizing on the emerging field of biotechnology and growing concern about water pollution, Bio-Care has developed a service that offers to restaurants and food services an environmentally safe way of eliminating one of their worst problems: clogged drainage lines.

At first glance, this service doesn't sound like much more than a glorified plumbing service, but Bio-Care executives persuasively argue that it is much, much more. Even if it were only that, it would not be a bad franchise to consider; after all, plumbers and Mr. Rooter®-type services often earn extremely high profits. Bio-Care plans to use its "grease-gobbling" bacteria service as a *platform business,* that is, it plans to use its degreasing service as a "foot-in-the-door" through which its franchisees will eventually offer a broad and deep package of environmentally safe services for restaurants, hospitals, schools, etc. Its concept is that once you successfully sell your subscription-based drainage cleaning and monitoring service, you make repeat sales to the same customer by adding low-cost pest control, fire extinguisher, and other similar services. Since your technician already calls on the establishment once a week, he or she can easily spend a few extra minutes doing the other services as they are required.

The establishment owner realizes numerous advantages: one-stop shopping for health and safety services required by law; lower costs than from using different services with their own overheads to pay (you cover your overhead with the drainage cleaning service); fewer problems with health and safety inspectors; and more sales and higher profits because customers are happier with a healthier and more pleasant atmosphere. However, launching the expanded platform business remains in Bio-Care's future.

Today, Bio-Care's franchised drainage and degreasing franchise works like this: on a fixed-fee, subscription basis, you sell an environmentally safe, biotechnology-based drainage-cleaning and drainage-monitoring service to restaurants, hospitals, schools, nursing homes, and any large commercial kitchen that faces a grease-clogged drainage problem. You charge between $150 and $300 per month, or between $1,800 and $3,600 per year, with $2,400 an average annual cost per establishment.

Once a week, your technician treats each restaurant's drainage line with a lightweight packet of potent, but safe, bacteria. The technician simply drops a packet down each drain in the restaurant's kitchen, and the hungry, grease-gobbling bacteria do the rest. The bacteria digest the grease, thereby sharply reducing the number of calls per year a restaurant must make to a drain-cleaning or grease-pumping service; this saves the restaurant owner hundreds of dollars a month in service costs and additional profits. Bio-Care estimates that you can reduce by one-half, from 12 to 6, the number of drainage cleaning/pumping service calls per year.

Your technician then monitors kitchen procedures and recommends changes to the restaurant owner. You also act the intermediary if an emergency does arise; you call the drain cleaning service. The drain-cleaning service charges you a discounted price, say $45, and you profit by charging the restaurant a slight discount from the regular price, say $60 to $65.

What are you doing while your technician does the work? You are selling the service to restaurants and food service operations, and you are managing the business. Bio-Care advises you to operate the business from your home at first to save thousands of dollars in annual office expenses. You can also work as your own technician at first and hire someone as you increase your sales, but Bio-Care executives prefer a salesperson or manager as a franchise buyer. They believe a franchisee spends his or her time more profitably by signing new clients.

Speculative Service

All this sounds very lucrative, and it has tremendous potential. However, Bio-Care is a new company, although it is managed by high-powered, experienced franchise executives and has the financial backing of the venture capital arm of the huge W. R. Grace chemical manufacturer, Grace/Horn Ventures Group. Its accounting firm, prestigious Arthur Anderson, notes in Bio-Care's UFOC (Uniform Franchise Offering Circular) that the company was in development stage at the end of 1988. Anderson added to Bio-Care's

September 30, 1988 financial statement, (the most recent available) the following:

> ". . . the Company is in the process of establishing its channels of distribution, which include franchising, and has not yet reached a level of revenues sufficient to fund its operations. As a result, it remains in the development stage. The Company is subject to a number of risks, including competition from larger companies with greater financial resources and the need for additional financing. There can be no assurance that additional financing will be available."

Since the firm issued this caveat, Bio-Care has obtained more than $500,000 in new financing, has made a significant push into selling its master regional franchises, and has introduced its first consumer product and service. The consumer marketing plan is based on a subscription service designed to appeal to the 15 million homeowners with septic tanks. It uses a variation of its commercial bacteria product to help clean septic tanks; once a month, Bio-Care ships a packet to each subscriber's home; the homeowner drops the packet into the toilet and flushes. Bio-Care estimates its bacteria-based product and service can reduce by half the number of septic-tank-cleaning calls a homeowner must make.

Although this franchise remains speculative, it is included in this book because it offers a significant profit potential since it costs relatively little to start this business.

How Much It Costs

Bio-Care primarily sells through a three-tier system:

Master franchise: $60,000 fee and $20,000 start-up costs for a territory capable of supporting 20 to 25 Bio-Care franchise operations. The master franchise concept is balanced very favorably to the buyer: Bio-Care gives you 100 percent of your first four franchisees so you can immediately recoup your total start-up cost. You also receive 60 percent of the royalty payments. After the first four franchises, you receive half of each franchise fee and the same 60 percent share of the royalty payments. Bio-Care obviously designed this lucrative master franchise structure to encourage rapid master franchise acquisitions. But the master franchise must not only sell to but also support unit franchisees with training and on-going services.

Area franchise: For those who want to buy multiple-unit territories from the master franchisee.

Unit territory franchise: For individual franchise owners, whose fees equal $20,000.

You must pay a 10 percent monthly royalty fee of gross revenues. But Bio-Care does not charge an advertising fee or any other percentage fee. However, in the future, if the unit franchises within any region agree, each unit will have to contribute 5 percent to a regional or national advertising fund. This cost does not exist yet and should not for several years.

You must also spend the greater of $100 per month or 1 percent of your gross revenues on local advertising, in addition to having a Yellow Pages ad listing.

Your total initial investment should fall into the ranges given in the following table:

	Low	High
Expenses		
Franchise fee	$20,000	$20,000
Initial equipment	4,000	5,000
Deposits	600	800
Insurance (6 mos.)	300	400
Marketing materials	500	750
Initial ads and promos	1,500	2,000
Product cost	500	700
Accounting services	150	250
Training travel	1,600	2,000
Miscellaneous	250	500
Subtotal	$29,650	$32,800
Working Capital Costs		
Rent[a]	0	0
Labor	4,000	8,000
Marketing	150	200
Auto/van lease/purchase	2,500	3,000
Uniforms	40	50
Supplies	200	250
Reserve	2,000	2,500
Subtotal	$ 8,890	$14,000
Total	$39,540	$46,800

a. You should begin this operation from your home and move into an executive office location within a year or two. You should save $10,000 to $15,000 in first-year expenses working from home.

Frankly, these statements are among the most reasonable this author has seen in any franchisor's documents. The costs cited provide liberal, even generous, estimates so that you can avoid surprises.

Obligations to Purchase

Bio-Care has exclusive rights to patented biotechnology products which another firm makes, so you must buy your "grease gobblers" from Bio-Care. You can expect these purchases to equal up to 16 percent of your annual operating expenses.

You can expect your total monthly operating expenses to equal between $3,500 and $4,000 by the end of the first year. This amount includes a technician's salary. Overall, however, your expenses should not be excessive, and you receive a great deal of training and support.

What You Get

Bio-Care offers a truly unique territory; it is based on the number of restaurants in a geographic area. With more than 500,000 restaurants in the U.S., each unit territory encompasses between 500 and 550 restaurants. Clearly, Bio-Care wants to establish about 1,000 franchises. Although restaurants make up your best and largest market, you can still sell to hospitals, schools, universities, nursing homes, and any other facility with a commercial food-service operation; all these types of organizations are potential customers. Smart franchise buyers will identify areas not only with many large restaurants but also those with diverse ancillary food-service operations so that they can make added sales and profits.

Besides the unique territory, you receive up to 14 days of training at Bio-Care's company location. By the way, the company location signed up 200 customers during its first year of operation. You may find it difficult to duplicate this feat, however, and the company does not claim that you should or will do so.

You also receive field-training in making actual service and sales calls for at least one week after your start. And you receive the usual gamut of operations manuals, advertising and promotional materials, telephone support, etc.

Primarily, you receive the opportunity to start as one of the first Bio-Care franchisees and receive the lavish attention that most early franchisees receive. Bio-Care will invest much effort to help you succeed, an advantage franchisees who buy five years from now may not receive.

How Much Can You Make?

Bio-Care's essential financial advantage comes from its nature as a subscription service. Company executives describe it as a cash flow business that is simple to sell and one that provides steady profits with no seasonal downturns, such as those that regular septic cleaning, plumbing, or degreasing firms experience. It is also an 8 A.M. to 5 P.M. business; any nighttime or weekend emergencies are farmed out to a Mr. Rooter-type service.

You can expect to earn $150 to $300 per month per restaurant. You can expect to reach 15 percent market penetration—that is, you can expect to sign up 15 percent of all restaurants in your territory—within several years. A conservative income estimate is of gross revenues of $7,500 per month, which is based on 50 customers paying $150 per month by the end of the second year. A high expense estimate of $4,000 per month leaves a net pre-tax income of $3,500 per month, or $42,000 per year, by the end of the second year.

An optimistic three- to five-year growth estimate would result in 80 customers paying $300 per month for a gross income of $24,000 per month by the end of the fifth year. This operations level would require two technicians and, probably, an office, so your expenses could equal $11,000 per month for a net pre-tax income of $13,000 per month, or $156,000 per year. Your cash ROI should begin to exceed 100 percent by the end of your second year.

Not bad at all for selling "grease-gobbling" packets that make both restaurant owners and customers happy with a cleaner, safer, healthier eating place and also contribute a little to a cleaner environment!

MAIL BOXES ETC. USA

Mail Boxes Etc. USA
Suite 100
5555 Oberlin Drive
San Diego, CA 92121
(619) 452-1553
(619) 452-9937, FAX

Mail Boxes Etc. (MBE) was one of the most rapidly expanding franchises in the country during 1989, adding almost 300 new franchises. It expected to continue this rapid growth pace during 1990 and 1991. Its growth was spurred by an aggressive regional and area development plan and a very sophisticated promotional program. MBE executives predict the company will exceed 2,500 franchises by 1995, creating significant opportunities for potential franchisees.

By the end of 1989, MBE had more than 1,050 franchises in operation, a phenomenal growth rate since 1987 when it had only 350 franchises. MBE's growth was led by about 115 area development franchisees in 46 states, Puerto Rico, Canada, and several foreign countries.

Of the franchisees, 41 percent were married partners and 30 percent were individual women owners—making it a leading company for women franchisees. More important, some 20 percent of the area franchisees were women, giving them a serious voice in how MBE grows.

MBE has been consistently rated either first or in the Top Five in its category in magazines such as *Venture, Entrepreneur, Women's Enterprise,* and similar business publications. In *Entrepreneur's* annual Top 500, it was rated 40th out of the Top 500, and the 16th fastest growing franchise.

A Timely Idea

MBE's concept is one which makes business success relatively easy—an idea whose time has arrived. MBE offers an inexpensive alternative to the U.S. Postal Service by offering more up-to-date and better quality services at reasonable prices. Its executives contend that MBE will become "the 7-Eleven of business services." In addition to 24-hour access to personal mail boxes, the franchise offers unlimited hold-mail service, mail forwarding to vacation addresses, and a telephone number to call and find out if you have mail waiting for you. All these are services the USPS does not offer or offers only in a limited manner.

As important, MBE's business services, especially overnight package delivery and facsimile transmission, have continued to explode. These services cost very little to perform, and they form incredibly profitable centers: a fax transmission gives as much as 75 to 80 percent net profit; and a $3 service charge to hand a package to UPS or Federal Express is almost all net profit.

During 1990, MBE has launched a potentially explosive growth opportunity: an electronic income tax return and "instant" tax refund program. Although franchisees do not prepare tax returns as H & R Block or an accountant do, they will electronically transmit individual tax returns to the IRS for a small fee, about $10 or so. If the person wants an "instant" tax refund, MBE acts as a loan broker between the individual and Greenwood Trust Company, the Sears and Discover card bank. The bank gives the franchisee a small finder's fee. With electronic tax returns likely to become the wave of the future, MBE franchisees may earn significant profits from this practically pure profit service.

The typical MBE "service center" is located in a strip shopping center in a 1,200- to 1,500-square-foot facility. Each store offers mail box services, parcel shipping, packing and receiving, telephone message services, secretarial services, office supplies, packing materials, and small business communications, including facsimile, telex, cable grams, Mailgrams, telegrams, and electronic funds transfers. The store also sells stationery, supplies, stamps, keys, passport photos, and a film-processing service.

Franchise Territory

For a typical individual franchise, the minimum population area is 25,000, while area franchises include a minimum of $500,000. Note that a securities

prospectus said—Mail Boxes Etc. is a public company—that the usual territory had a minimum population of 30,000, but the UFOC issued in June,
1986, states that the minimum population area is 25,000, the figure used
here. A new franchisee interviewed for this book said, however, that his territory includes about 30,000 people.

Area franchisees receive the exclusive right to sell individual outlets in
their area and earn substantial commissions in return for start-up assistance, training and on-going support.

How Much It Costs

The fee for an individual franchise is $19,500, an increase of 30 percent
since 1987. However, in late 1989, MBE announced it would begin to
finance almost three-quarters of the franchise fee. MBE will accept a
$5,000 down payment and finance the remainder of the fee, $14,500, for
up to five years.

Minimum start-up costs, the company estimates, range from $43,345
to $64,767, but that range does *not* include $10,000 to $15,000 for several
months of cash flow. The working capital estimate does not include any
money for living expenses, unlike many other franchisees' estimates. Nor
does the estimate include payments for debt service or installment loans, nor
$3,000 to $5,000 for grand opening advertising and promotion. It also does
not include training travel costs to San Diego for you and one other person
for the two-week training program, a total averaging between $1,000 and
$1,500.

You do best to add at least $18,000 to $30,000 more to the company's
estimate. (Note how closely you have to consider these subtle differences
among different franchises' estimated start-up costs. One may include every conceivable expense or cost, while another may deliberately leave out
costs that amount to 30 to 40 percent of their so-called "initial investment"
estimate.)

By the way, Mail Boxes Etc.'s UFOC says, in a statement rare among
franchises, that corporate officers, directors, and key management employees can buy franchises for themselves or their immediate families just
for a 50 percent discount from the regular fee. By the way, this has
changed; in 1987, an earlier UFOC stated that franchise executives could
buy an outlet for a $4,500 fee, so the new policy is more fair to individual
buyers.

If you, as an individual franchisee, buy a second franchise, you receive
a $3,000 or 15.4 percent discount, and a $5,000 or 25.6 percent discount on
third and subsequent franchises.

The table on page 217 shows in detail the MBE estimate of start-up costs.

MAIL BOXES ETC. USA, INC., ESTIMATED START-UP COSTS

	Low	High
I. Franchise Fee (Payable to franchisor)		
franchise fee total	$19,500	$19,500
Training fee (MBE University)	1,300	1,300
II. Leasehold Improvements (Payable to franchisor or contractors of franchisee's choice)		
Construction build-out (framing, cabinetry, electrical, paint, and carpet: See Note 1)	$10,500	$20,500
Exterior sign (See Note 2)	1,800	3,000
Interior graphics and window signs	1,500	1,500
Construction management fee (Optional)	1,500	2,000
Leasehold Improvements Total	$15,300	$27,000
III. Supplies and Inventory (Payable to franchisor or supplier of franchisee's choice: See Note 3)		
Miscellaneous equipment, supplies, and inventory (See Notes 6 and 7)	$ 2,500	$ 5,000
Office supplies inventory and fixtures (Optional)	1,500	3,000
Freight and shipping charges (Based upon distance)	250	500
Key display and blanks	480	687
Supplies and Inventory Total	$ 4,730	$ 9,187
IV. Deposits (Payable to suppliers of franchisee's choice)		
Copier rental (Refundable, See Note 9)	$ 330	$ 450
Security deposit leased equipment (See Note 6)	365	500
Security deposit leasehold (Last month, See Note 8)	700	2,000
Telephone deposit	100	300
Utility deposit (Refundable, See Note 4)	100	300
UPS deposit (Refundable, See Notes 4 and 5)	0	1,000
Deposits Total	$ 1,595	$ 4,550
V. Prepaid Business Expenses (Payable to franchisor or suppliers of franchisee's choice)		
Business liability insurance premium (1M–$300,000 coverage)	$ 500	$ 750
Prepaid rent (First month, See Note 8)	700	2,000
Business license fee	25	50
Prepaid postal caller service (6 months)	130	130
Miscellaneous expenses	400	600
Leased or rented equipment (See Note 6)	365	500
Regional ad association membership	100	500
Prepaid Business Expenses Total	$ 2,220	$ 4,530
Total Estimated Start-Up Costs	$44,645	$66,067

Important Note:

The start-up costs specified above are the costs expected to be incurred in the opening of an MBE facility. It should be noted, however, that one cannot expect to succeed in any new business venture without sufficient working capital. *Franchisee should plan to have $10,000 to $15,000 in working capital available to support negative cash flow which is usually experienced in the first several months of operation of any new business. Working capital does not include any sums necessary for living or personal expenses. The estimated sum is for expenses of the new business only. Payments for debt service, if any, are in addition to the working capital estimates. An additional $3,000.00 to $5,000.00 should be available for grand opening promotional activities* required to get the business off to a good start. Please note that one of the primary causes of new business failures is the lack of adequate working capital.

All of the above-estimated expenditures are non-refundable, unless otherwise noted.

1. For approximately 1,000-square-foot leasehold facility with HVAC, lighting fixtures, electrical outlets, and telephone wiring installed. Construction costs in some areas of the country may exceed these estimates.
2. Dependent upon requirements of landlord and/or local specifications.
3. Add state sales tax, where appropriate.
4. Varies in accordance with Center projection of monthly volume and is generally refundable after 90–180 days with establishment of good credit.
5. Deposits will vary from region to region and may range from $0.00 to $1,000.00 or more.
6. Monthly lease costs are subject to change as a function of equipment price changes and fluctuations in interest rates. This estimate is based on the franchisee leasing the following equipment: mail boxes (250 openings and numbers—leased); 30-key cash register; passport photo camera and tripod (leased); fax machine; copy machine (rented); electronic typewriter (leased); stamp vending machine; MBE Business Systems: Hardware/MBE-1200 AT compatible computer; MBE Software Package.
7. The franchisee may elect to purchase the mandatory lease equipment at an additional cost of approximately $12,500.
8. Leasehold deposits and monthly costs in certain areas may exceed these estimates.
9. Refundable and applied equally to the first three monthly invoices, less the installation charge of $60.00. Purchase of the copier is approximately $3,400.00.

THERE ARE NO OTHER DIRECT OR INDIRECT PAYMENTS IN CONJUNCTION WITH THE PURCHASE OF THE FRANCHISE.

Area Franchise Fee

The price for an area franchise ranges from a nickel to a dime per person, or $25,000 to $50,000, a bargain compared to the individual price. You must also buy and operate one $15,000 franchise as well. But you only have to pay half (50 percent) of the area fee in cash; you can finance the other half at market interest rates for three years. You also face stiff expansion requirements. You must open at least two new franchises per year during the 10-year term of the agreement. Most area franchisees, however, sell franchises to other individuals at a much faster pace. They receive up to half of the initial franchise fee from MBE and up to half of the on-going royalty payments. If an area developer sells the maximum of about 20 franchises in his or her area, then the potential income from shared royalty fees alone is phenomenal, on the order of $120,000 to $150,000 per year after three to five years of work.

Area franchisees can do very well from franchise and royalty fees. The area rep receives 40 percent or $6,000 of each individual franchise fee, and the company divides the on-going royalties in half. With very substantial average revenues, an area franchisee can make very substantial returns on his or her investment in just a few years.

Other Fees and Costs

More importantly, you pay a reasonably small 5 percent royalty on gross revenues and a 2 percent advertising fee. The good thing about the ad fee is that half of it is used to your direct benefit in area advertising programs. You are also required to spend an additional 1 percent of your gross revenues on your own local advertising plans.

You also have to join a regional advertising cooperative group and contribute up to $5,000 per year for membership and other fees. This amount does not include the actual costs for advertising, public relations, and promotions for that region.

What You Get

MBE offers a feature-filled program:

- A reputation and market presence that has become quite phenomenal since 1987. MBE now accounts for one-fifth of all revenues in this industry, and its market share continues to increase.
- A 10-year term renewable for additional 10-year terms, an excellent opportunity to build long-term equity. The renewal fee is equal to 25 percent of the then-current franchise fee. And you have one of the easiest termination policies among the 50 franchises in this book: you need only give 180 days (six months) notice to cancel the contract.
- Site selection assistance with evaluation and lease negotiation, including a visit, if necessary.

- Construction management. MBE gives you all of the necessary leasehold improvement designs and specifications, but for 10 percent of the construction cost, or a maximum of $2,000, MBE representatives will manage the leasehold build-out for you.
- A minimum two-week training program for two people, either at headquarters or with an experienced area franchisee. And you spend five days working in your area franchise developer's store to learn actual operations. Additional training costs you a per-day fee plus expenses.
- Comprehensive advertising and promotion materials. The company also wants area and region franchises to form cooperative advertising groups.
- Volume purchasing discounts through the corporate office.
- The usual panoply of support staff, newsletters, hot lines, and the like.

How Much Can You Make?

Although the company does not want any earnings figures quoted, either its own or those of its franchisees, this book's specific purpose is to identify the most profitable franchises from the point of view of the franchise buyer, not the company itself. MBE is a profitable, well-managed company, but more importantly, its franchise buyers can earn very significant returns on investment, according to several publications. You are best served if you have some reasonable way to determine how much you can earn before you take the plunge into a franchise.

Even so, each MBE franchise offers such a wide range of services and prices—each franchise is free to set its own prices for its services and products—that determining actual income and ROI is difficult. *Venture* magazine reported that MBE franchisees received an average two-year ROI of about 50 percent.

The company's own published figures show that during its fiscal year 1989, 831 operational franchises grossed $235.4 million, for an average gross income of $283,273. That figure includes new as well as established franchises, so clearly after several years, your results should exceed this figure.

One new MBE franchisee reported that, in late 1989, his store quickly fulfilled the financial projections that MBE gave him after he bought the franchise. Of course, MBE cannot give you financial projections before you buy because the FTC disclosure rule prohibits it.

Prices vary widely for each service, but here are some of the more common ones so that you can get an idea of how you would accumulate average gross revenues estimated at $283,000.

Mail box rental. Rentals are charged at $10 to $25 per month. Each center has 250 mailboxes, for a potential total revenue between $30,000 and

$75,000 per year. Most MBE franchisees sell these as part of a package of services, including rental, fax transmission, etc.

Parcel shipping. Most firms charge packing charges of $2 to $5 dollars— or more, depending on the size and complexity of the package. You would also receive revenues from each service—UPS, Federal Express, etc.—for whom you acted as agent.

Business services. Typing is usually charged at $1.50 to $3 per page. You would pay a good secretary $7 to $15 an hour, and he or she can type 12 to 15 pages an hours depending on location, so you can net up to 50 percent on each typing job. Telephone message services cost $12 to $30 per month. Some MBE franchises add desktop publishing services with personal computers and laser printers.

Communications services. Overnight mail charges average $8.50 to $15 per package of about 30 sheets, so telex, fax, and similar services cost proportionally more. Your net profits on these services should be in the 75 to 95 percent range.

Supplies and convenience item sales. You can also earn 40 to 100 percent markups on most materials, stationery, and supplies, except on stamps.

With this multiplicity of profit centers, you can see how your revenues can quickly mount up. Expect most of your first year to be spent earning back your investment. Provide a small salary for your living expenses, and then move into significant returns during your second year as you retire short-term debts and increase sales volumes.

You should net—before taxes—between 25 and 45 percent of your gross, or between $70,000 and $127,000 by the end of your third year.

Important Notes

One of the secrets to success is getting off to a fast start. MBE is growing so fast, however, that by late 1989, it was stretching its support staff very thin. The new franchisee interviewed for this book noted that his only problem was getting adequate support from the national support team. His area developer was helpful, but the national group was so busy that its members could not keep up with the demand for their help.

Although MBE won or made small settlements on several small lawsuits, it did lose one very important suit tied to its 1988 sale of common stock. In September, 1989, a jury found that MBE and some of its officers had misled someone named Nancy Tash by failing to disclose material information during the stock sale. The jury awarded judgments of $2.5 million against MBE and $1.5 million against its president, A. W. (Tony) De Sio, to Ms. Tash. By late 1989, MBE had not disclosed whether it would appeal the jury verdict.

Although this suit has nothing to do with how well its franchisees do, this is pertinent information you may wish to consider before you buy.

Fortunately, MBE franchisees appear to enjoy very high success rates. Before 1989, only 20 franchises closed: five company units; the franchisor closed eight for non-payment; and the company reacquired seven franchises. Some 73 franchisees either sold or transferred their stores to another person. The number may include the following categories: some stores owned by company executives; some early franchisees were taking their equity profits and selling out; or some were failing, and the company helped them to sell. The total of 93 equals 11.2 percent, or about 3.7 percent per year—about the average for franchise failures.

In any case, Mail Boxes Etc. appears to constitute a profitable trend towards "convenience business and retail service centers" that may take the place of traditional and separate services, including the USPS, the typing service, the telephone answering service, Western Union, and the like.

HAIRCRAFTERS AND GREAT EXPECTATIONS HAIR SALONS

CutCo Industries, Inc.
125 South Service Road
Jericho, NY 11753
(516) 334-8400

CutCo Industries offers investors and sophisticated owners of hair salons an excellent opportunity to make remarkably high profits. One franchisee, for example, owns 35 Great Expectations' and Haircrafters' franchises in Florida, and his stores grossed more than $7 million during 1989. The franchisee certainly has an annual income in the high six figures, if not more than one million dollars.

CutCo's two franchise offerings have been consistently rated among the *Entrepreneur* magazine Top 10 hair salon franchises for the past six or seven years.

The average CutCo franchisee owns four locations, and the company emphasizes a clustered marketing technique, so the fixed costs of management and advertising expenses can be spread among more units, thereby making each unit's profit margin greater. For example, it is as easy to buy one advertisement identifying 20 locations as it is to pay the same amount identifying one or two. And you can get much lower ad rates with volume buys as well. It could add an extra one-half or one percent to your bottom line. Thus, you extend your market reach at no extra costs. Of course, opening additional franchises is less costly, and an owner is more likely to get a bank or investor to loan him more money for a chain of salons. But CutCo does not impose strict requirements on how many salons you must open in any given territory; rather, it persuades investors with very impressive figures.

In fact, it offers a 50 percent franchise fee discount on what executives call "bloc franchises" that give exclusive rights to large territories. Within these territories, you agree to open as few as three or as many as 20 salons within three years; company executives do say they give two-year extensions, but rarely. They want rapid growth. The territories are based on county boundaries, and territories which require a large number of new shops tend to be located in metropolitan areas.

The attraction of the hair salon business is that it is relatively recession-proof—you could actually do better because women tend to get their hair done more during recessions. This is not a sexist remark, but one proven by actual market figures. It is a clean business with no accounts receivables—all cash and credit cards. You have minimal inventories of retail items, and franchises are grabbing ever larger shares of the hair salon marketplace. The number of salons has fallen rapidly since the 1970s, but the number of franchised operations has soared.

CutCo Industries has more than 675 operating franchises owned by about 150 individuals or investor owners. It offers two franchises: *Great Expectations,* an up-scale, Yuppie-oriented hair salon usually located in regional shopping malls in more than 210 cities; and *Haircrafters,* a family-oriented, value-priced franchise located in local or area strip shopping centers. During 1989, CutCo added about 45 salons, most of which were owned by existing franchisees. CutCo, a prosperous 32-year-old company, can afford to be choosy about its new franchisees.

How Much It Costs

Each of the two franchises has a $20,000 franchise fee. If you own three or more salons, you pay a reduced franchise fee of $15,000, a 25 percent savings, for each additional salon. This gives existing owners another incentive to expand rapidly.

Start-up costs range from $83,000 to $171,500 for Great Expectations salons, while Haircrafters costs range from $73,000 to $126,500. The high end exceeds this book's limit, but CutCo reports that most new franchisees spend less than $100,000. As they expand, they tend to open larger, more expensive salons.

Estimated Start-Up Costs

These are reasonable figures, especially the liberal provisions for miscellaneous start-up costs. As usual, you have to pay for your travel and room and

Haircrafters	Category	Great Expectations
$20,000	Franchise fee	$20,000
25–50,000	Lease improvements	35–90,000
0–3,500	Site acquisition	0–3,500
0–5,000	Lease deposit	0–5,000
15–25,000	Fixtures	15–30,000
3,000	Opening inventory	3,000
10–20,000	Miscellaneous	10–20,000
$73,000–$126,500	Total Cost Ranges	$83,000–$171,500

board expenses during your extensive training period. Special considerations include the following:

CutCo will often lease the space and sublease it to the franchisee in a straight pass-through arrangement.

CutCo will manage the construction of your leasehold improvements, but charge a minimum equal to 10 percent of the first $25,000 and 5 percent of all additional costs. You can expect the fee to range from $2,500 to $6,250.

The company sells private-label hair care products and acts as a Redken hair and beauty care products distributor. You are not required to buy these products, but the markups are so good and the marketing is so easy that most franchisees have turned the sales of these products into new, no-cost profit centers.

The company requires the usual insurance coverages, plus salon operators' malpractice insurance.

Royalties and Fees

The royalty structure is straightforward: 6 percent of your weekly gross sales, with a $140 weekly minimum for the first year. You also pay a 2 percent advertising fee to the company's Cooperative National Advertising Fund. CutCo has established an advertising trust managed by its franchisees and corporate officers.

Available Financing

CutCo has also made financing arrangements on behalf of its franchisees. Three lending companies will make loans at market rates in amounts directly related to your credit-worthiness, collateral, and available security. Recently, these loans have been given for amounts ranging from $20,000 to

$200,000 at interest rates 4.5 to 5.5 percent over the prime lending rate. CutCo will also help you apply for a Small Business Administration loan.

And in some circumstances, the company may finance the franchise fee for two years. Repayment is in 24 monthly installments at interest rates equal to the prime rate, or about $800 per month for 24 months.

What You Get

Franchisees, especially investors and businesspeople, receive a remarkable opportunity to recoup their investment and make large profits within the first two years. They also benefit from depreciation allowances on the equipment and leasehold construction costs.

Under the "bloc franchise" arrangement, you receive a large exclusive territory, and the company says that its policy is to avoid establishing company-owned or competing franchises in a market crammed with competing hair salon franchises. This also means that it may allow a Haircrafters to be opened near a Great Expectations salon because CutCo maintains that the two franchises reach different markets.

You also get a very good 15-year term with up to three five-year renewals. This allows you to build significant equity and resale value. Nor do you have to pay a renewal fee. This saves you thousands of dollars as compared to other franchises.

Training lasts from one to two weeks at an existing, company-owned or franchised location near yours, thereby reducing your travel expenses. You can bring a store manager with you, but you are responsible for his or her expenses.

CutCo also offers a sophisticated support program proven in more than 20 years experience as a franchisor.

How Much Can You Make?

In its newsletter, CutCo has published some remarkable, but authentic, gross income figures for its Top 10 franchises. During 1988, the seventh-best store grossed more than $500,000, and the Top Twenty all grossed more than $300,000 each. A nine-month-old shop achieved $10,000 per week in sales. The average gross sales for the franchisee who own 35 Florida salons was $205,000 each, with his best salon grossing more than $500,000. Many salons report healthy gross sales of retail items, such as hair care products, in the $8,000 to $13,000 range, with 50 percent net profits.

Clearly, you should net 25 to 35 percent from an individual salon after just one year, and you should increase that net to 35 to 45 percent for a multi-unit operation.

Although the start-up costs are high, you can use the available financing plans to reduce your cash costs and let the business pay for itself. Investors ranging from dentists to lawyers to engineers to husband-and-wife teams have found that CutCo's opportunities provide excellent short- and long-term rewards.

COST CUTTERS FAMILY
HAIR CARE SHOPS

Executive Vice President
Franchise Development
Cost Cutters Family Hair Care Shops
300 Industrial Boulevard, N.E.
Minneapolis, MN 55413
(612) 331-8500

Cost Cutters Family Hair Care Shops was one of the fastest growing hair-cutting franchises during 1989. It provides low-cost, "no frills" hair care services for men, women, and children. Each service— cut, blow dry, perm, etc.— is offered at a separate price. For additional profit centers, it sells a full line of accessories, hair care products, merchandise, and appliances, such as blow dryers. This franchise's main advantages include:

- Relatively low start-up costs
- All cash business with no receivables, but perhaps some credit cards
- Ability to keep your present employment
- No hair care experience needed

The franchise's rapid growth is based on development agreements under which a franchisee agrees to open a predefined number of shops within a given period of time. Cost Cutters bases its franchises on territories with a population of about 30,000 per unit. Cost Cutters' approach appeals to a middle-class market, so be sure to locate your franchise in an area with middle-class, cost-conscious families.

How Much It Costs

Cost Cutters is very open with information about start-up costs. It gives one of the better estimates of your total initial cash investment. It states that the average total start-up investment is $55,000, with a range from $54,880 to $76,700. The table below shows these estimates:

	Low Estimate	High Estimate
Initial franchise fee[a]	$19,500	$19,500
Opening advertising	1,000	2,500
Furniture, fixtures	10,860	15,000
Leasehold improvements	12,000	23,200
Initial inventory	1,300	2,500
Working capital	10,000	14,000
Total	$54,660	$76,700

a. Second unit fee equals $17,500; third unit, $15,000; and fourth and subsequent units, $12,500.

Costs Explained

You must buy the furniture and fixtures prescribed by the franchise company, but you can obtain them from any approved source. You must buy or lease at least 900 square feet of space and have at least 8 to 12 hairstylists on staff—several full-time and the rest part-time. You are also required to hire a manager and are encouraged to hire a receptionist as well.

The leasehold improvement costs vary so widely because Cost Cutters has found that the cost depends directly on the size and location of available space. You could take over an existing hair shop, or you could lease brand new space and have to pay for everything, including having the floors laid and the electrical outlets installed.

The working capital estimates are liberal; you will probably spend the funds on the following: (1) wages and travel expenses during training; (2) permits and licenses; (3) lease and utility deposits; (4) lease down payments; (5) insurance premiums; (6) Yellow Pages ads; and (7) miscellaneous operating costs. These costs will vary from place to place, depending on many factors.

You are required to spend between $1,000 and $2,500 on your initial advertising. You are required to buy liability, products liability, malpractice, personal property, automobile liability, and other necessary insurance coverages.

Royalties, Fees, and Payments

In addition to your initial investment, you pay a weekly continuing fee of 4 percent of your gross revenues. After the first year, you have to pay a minimum weekly fee of $75. But you also must pay a weekly advertising fee of 4 percent and spend, each quarter, at least 1 percent of your gross revenues for local media advertising and promotion.

You are required to attend and pay for the cost of the trip to one national meeting each year.

Although not *required* to do so, you can buy all of your supplies, hair care products, appliances, furniture and fixtures, etc., from the franchise company. It does make a profit on them.

What You Get

In return for your franchise fee, you receive a turnkey package of approved plans and specifications, approved sources' lists, written development schedule, and extensive training, which consists of at least three days of classroom and on-the-job instruction. Cost Cutters then sends a representative to help you for five days as you get started. The company also offers advanced training seminars at its center in Minneapolis, and it will send a trainer to your franchise to give a customized training program at extra cost.

You do *not* receive an exclusive territory unless you enter into a Development Agreement; that is, you agree to develop a larger territory during a specific time period. You must open one Cost Cutters' shop for every 30,000 people in that territory. The term of the standard franchise agreement is 15 years, but the Development Agreement term ranges from 1 to 10 years. Its length depends on the number of units you plan to open. However, if you renew a franchise agreement, you do not pay a renewal fee.

How Much Can You Make?

In its UFOC, Cost Cutters provides one of the most complete discussions of potential earnings of any of the franchises described in this book. It gives a pages-long chart that lists the unaudited gross sales of all of its franchises since the year each shop opened. The figures show that the business tends to fluctuate up and down, but that many franchisees quickly experience strong growth. Others show small dips and small increases from year to year. The most successful units grow from about $110,000 per year to more than $325,000 per year within several years. On average, the units tend to grow from about $41,000 per year to about $100,000 per year within several years. Sales gains tend to fall in the 20 to 40 percent per year range, and sales declines tend to be in the 8 percent to 20 percent range. All in all, no one loses his shirt, and most do very, very well.

A Cost Cutters' projection model—which does not guarantee success or any income figures—shows that you can expect to lose money (about $12,800 on sales of $96,000) during your first year, but start returning a good return by the second month of your second year. The model makes some assumptions that do not seem to apply in practice. First, it assumes that your start-up costs will total $46,700; and second, that sales will not increase after your second year. With this conservative approach, it is clear that the actual returns experienced by the vast majority of franchisees are substantially better than those in the fictitious model. As your sales exceed the model's estimates, your profits and ROI increase. According to a cash flow model, your cumulative ROI, although a negative 20 percent during the first year, quickly soars to almost 34 percent by the end of your second year, and reaches 147 percent by the end of your fourth year.

Given below are Cost Cutters' projection models and the assumptions behind them.

Cost Cutter Projections[a]

First Year

Total sales	$ 95,800
Cost of sales	60,287
Gross profit	35,513
Operating expenses	48,289
Profit/deficit	(12,776)

Second Year

Total sales	$146,000
Cost of sales	78,840
Gross profit	67,160
Operating expenses	45,927
Profit	21,233

Third Year

Total sales	$150,000
Cost of sales	81,000
Gross profit	69,000
Operating expenses	46,167
Profit	22,833

a. This projection is based on a one-shop model for the first three years of operation. Another set of figures shows that your cumulative earnings after three years should yield a cumulative return on investment of 147 percent, with a net cash flow of $68,631.

FOUR SEASONS GREENHOUSES
DESIGN & REMODELING CENTERS

Four Seasons Greenhouses
Design & Remodeling Centers
5005 Veterans Memorial Highway
Holbrook, NY 11741
(800) 521-0179
(516) 563-4000

Four Seasons Greenhouses is one of the decade's leading franchise success stories, growing from a $2,000 investment by a construction worker to a network of more than 270 franchised Four Seasons Greenhouse showrooms worldwide. A very positive, up-scale image has resulted from its pervasive national advertising campaign—accomplished *without* an advertising fee that franchisees pay—in all leading magazines aimed at affluent Baby Boomers, the wealthy, and significant commercial accounts.

The company has transformed what was once a market strategy aimed at energy-conscious consumers into a strategy aimed at making a greenhouse practically a remodeling "necessity" for a home, restaurant, or office structure. If you need any more evidence of its success as a restaurant concept, look at most of the leading fast-food and mid-scale restaurants, such as Burger King, Ryan's Family Steakhouses, and TGI Friday's, to name just three leading chains. During the past several years, they all have rushed to add greenhouses to their facilities.

The market for home remodeling in itself is enormous, about $80 billion a year, and homeowners have some $4 trillion in equity with which they can finance home improvements. During 1989, homeowners added more than 1.5 million rooms to their homes, more than 3.6 million kitchens, and more than 4.1 million bathrooms. More than 4 million existing homes were resold during 1989, and more than 40 million homes are more than 25-years-old. All of these are excellent candidates for greenhouse additions.

Equally important today are Four Seasons' commercial and office remodeling and construction sales. And a recent report by John Naisbitt shows that the market for franchises in construction and home services, remodeling, and home repair, etc., has grown an average of 20 percent per year during the past five years (1986–1991) and should grow at a similar high rate during the next five years.

Four Seasons franchises are based on the "remodeling center and showroom" concept. You open a showroom that builds Four Seasons products into the structure and use it to display both residential and commercial product lines to potential customers. You also make direct sales calls to architects, developers, and major construction firms. It is unlikely that making direct sales pitches to homeowners is a good way to sell.

The product line includes nine models of wood- and aluminum-framed solariums, two patio rooms, and a line of wood and glass doors. You also sell related products, such as skylights, windows, and store fronts, and some franchisees sell luxury add-ons, such as hot tubs, spas, and ceramic tile floors and walls. Often, you work with quality subcontractors who install your product line and your add-ons. You get customer referrals from them, too.

What It Costs

Four Seasons offers three levels of franchise fees, which are based on market potential and population:

- $20,000 for a full franchise for a major metropolitan area like Boston.
- $10,000 for a mini-franchise in a smaller area like Utica, New York.
- $5,000 for a rural franchise in an area like Great Falls, Montana.

Four Seasons expects a full franchisee to set up a free-standing location and devote full-time to the business. But it encourages its rural franchisees to incorporate the greenhouse business into an existing business, such as home remodeling, repair, or construction.

Total start-up costs, including the fee, but not including a required start-up product package, ranges from as low as $13,500 for the rural franchise to $100,000 for a full franchise.

Four Seasons' UFOC includes the following expenses in its estimate: franchise fee, displays, signage, leasehold improvements, first month's lease and two months' deposit, training travel, furnishings and fixtures, and working capital.

You may have to pay some additional costs:

- Zoning variance approvals for your showroom center;
- Down payments on vacant commercial land, if you buy and build your center on your own land;
- Points and closing costs on such a purchase;
- Legal and accounting fees;
- Office supplies;
- Lead follow-through sales materials and aids, purchased from Four Seasons;
- Construction fee; and
- Site selection fees.

You also must buy a start-up product package which averages about $15,000 for a full franchise, about $7,500 for a mini-franchise, but much less for a rural franchise.

Beneficial Royalty Structure

Four Seasons offers a very good royalty structure. You do not pay any royalties on products you purchase from Four Seasons. You pay a low 2.5 percent royalty on other products that you do not buy from Four Seasons, such as ceramic tiles, hot tubs, and the like.

As mentioned, you do *not* pay an advertising fee, despite the fact that Four Seasons spends at least 2.5 percent of its own revenues on a very good national advertising campaign. This campaign generates hundred of thousands of leads for its franchisees each year. This remarkable system will be described below.

Perhaps your largest on-going cost will be that you have to buy almost all of your products from Four Seasons. You are restricted to offering its product line. In this way, Four Seasons is more like an auto dealership or a beverage franchise than a business-format franchise.

What You Get

In exchange for the franchise fee and start-up product package purchase, you receive a complete turnkey operation.

Exclusive territory in a demographically sound area. Look for a territory with lots of chain restaurants, affluent homes, and professional office space.

Marvelous lead generation system. All of Four Seasons ads are geared to generate coupon responses. Four Seasons automates the hundreds of thousands of leads it receives each year. The company not only sends each lead a sophisticated color catalog but also it refers all of the leads from your territory to you so that you can follow through and make a sale. Your name also appears on the catalog sent to the customers, so they can call you on their own. This is probably the most sophisticated lead generation system of any franchise in the country.

Cooperative advertising allowance. Four Seasons also helps you pay for your own ad program. Four Seasons, remarkably, will pay you 5 percent of your *gross purchases* of Four Seasons products for your own advertising campaign. This is called a 100 percent cooperative advertising program because Four Seasons pays the full cost of the ad up to the 5 percent limit. For example, if you buy from Four Seasons $500,000 worth of greenhouses per year, Four Seasons will give you $25,000 for your local advertising budget. You can use it to advertise as you please.

Professional sales tools. The company does have one of the best sales presentations of any in the business.

Training. Four Seasons concentrates on training the franchisee to be a good business manager and salesperson and suggests that you hire an experienced construction manager to supervise installations. You can also work with subcontractors.

National accounts program. Four Seasons itself pursues an aggressive national accounts sales program, but it does offer each account and the local franchisee the opportunity to work together. Hotel chains, supermarkets, fast-food franchises, large builders and developers, etc., all have national account status. The Four Seasons' operation is truly impressive.

How Much Can You Make?

Company executives reported that during 1988, the average gross sales volume for Four Seasons' full franchises one-year-old or older equalled $759,000. That should mean a net per-tax profit in the $150,000 to $200,000 range for a full franchisee in a metropolitan area. During 1988, Four Seasons' franchisees reported system-wide volume of about $150 million, or about $625,000 each. This figure includes new franchisees, who tend to drag the average down. This is a strong rate, totaling 58 percent during the four years between 1985 and 1988. You should easily recoup your investment within 18 months and begin to realize 100 percent or greater annual ROIs by the end of your third year.

Here's how you should calculate it for each sale. The average residential greenhouse addition costs $10,000 to $15,000, with $12,000 a likely average. Four Seasons executives say that you make a 40 to 42 percent gross profit on each sale and each installation. On a $12,000 home solarium, you will gross about $4,800 on average, just for the product. If you do the installation, you can make even more, probably about another $1,000. Of course, as you buy more greenhouses from Four Seasons each quarter, it is likely that your discount—and your gross margin—will increase.

After you subtract your overhead from that $5,800, you should net about 30 to 40 percent, or between $1,740 and $2,320 on an average sale and installation. This is a reasonable, but not an excellent profit for the difficult and time-consuming "onesy-twosey" sales to homeowners. Instead, the company advises you to spend your time selling to developers building dozens or hundreds of houses: for example, convince them to build a greenhouse into their designs. Then, you can arrange for Four Seasons to ship the greenhouses to the builders and let them worry about installation. You can also sell commercial accounts and keep your crews busy retrofitting all of the fast-food franchise outlets in your area. With commercial accounts, your net profits should soar.

8

Franchises with Fees Greater Than $20,000

Tri-Mark Publishing Co., Inc.
Travel Agents International, Inc.
American Advertising
  Distributors, Inc.
Priority Management Systems, Inc.
Ceiling Doctor International, Inc.

Monograms Plus
General Business Services, Inc.
Uniglobe Travel International, Inc.
ProFusion Systems, Inc.
Press Box News
Dynamark Security Centers, Inc.

Tri-Mark Publishing Co., Inc.

Tri-Mark Publishing Co., Inc.
184 Quigley Boulevard
P.O. Box 10530
Wilmington, DE 19850-0530
(800) TRI-MARK (874-6275)
(302) 322-2143

Tri-Mark offers a direct-mail marketing program through which you sell direct-mail advertising to local merchants in an exclusive territory. Tri-Mark handles all printing and direct-mail services. You pay Tri-Mark for these services, but you do not pay any other royalties or fees against your income. Tri-Mark makes its profits by providing you with on-going advertising, printing, and mailing services; you earn income by selling direct-mail advertisements, emphasizing coupons, and collecting payment.

If you can learn to sell advertising to local merchants and professional services, such as dry cleaners, opticians, cleaning services, pizza parlors, sandwich shops, restaurants, etc., you can do very well in this business. The business is a very competitive one because your clients are already barraged by ad salespeople from local shoppers, weekly newspapers, other direct-mail franchises and services, local radio stations, daily newspapers, local magazines, TV magazine giveaways, and many more.

Your advantage over most of the competition is that you can promise precisely targeted mailings to at least 10,000 homes at a very low cost per household. Your clients can easily measure the results by simply counting the number of coupons their new customers bring in during the redemption period. And Tri-Mark provides a high-quality, professional direct-mail "piece," that is, the envelope is filled with noncompeting advertisements.

Your *business* advantage is that you can run this business from your home and keep your overhead very low. You can work part-time or full-time; Tri-Mark does not care as long as you meet its sales quota.

The ROI and income potential are very substantial, with Tri-Mark's leading franchisees reporting gross incomes of more than $360,000 during 1989. This is a 1,000 to 1,200 percent return on their original investment. Before you get too excited, however, understand that most of Tri-Mark's more than 60 franchisees do not make nearly that rate of return.

Special Situation

In a dispute with a former franchise salesperson, Tri-Mark filed for Chapter 11 bankruptcy in early October, 1988. Filing a Chapter 11 bankruptcy petition allows a company to continue to operate while it reorganizes and negotiates settlements or payment arrangements with its creditors. In this case, Tri-Mark had $2.83 million in assets and $3.2 million in liabilities, so Tri-Mark's financial health was not at issue in this filing.

Rather, it meant that Tri-Mark arranged to protect its assets from the former salesperson in a dispute over payment of the salesperson's commissions. Tri-Mark executives noted in a letter to franchisees that, although they had vigorously contested the former salesperson's lawsuit, a jury had awarded him a $125,000 judgment. They added that they had paid the salesperson $85,000 and had tried to negotiate arrangements to pay the remaining $40,000. But the salesperson apparently went to work for a competitor and filed for an execution judgment. The executives maintained that they expected to emerge from the Chapter 11 in early 1990 or earlier, as they pay the $40,000 owed to the former salesperson.

Tri-Mark's executives said they were trying to arrange to sell their real estate assets valued at more than $2 million. The company has also opened an escrow account with a bank to make sure its franchisees' printings and mailings are done on time and to reassure the franchisees.

Before the matter came to a head in October, 1989, one-third of Tri-Mark's franchisees had stopped making payments to the company and had been dropped as formal franchisees. With the Chapter 11 filing, Tri-Mark executives said they would vigorously pursue these franchisees to encourage them to return to the system and pay the money they owe the company.

Tri-Mark was very forthcoming about its situation and appears to be making serious efforts to resolve these problems and to emerge again as a strong company by mid-1990. Potential franchise buyers should be careful, but Tri-Mark's openness and commitment to survival and future growth could mean that new franchisees will obtain more help and support than they otherwise might. Of course, the company must have the financial resources to provide that assistance. You should have your attorney review any Chapter 11 reorganization plans and your accountant review any financial statements issued during or after the Chapter 11 process ends.

How Much It Costs

Technically, Tri-Mark charges only a $1 license fee, but actually, the total fees for a liberal support program range from $19,900 to $28,900, $5,000 less in 1990 than in 1987, perhaps a reflection of its difficulties. The fee depends on how many "mailable homes"—an important concept to consider—are in your territory. The fee structure is the following:

Up to 150,000 mailable homes	$19,900
151,000 to 200,000	22,900
201,000 to 250,000	25,900
251,000 to 300,000	28,900

After you get started, you can buy more territory contiguous to your original area for a fee of $100 per 1,000 homes. The term "mailable home" means a household with an income above $12,500 and receiving mail. Market research studies show that homes with incomes below $12,500 do *not* redeem direct-mail coupons very often. A mailing to such a home would be wasted and of no benefit to you, the advertising client, or to Tri-Mark. This distinction is an important one compared to other advertising business opportunities. In advertising, knowing and appealing to customer demographics (their age, income, occupation, etc.) and psychographics (their attitudes and beliefs, which create buying habits) make advertising precise and worthwhile.

Your ultimate goal would be to advertise only to perfect prospects and turn each of those prospects into a customer. With direct mail, such as Tri-Mark, you can more accurately target your clients' audience of customers than with any other advertising medium.

Other Costs and Fees

Although Tri-Mark does not charge any royalty or ad fees, or the like, you do have to make purchases from the company, including:

- Cost of preparing, printing, and mailing the inserts, plus the costs for envelopes and labels, with the total cost estimated at $1,500 to $3,500 for a typical mailing to 10,000 homes. The actual cost depends on how many ad inserts will go into each direct-mail envelope. Of course, the more inserts, the more money you make, too.
- A $25 to $75 per 10,000-piece inserting charge for preprinted inserts—prepared ads that you or a client want put into the mailing envelope. You also must pay to ship the inserts to Tri-Mark for insertion.

Additional Start-Up Costs

You face additional start-up costs that depend largely on whether you work from home or not. They include the following categories, with estimated cost ranges also given:

Description	Low Estimate	High Estimate
Office lease[a]	$ 600	$2,500
Office furniture	300	2,500
Telephone[b]	0	500
Postage permit	40	40
Accountant[c]	160	500
Auto insurance[d]	100	500
Sales personnel	100	2,000
Total[e]	$1,300	$8,540

a. If you work at home, you save this and most other costs as well.
b. You can use your own phone, unless you advertise in the Yellow Pages or similar business directory. If you do, you will probably need to have a business phone installed.
c. Tri-Mark estimates these figures as monthly charges.
d. You can use your own car and avoid most of this cost.
e. Does not include any money for working capital or living expenses for a month or two. Add a reasonable figure, such as $3,000 to $5,000, for those costs.

Tri-Mark says that most franchisees spend between $3,000 and $5,000 to get started *before* they add in working capital. Your working capital, as noted, will be used for telephone charges, gas for your automobile—this is largely a direct-sales, door-to-door effort—and living expenses, as well as for additional office supplies, business cards, brochures, and other sales materials, when your initial supply from Tri-Mark runs out.

Sales Quotas

Tri-Mark has, and enforces, a strict sales quota. You must make a minimum purchase of five "distributions," that is, mailings to at least 10,000 homes, every six months. You must begin selling your territory within 90 days of signing the franchise agreement and generate mailings to 50,000 homes every six months to keep the franchise active. And you can only sell ads to businesses physically located within your territory. It appears that you can sell ads to local franchisees of national companies without conflicting with Tri-Mark's national accounts program that is described below.

Tri-Mark says that the average distribution costs $1,800 plus postage, and the average annual payment to the franchise company per year has been $18,000 for 10 distributions plus $8,100 for postage. (This figure will go up since postage costs keep rising; you raise your ad rates to cover postal cost increases.) If you do not meet the minimum quota, the company has the right to terminate the agreement, and it will.

Franchisor's National Accounts

Tri-Mark also reserves several rights that raise questions. Most importantly, it reserves the right to put its own advertisements into each package *without* paying you a commission. These include ads for its printing services, such as personalized labels, business cards, stationery, or mail-order products. However, you can put your own inserts into the package and pay only the insertion charge, as discussed above.

More importantly, Tri-Mark has an extensive national account sales program that can greatly benefit you. A national account is defined as one that has a national address, uses a business reply-card insert, is not affiliated with any retail store, and mails at least 100,000 pieces per year.

Although you cannot sell national accounts (only home office reps can), you earn commissions on them in two ways:

1. From national account sales made by the company. You receive 70 percent of the proceeds— a very liberal payment plan; Tri-Mark receives 20 percent; and 5 percent goes to the franchisee in whose territory the national account is located.

2. For a national account lead that you generate. The remaining 5 percent of the total listed above goes to the franchisee that generates a national account lead; as a franchisee, you get the full 10 percent if you generate the lead, *and* the lead is located in your territory.

Tri-Mark does not give you direct cash payments from its national account sales; instead, it gives you a credit against your outstanding balance with the company.

What You Get

Tri-Mark provides a liberal training and support program, which is paid for by its fairly high franchise fee.

Indefinite term. It can be an excellent feature for you. As long as you meet the minimum quota, the agreement stays in effect as long as you want it to. The indefinite term can also be thought of as a blessing or a curse—a blessing if you are dedicated to building up the business, and a curse if you want to work part-time and have a difficult time meeting your quotas. There is no provision for a lower quota for part-time franchisees.

Training. You get five days of training at the home office and five days of field training. This training is valued at $5,000. Tri-Mark even pays all of the transportation and room-and-board costs for one person to be trained. If you bring anyone else to the home office, you or the other person is responsible for the additional expenses. Who pays the minimal additional cost of lodging when two share a room was not discussed in the company's UFOC.

Supplies and materials. This includes an initial mailing to 1,000 local businesses advertising your services, as well as the usual kits, brochures, manuals, stationery, etc.

Field assistance program. If needed, a field trainer will work with you for up to five days after your home-office training to teach you local market analysis, selling skills, goal setting, and office management techniques.

How Much Can You Make?

The table at the end of this chapter shows sample gross margins based on the number of inserts that go into each mailing. According to these figures, you charge $375 per 10,000 homes, a per home charge of 3.75 cents. Your profits climb in direct proportion to the number of ads inserted into each mailing.

You earn what are essentially 47 percent commissions, after you pay Tri-Mark for its services. Those commissions make up your gross margin, from which you must subtract your operating expenses and a portion of your initial investment before you can determine your net profit.

The figures in the table should be used as guides, not gospel. For example, if you sell multiple insertions to one customer, you will have to offer significant discounts, often 15 to 20 percent, reducing your potential gross, but increasing your current income. You can see from the table that selling the minimum number of insertions will net you just $206, if each customer pays $375. If you do this five times a year, the $2,472 annual gross margin is hardly worth the effort. It would take years to earn any ROI on that. Therefore, you have to keep your overhead low, and you must sell aggressively.

From these figures, it appears that this franchise has very little potential as a part-time effort, if your goal is to earn high returns relatively quickly.

However, top sellers can do very well. Tri-Mark's in-house newsletter reports that the 1988 purchase volume of its Top 10 franchisees ranged from $142,000 to $364,000. One franchisee has reported that his first-year sales were just $43,000, but he built his total sales volume over six years to more than $750,000; he paid about half of that to Tri-Mark for its services, so he grossed more than $380,000. With net margins, after expenses in the 25 to 35 percent range, he should earn a net income between $95,000 and $133,000. The average franchisee, however, should earn net incomes between $30,000 and $50,000 after two years. This will build a steadily strong ROI if you keep your total start-up costs below $30,000.

Sample Gross Margin Residential Mailing

Customers	Suggested Retail Price	Approximate Billing from Tri-Mark	Franchisee's Gross Margin
6	$2,250	$2,044	$ 206
7	2,625	2,153	472
8	3,000	2,262	738
9	3,375	2,371	1,004
10	3,750	2,480	1,270
11	4,125	2,589	1,536
12	4,500	2,698	1,802
13	4,875	2,807	2,068
14	5,250	2,916	2,334
15	5,625	3,025	2,600
16	6,000	3,134	2,866
17	6,375	3,243	3,132
18	6,750	3,352	3,398
19	7,125	3,461	3,664
20	7,500	3,570	3,930
21	7,875	3,679	4,196
22	8,250	3,788	4,462
23	8,625	3,897	4,728
24	9,000	4,006	4,994

The above figures are based on the following costs:

Fixed Costs (per Mailing)		Variable Cost (per Customer)	
Postage	$1,010	Printing, Cutting,	
Envelopes	190	Plates, & Artwork	$ 84
Addressing	190	Insertion	25
Total	$1,390	Total	$109

TRAVEL AGENTS INTERNATIONAL, INC.

Travel Agents International, Inc.
111 Second Avenue N.E.
15th Floor
St. Petersburg, FL 33731-8905
(813) 895-8241
(813) 894-6318 FAX
Telex 8100080165

Travel Agents International is the second largest travel agency franchise, and during the mid-1980s, it was the fastest growing travel franchise, according to *Venture* magazine. By the end of 1989, it had 360 operational franchises in 39 states, with 40 operational in Canada. It plans to open 45 to 50 more during 1990 and each year thereafter.

In December, 1988, *Venture* rated it the 70th fastest growing franchise. The January 1989 issue of *Entrepreneur* magazine rated it 90th among the top 500 franchises in the U.S. and the 38th fastest growing franchise in Canada. And *Florida Trend* magazine rated it the 20th best of the top 200 companies in Florida in a 1989 issue.

Unlike other travel agency franchises or large travel agencies, this company emphasizes customized family vacation bargains, which include the following: cruise ship discounts; group travel and tours; hotel and car rental discounts, and the like. It supports these emphases with co-op advertising, group space bookings, higher commissions, payment overrides, and other techniques that raise a franchisee's net income.

Its corporate travel program is based on a guarantee that it will arrange the lowest air fare for the business traveler or reimburse the difference between the fare paid and the lowest available fare. Faced with a massive consolidation of services within the corporate/commercial marketplace, TAI has responded by setting up a corporate accounts program in which individual franchisees service the local branches of major corporations. And, it has responded to the challenge of Uniglobe by acquiring a 40-office Canadian travel agency franchise, Travel Servicenters Systems, Inc. (TSS).

TAI was very forthcoming with financial information and earnings projections based on *industry,* not franchise, averages. During 1988, its existing 350 offices grossed more than $450 million in annual travel sales; that almost doubled the 1986 total of $250 million. The average office grossed more than $1.4 million in booking volume, with average gross commissions of about $150,000 to $200,000 per office.

With this success, TAI expanded aggressively into Canada during the late 1980s, concentrating its efforts on Quebec, Montreal, Toronto, Vancouver, and similar population centers. Now, TAI executives say they are slowing their pace a bit and screening their potential franchisees much more closely than before. TAI uses a "success matrix" to judge a franchisee's potential before TAI allows someone to join its system. TAI also says that the average owners are middle-aged couples who dream of starting their own business, but who are willing to work hard and have a desire to succeed.

TAI plans to enter so-called minor, under-served markets—cities with 50,000 to 100,000 people—and state and regional markets, where fewer travel agencies already exist compared to major cities. TAI is actively searching for franchisees in California and the Midwest, but has many locations in the Southeast and the East.

In its markets, franchisees focus on the vacation, leisure travel, and discount travel markets. They also aim their services at the 20 million people and 50 percent of the traveling population that do not now use travel agencies.

How Much It Costs

TAI charges a total fee of $44,500, a $5,000 increase since 1986. Of that, about half covers the franchise fee, and the other half pays for the cost of office furniture, supplies, and materials package. It will also negotiate—case-by-case—discounts on these fees for conversion franchises, existing independent travel agencies who join TAI's network. Existing franchises opening a second office may qualify for a fee as low as $4,900.

Total Start-Up Costs

TAI estimates these total start-up costs as follows. (The author sometimes adds a range of costs in certain categories and additional costs not mentioned in the UFOC.)

Description	Low Estimate	High Estimate
Total fee	$44,500	$ 44,500
Airline reservation system[a]	700	1,000
Lease deposits[b]	1,500	3,000
Leasehold improvement	750	3,500
Signage[c]	100	5,000
Carpeting	1,000	2,000
Grand opening ads[d]	1,500	3,000
Trade association memberships	600	700
ARC bonding required/ins.	1,700	1,700
Office supplies	500	2,500
Telephone/utility deposits	300	750
Working capital[e]	33,850	64,750
Travel/training expenses[f]	850	1,300
Total	$87,850	$133,700

a. Not charged for first eight months with System One Inc. reservation system.
b. Based on a requirement of a 600-square-foot office.
c. Wide range depends on use of interior or outside signage. Franchise fees paid to TAI covers the cost of two inside signs.
d. TAI's estimate, but not required, although advisable.
e. Liberal estimates to cover salaries and miscellaneous expenses for the first six months of operation.
f. Author adds this low estimate for one person to spend nine days at TAI's St. Petersburg headquarters. TAI estimates a cost ranging from $90 to $140 per day per person.

Royalties and Advertising Fees

You pay a variety of royalty and advertising fees:

A. Royalty
    $485 per month for first 12 months
    $585 per month for months 13–24
    $785 per month for months 25–36
    Annual adjustments on Sept. 1 of each year after your first 36 months.
B. Advertising fees. You face several types:

1. $115 per month for the first two years to cover the cost of the monthly newspaper, "Travel Agents International News," sent to everyone on a mailing list that you give to the franchisor. The amount increases to $230 per month after two years.
2. $75 per month for a TAI National Product Development Fund for complete advertising and promotional materials.
3. $400 per month into a Regional/National Advertising and Promotional Fund. This money is used for national television and regional television, radio, and print media advertising. This amount is adjusted annually on September 1.

Other Required Payments

You can anticipate monthly lease payments of $350 to $500 per month for the use of an airline reservation system. TAI recommends System One, an unaffiliated service supplier, because it gives you your first eight months usage free. This payment is estimated to equal between 5 and 7 percent of your annual operating cost.

You also must use Travel Computer Systems' software package at a monthly lease and maintenance payment of about $220 per month for five years. This package will account for between 2 and 3 percent of your annual operating cost.

What You Get

In return for the franchise fee, you receive a wide range of services and support:

Term of agreement. The initial term is a healthy 10 years, and you can renew for two more 10-year terms. The total of 30 years gives you plenty of time to build a prosperous business with high resale value.

Furniture package. You get enough desks, chairs, computer stands, and the like, to furnish a three-person, 600-square-foot office space. You also get adequate supplies of stationery, travel brochures, and the like. TAI provides a very thorough list of the furniture and materials you will receive.

$5,000 donation. TAI contributes $5,000 of your franchise fee to its national/regional ad fund to help support your grand opening effort.

Exclusive territory. You get an exclusive, but limited, territory with two exceptions. If you locate in a regional shopping mall or in a downtown business district of a major metropolitan area, you do not get exclusive territories. If you operate within a metropolitan statistical area with more than 250,000 people, you do get an exclusive territory. Otherwise, you can get a territory with a 1.5-mile driving radius, inside which TAI will not open a competing franchise. But if you open a franchise outside of a regional mall, and someone else wants to put an office in that mall, TAI reserves the right to do so, although the company will probably offer you the opportunity first.

Training program. As owner, you take a 10-day training course in all aspects of management, operations, and sales, while a manager or staff person takes a five-day course in marketing, selling, and basic operations.

Employment support. TAI also helps you hire an "ARC qualifier" as part of your opening staff. This person is vital because he or she is "licensed" to book reservations and receive commissions on the national airline reservation systems.

On-site assistance. A TAI staff member will work with you for two days during your first month of operation.

Continuing education. Seminars, occasional visits, and the like, are provided by regional managers.

Corporate marketing program.

Discounted promotional items.

Franchisee Advisory Committee. Made of current franchisees with at least two years experience, this group advises TAI about all of its proposed marketing plans and structural changes.

Publications. This includes the free newspapers sent to clients and prospects and an in-house newsletter.

TAI's program is a very good and complete one for the travel industry. Note that during the three years before the end of 1989, only 38 franchises went out of business: 23 for failure to comply with standards (non-payment of royalties and ad fees); seven for other reasons; four were not renewed; and four were repurchased.

How Much Can You Make?

TAI, in previously published articles, has discussed how much its franchisees earn. It appears that, based on industry averages, you should begin to show a healthy 31 percent gross pre-tax profit by the end of your third year. TAI does say that the first-year industry average sales volume is below the average achieved by TAI's new franchisees. If the average TAI franchisee grosses about $1.4 million in commissionable sales, then you should gross about $150,000 to $175,000, with net pre-tax profits of $30,000. That does include a salary for you in the $25,000 to $35,000 range.

TAI also gives an estimated range of monthly expenses based on its nine years of experience in franchising. The range, reproduced below, is $4,708 to $7,653. This means that, based on 12 percent commissions, you

Estimated Monthly Expenses (Prepared 2/89)
First Eight Months

		Amount/Estimated Range	
No.	Item	Low Range	High Range
1	Payroll—Manager	$1,200	$1,800
2	Payroll—Agent	600	1,000
3	Payroll—Taxes	150	200
4	Employee Benefits	100	150
5	Rent	800	1,750
6	Utilities	100	300
7	Telephone	250	400
8	Office Supplies	50	50
9	Advertising	205	500
10	Entertainment	50	50
11	Postage	25	100
12	Subscriptions, dues, etc.	75	100
13	Insurance	100	150
14	Miscellaneous	100	200
15	Monthly Royalty Fees	485	485
16	Accounting Service $155/Monthly—Software $63/Monthly—Maintenance	218	218
17	Computers	00	00
18	Travel	200	200
	Total Estimated Monthly Expenses	$4,708	$7,653

Table Notes:
1. For the first eight months, there is no computer charge for Texas-Air SYSTEM-ONE.
2. It is common for an agency to open with a qualifier and the franchisee. In that instance, the expense for an agent ($600—$1,000) can be eliminated.
3. This expense sheet does not include an owner's draw.
4. These expenses are based upon our experience over the past six years. Travel Agents International in no way guarantees that if you are awarded a franchise that your costs will definitely be within this estimated range.

---

must sell services worth at least $40,000 to $65,000 per month before you begin to show any profit, much less earn a return on your investment. And that range includes only a small salary or draw for the owner.

So, it would appear that you can expect a TAI franchise to grow relatively quickly, but you cannot expect a sizable return on your investment, on average, until the third year. But this is far better than most independent travel agents, who often earn minimal salaries and struggle to survive. Your chances of success with a travel agency are much greater with a franchise than if you go it alone.

AMERICAN ADVERTISING DISTRIBUTORS, INC.

American Advertising Distributors, Inc.
234 South Extension
Mesa, AZ 85202
(800) 528-8249
(602) 964-9393

American Advertising Distributors, Inc., (AAD), is the fastest growing and, perhaps, most service-oriented of the cooperative direct mail franchisors. Its mail quotas are somewhat less strict than others, its franchise fees are somewhat lower, and most of its management team started out as franchisees for the company.

AAD has gone through turmoil in its 10-year history with two changes of ownership, most recently in 1984, when the former franchisees and some professional managers bought the company from a large California wine company. Since then, the company has expanded very rapidly, and is now adding two new franchisees per month, the limit that its training department can handle. By late 1989, that meant there were about 120 AAD franchisees around the country.

Very importantly, AAD's UFOC does not list any lawsuits or litigation during the past three years, although it does show that about five franchisees fail each year because they do not meet AAD's sales quotas. AAD tends to reacquire about one-third of the failures. AAD shows very strong financial growth, almost all attributable to its franchisees' sales increases. The company's sales have grown at a compound annual rate of about 20 percent from $2.7 million during 1981 to about $14 million during 1987. AAD was rated the leading direct mail ad franchise by both Dan Dorfman's syndicated column and *Entrepreneur* magazine.

About 40 percent of AAD's franchisees are existing small business, with another 40 percent husband-and-wife teams, and the rest sole proprietors. Experienced salespeople tend to do best, but anyone can succeed because it is such a low-overhead business with no inventory and no retail location.

The success of direct mail franchises rests on one premise: generating new and repeat customers for small businesses and professional services in the local community. AAD has identified more than 162 types of businesses and professionals who can benefit from direct mail services. The results they obtain are self-evident because almost three-quarters of a franchisees' clients are repeat customers, a very high percentage for any kind of direct mail operation. The relatively low cost of the advertising for the targeted coverage means that the local small businessperson quickly understands the value he or she receives.

How Much It Costs

The franchise fee equals $23,500 and more based on this territory formula:

Residences	Franchise Fee
0 to 80,000	$23,500
More than 80,000	$200 per 1,000 residences

You should note that a territory consists of "mailable homes"—excluded are low-income households which do not have enough disposable income and do not usually respond to direct mail pieces. (A useful rule-of-thumb for almost any service franchise is to determine the number of people living at or near the poverty level. They will not be customers for personal services, direct mail solicitations, and the like. They will tend, however, to be good markets for fast-food franchises, as is evidenced by the success of many fast-food restaurants in inner city neighborhoods across the country.)

Additional Costs and Royalty Fees

Of course, you must also pay AAD for the cost of preparing and mailing your ads. An average 16-insert mailing costs $2,515 for artwork, printing, inserting, envelopes, and mailing list. You also must pay a postage and royalty fee of $18.00 per 1,000 residences—$180.00 for a 10,000-piece mailing, or about $360.00 for a 20,000-piece mailing. This fee has increased about 9.9 percent since 1987. Other direct mail opportunities do not necessarily charge a royalty.

Mailing Quotas

AAD also has mailing quotas you must meet, although they do not appear as strict as similar franchises. You are required to do one mailing to at least 10,000 residences within six months of start-up. After that, and within the next 12 months, you are required to conduct four mailings to at least 20,000 residences, each with no more than 12 weeks between each mailing. And after your fifth mailing, you must mail at least 120,000 pieces per year to keep your franchise active.

Franchisor's Rights

AAD reserves the right to place a number of inserts equal to the number you have sold in each envelope at no cost. Of course, the franchisor pays its own preparation, printing, and inserting costs. The pieces inserted by the franchisor cannot compete with any of your clients' pieces. In addition, you can categorically refuse permission to allow the franchisor to "insert." However, you then have to pay AAD a fee equal to the lowest advertisement rate you charge a customer. This is an expensive penalty, and franchisees rarely execute this option.

The coupons the franchisor inserts are "national accounts." The revenues secured from national accounts help offset AAD's overhead expenses. National accounts that the local franchisee secures and places in the program can become major revenue producers for the individual franchisee, company executives say.

Financing Arrangements

Normally, AAD does not provide financing, but in limited cases, it has financed the franchise fee for a short period for three types of people: (1) existing franchisees seeking to expand; (2) a former employer of the company; or (3) a former employer of an existing franchisee.

Start-Up Costs and Total Investment

Besides the franchise fee, you also must spend about $10,000 or more in what AAD calls working capital to open your doors. You should also expect about $550 in monthly operating expenses, if you work by yourself. One good thing is that you can run this business out of your home or any kind of office space. One company executive who started as an AAD franchisee paid $130 per month for 130 square feet of space in a basement, but built his franchise to $450,000 per year.

The start-up cost estimates include:

Category	Low End	High End
Franchise fee[a]	$23,500	$34,500
Furnishings	1,000	2,000
Deposits	200	750
Travel expenses[b]	250	500
Operating expenses[c]	8,800	9,800
Lease deposits[d]	200	750
Total[e]	$33,950	$48,300

a. The high end represents a territory of about 135,000 mailable homes.
b. AAD pays $600 towards your room and board expenses during two weeks of training in Arizona, and all of the cost of a round-trip coach air fare for one person.
c. AAD says this should cover salaries, permits, and licenses, and operating expenses for the first few months. You should add the cost of insurance if you rent any space.
d. AAD does not require office space, but if you choose to rent space, rent inexpensive space with easy access and good parking. You probably do not need more than a small office.
e. This figure does not include any money for wages for assistants or additional salespeople. Most franchisees start on their own, and hire assistants and salespeople as their results improve. To keep your overhead down, you can hire freelance artists to help do ad layouts, have part-time assistants, and pay a salesperson only on a commissions basis.

What You Get

You receive one of the best support systems among direct mail franchises. A recent article in *Franchise* magazine emphasized AAD's commitment to service towards its franchisees. You also receive:

Term. A 10-year franchise agreement with additional five-year renewals for a charge of just $100, a very low cost. You can also cancel the agreement with 90 days' notice as well, a liberal provision.
Territory. You receive an exclusive territory based on county and mu-

nicipal boundaries. Be sure you very carefully examine the proposed territory. Literally, drive the territory when you receive the company's proposed boundary map to make sure you are getting quality households and potential advertisers. Negotiate for better boundaries, research the demographics of census tracts in your local library, and do whatever else you can since these boundaries will do much to determine your future success.

Training. You receive two weeks of training at AAD'S Mesa, Arizona, headquarters and two weeks of on-the-job training in your territory or a nearby existing territory. As noted, the company pays up to $600 for room and board for one person and the round-trip coach air fare. The training emphasizes, as it should, selling and proven sales techniques.

On-going support. According to several articles, franchisees themselves praise AAD's management for its empathy and concern for their operations. It includes toll-free numbers and new sales techniques, but more importantly, AAD managers encourage a close rapport with their franchisees because most of them have been in the franchisee's shoes.

How Much Can You Make?

On the high end, four AAD franchises grossed more than $1 million in sales during 1987. After they paid their printing costs, royalties, and fees, their gross profits were at least $400,000 before operating expenses, for a 40 percent gross margin. An additional 15 to 20 franchisees grossed more than $500,000, probably giving them about $200,000 gross profits before they deduct their expenses.

AAD recommends ad rates, but you are free to set rates according to market conditions. Obviously, a mailing to 10,000 homes with an average income of $40,000 is more valuable than one to homes with an average income of $20,000; the former socioeconomic group simply tends to have more disposable income—money to spend on consumer goods and services.

According to AAD's franchise insert charges, you cannot begin to make any substantial profits with fewer than 12 inserts per mailing. The cost of 12 inserts is $2,105, plus a royalty of $180, and postage of about $1,010. Your total costs would be $3,205; if you charge $450 per insertion, your gross revenues would be $5,400, and your gross income after costs would equal $2,195 for just one 12x-insert mailing to 10,000 homes. That's before you deduct your expenses, so your net income would only equal about $1,500.

Your average cost per insert drops dramatically as the number of inserts increases, and your postage and royalty costs remain constant. Yet, your ad rates also remain constant, and so your profits increase dramatically. For example, your average cost for six inserts is $439 each; for 20 inserts, just $225 each. Yet, you charge $450 for each insert; you would realize $9,000 from 20 inserts, but your printing costs would be just slightly more than double the cost for less than one-third the inserts (20 inserts for $8,015 compared to six inserts for $1,445). Your postage charge would double and your royalty would increase 150 percent, but you would still have a gross, after-cost income of about $4,795.

Your success in direct mail advertising depends solely on your selling skills and your ability to market your business. With average selling skills, you should easily recoup your investment in one year and start turning substantial ROIs for years to come.

PRIORITY MANAGEMENT SYSTEMS, INC.

Priority Management Systems, Inc.
U.S. Address:
Suite 1740
Koll Center Bellevue
500 108th Avenue, N.E.
Bellevue, WA 98004
(800) 221-9031
(206) 454-7686

Canadian Headquarters:
601 West Broadway
Vancouver, British Columbia
Canada V5Z 4C2
(800) 663-1157
(604) 879-6121

Priority Management Systems, Inc., the Canadian-owned and most rapidly growing management training franchise, offers two types of businesses in one: (1) a time management and personal productivity training and consulting service; and (2) a repeat product sales and marketing operation. You work as a trainer and consultant and receive $300 to $400 per attendee fees, but you realize practically free profits with your repeat sales of the time management products and materials that your seminar participants must buy to use their new skills most productively and effectively.

For example, Andrew Sherwood, the company's Toronto, Ontario, franchisee grossed more than $750,000—working from the basement of his home—during 1988. He moved to an office during 1989 and grossed more than $1 million. Of that total, during 1988, more than $50,000 came from sales of consumable personal productivity materials, such as calendars, datebooks, notepads, and the like. Most of these revenues went straight to Sherwood's bottom line.

In 1989, *Entrepreneur* magazine rated Priority Management Systems as the leading business training franchise for the third straight year and ranked it as one of the top 25 new franchises. During 1987, PM's gross system-wide revenues exceeded $17 million, or more than $100,000 per franchise, and exceeded $24 million during 1988.

The Priority Management training system is called TIME:TEXT. It combines time management methods with materials that help your clients follow those methods. The materials—which you sell repeatedly—include meeting, project and communication planners, fax transmission sheets, notes and correspondence papers, financial planning kits, monthly priority lists, telephone directory, forward planners, and much more. You also sell vinyl, leather, or eel-skin briefcases, binders, and wallets with which your clients carry all of the material.

You have five basic TIME:TEXT systems to sell:

- General management and executive system
- Student edition for better study habits
- Real estate edition for tracking listings
- ProFile software package to manage time and sales territory
- Home Organizer edition for home time management

Of course, the most popular and profitable system—and your major market—is the one for business managers and executives. You sell the dollar benefits of the time savings and productivity gains to these companies in your area.

To succeed as a Priority Management franchisee, you must do four activities well:

1. Sell your system and its substantial benefits to businesses and organizations.
2. Conduct workshops to train your clients in the system.
3. Provide one-on-one follow-through consulting services after the workshop. This guaranteed, free follow-through service is your most valuable competitive edge over other management training systems.
4. Manage repeat sales of your materials. Priority Management executives want their franchisees to earn $50,000 or more per year from repeat sales within four years.

Actual results show most franchisees do much better. You arrange an annual or occasional reminder service through which you send renewal notices to your clients. The franchisor's goal is to achieve a 91 to 95 percent renewal rate, but the reorder rate seems to fluctuate between 55 and 75 percent. This rate is still strong enough to make substantial profits because the materials cost between $50 and $70 per year.

How Much It Costs

PM's franchise fee equals $29,500; that makes up the bulk of your start-up expenses because the company encourages you to work from your home for at least the first two years or so. Remember that Sherwood grossed more than $750,000 from his home during his fourth year in business. In Annapolis, MD, Dennis Mankin and a partner grossed more than $200,000 during their second full year working from their homes.

You also pay a 9 percent monthly royalty fee on gross revenues, or 9 percent of a minimum monthly quota, whichever is greater. The monthly quotas equal the following amounts:

Month of Agreement	Minimum Monthly Gross ($)
1–6	$2,000 ($180 min.)
7–12	3,000 ($270 min.)
13–18	4,000 ($360 min.)
19–24	5,000 ($450 min.)
25–end	6,000 ($540 min.)

You also have to pay a 1 percent advertising fee on gross revenues or the monthly quota ($20 to $60 per month). And you have to pay for a White Pages listing for your business name; this means you also have to install a telephone line. And PM may purchase local or regional Yellow Page ads on behalf of all franchises in the Yellow Pages area. You have to pay your proportional share of that annual cost.

Estimated Start-Up Costs

PM estimates your total start-up costs will range from $39,500 to $47,500, but that estimate is low because its working capital expenses estimate does not include your living expenses during the first three to six months. Nor does it include any office rental, office furniture, office machine, or similar expenses if you decide to rent office space or need to buy office furniture and equipment for your home office.

The following table estimates your PM start-up costs:

Expense Category	Low Estimate	High Estimate
Franchise fee	$29,500	$29,500
Opening inventory[a]	4,500	6,000
Working capital	5,500	12,000
Office expenses	1,000	3,500
Living expenses[b]	5,000	15,000
Total	$45,500	$66,000

a. Based on anticipated early sales volume.
b. Three to six months' average family expenses.

What You Get

For your substantial franchise fee, you receive a thoroughly proven and effective training method and very sophisticated sales and seminar workshop methods through which you sell your services. Of course, you receive a license for all of the names, products, and material which PM has developed, the business systems, and personal support from PM trainers and representatives. This author notes that the PM operation appears to be a very sophisticated, yet straightforward, one that attracts experienced sales managers, business executives, and professionals.

Your training consists of about two weeks at the firm's Vancouver, British Columbia, Canadian headquarters. You learn how to sell the service, present the seminars, provide follow-through consulting services, and make after-market materials sales. And PM sends a current franchisee to help you conduct your first two workshops. Of course, you pay the cost of your own training travel expenses, but PM pays the trainer to work with you.

Territory

PM wants to develop about 250 franchises in the U.S. and Canada. It places one or more PM franchises in major metropolitan areas where major organizations and corporations are located. For example, Mankin says that although he and his partner have the Washington-Baltimore, Maryland, territories, PM has another franchise which serves Washington and Northern Virginia because the population is so large (3.5 million) and the distances so great (60 to 75 miles from Baltimore to Northern Virginia). He says that more than enough business exists for the two franchisees to complement each other.

However, note that the PM franchise agreement does not grant exclusive territories. It states only that its current policy is to not establish more than one franchise for every 250,000 population in a major metropolitan area.

Mankin notes that, often, clients will be major national corporations with dozens of branches around the country. The client may want the local franchisee to travel into another franchisee's territory to train the client's employees in another state. When that overlap occurs, Mankin notes, local franchisees may informally agree to divide the fees or commissions to avoid conflict. But PM does not have a formal policy to deal with such overlapping sales.

Agreement Term

The original term lasts only five years, but you can renew for one additional five-year term under the agreement in effect in late 1989. This may change. Still, the duration seems a bit short if you're relatively young and want to build a career with the system.

Franchisee Status

By late 1989, PM had more than 120 franchises and was selling them in more than 30 states, Canada, Australia (seven), the United Kingdom (four), and Ireland. It was seeking more foreign master franchisees in Japan and Europe. Of that total, only two had been terminated for not paying royalties or not meeting quotas.

How Much Can You Make?

PM executives were very forthcoming about financial projections. The following table gives PM's profit-and-loss accounts for the first four years of the average franchisee's business operations. This table is a very exceptional and comprehensive document. Few other franchisors are willing to present comparable ones.

It shows that the average franchisee's profits skyrocket 500 percent from $25,000 to $127,000 by the end of the fourth year. Actual profits among franchisees range from $14,000 to more than $250,000 per year, but the average shows the excellent ROI potential from this service. Note, however, that profits count as your salary; the figures make no provision for your draw or a salary. In essence, your profits are your salary.

It also shows the phenomenal potential in repeat sales of materials; their sales should soar by almost 900 percent during the first four years, while your seminar business should grow "only" 400 percent.

In sum, for someone with selling, management training, or similar experience, PM offers a very strong opportunity to turn a substantial cash ROI by your fourth year.

Priority Management Systems, Inc.
Profit/Loss Account (in U.S. Dollars)

	Year 1	Year 2	Year 3	Year 4
UNIT SALES	200	384	540	778
NO. OF WORKSHOPS	12	22	25	36
CLIENTS	200	584	1,124	1,902
Sales				
WORKSHOPS	69,000	132,480	186,300	268,395
MATERIALS	9,912	28,365	57,107	90,600
	78,912	160,845	243,407	358,895
Direct Costs				
MATERIALS	26,115	59,024	95,055	143,298
ROYALTIES	7,891	16,085	24,341	35,890
	34,006	75,109	119,396	179,188
Gross Profit	**44,906**	**85,736**	**124,011**	**179,707**
Operating Costs				
Travel and promotion	6,200	7,570	12,000	12,000
Telephone	2,250	2,760	3,600	3,600
Wages		9,600	18,000	18,000
Insurance	890	890	890	890
Advertising	100	100	2,500	2,500
Hire of M. Room	1,200	2,200	2,500	3,600
Stationery	100	360	600	720
Catering Workshop	360	660	625	1,080
Bank Charge (Visa)	120	300	360	300
Miscellaneous	1,200	3,600	3,600	3,600
Accountant	750	750	750	750
Legal fees	500			
Bank interest	2,525	2,315	2,088	1,536
Depreciation	3,600	3,600	3,600	3,600
Car leasing, etc.			3,600	3,600
Total Operating Costs	19,795	34,705	51,113	52,176
Profit	**25,111**	**51,031**	**72,898**	**127,531**

CEILING DOCTOR INTERNATIONAL INC.

Ceiling Doctor International Inc.
2200 Lakeshore Blvd., West
Suite 105
Toronto, Ontario M8V 1A4 CANADA
(416) 253-4900

Ceiling Doctor® is a small, but very promising, Canadian franchise with tremendous potential in the U.S. It specializes in environmentally safe cleaning of acoustical tiles and ceiling materials and of exterior and interior walls. Ceiling Doctor concentrates on commercial buildings and institutions, which include office buildings, schools, factories, hospitals, and the like. The franchise's marketing advantage is this: it costs about 20 cents per square foot and a few hours to clean an acoustical tile ceiling, but it costs $1 to $2 per square foot and takes one week to replace an average tile ceiling. So, which commercial real estate managers would not prefer this service? Not many, certainly.

During early 1989, *Income Opportunities* magazine ranked Ceiling Doctor as one of the most promising franchises of the year. For three years in a row (1987 to 1989), *Women's Enterprise* magazine ranked Ceiling Doctor as one of the best franchises for women. By the end of 1989, Ceiling Doctor had 15 U.S. and 25 Canadian franchisees. These numbers mean that the opportunity is wide open in most of the best U.S. locations.

Of prime importance to franchisees is how Ceiling Doctor helps them save money and realize a profit from the beginning. Ceiling Doctor makes this franchise an ideal home-based business, too; it encourages you to work from your home for the first two years. It estimates you can save at least $12,000 per year on rent, utilities, business insurance, gasoline, and other costs associated with renting an office. As important, company executives tell their franchisees "to put the money they save into a certificate of deposit for two reasons. First, they have tangible proof they are profitable. And second, with that bank CD, they can obtain a loan or establish a line of credit for their receivables. Most important, they are happy to have the extra money. It reinforces their success, and it's there when they run into the slow months." This attitude reflects an apparently exceptional concern for your success.

Note, however, that Ceiling Doctor, with just 15 U.S. franchisees, goes head-to-head with several existing U.S. franchises, including two discussed in this book: Coustic-Glo and Wash on Wheels. Ceiling Doctor executives plan to grow relatively slowly and under control, with plans to add just 50 new franchises during 1990 and to reach a total of 300 franchises within five years. Ceiling Doctor sells its Canadian and U.S.

franchises only to individuals, but it has master franchise agreements for Ireland and Japan and is looking for other European, Asian, and South American master franchisees.

How Much It Costs

Ceiling Doctor's $20,500 franchise fee seems high for this kind of business. However, unlike similar competitors, Ceiling Doctor's fee *includes* the required equipment and supply package; moreover, the portion of the fee ascribed to training, materials preparation, company overhead, and the like, probably equals less than $7,500.

For this fee, you receive a very sizable, exclusive territory of between 500,000 and 600,000 people. If you want to add population or buy a larger territory—an entire metropolitan area the size of Atlanta, for example— you pay $1,650 for each additional 100,000 population. If you buy a smaller territory—such as Des Moines, Iowa, for example—you subtract $1,650 per 100,000 population below 500,000.

Ceiling Doctor has set up such large territories wisely, in this author's opinion, because you will need a large territory to develop a business that can reach gross sales in excess of a quarter of a million dollars a year. It reflects Ceiling Doctor's own experience and the franchisor's goals for your business.

You also must lease a van that meets Ceiling Doctor's specifications and uses Ceiling Doctor's logo, name signage, and decals on it. If you work out of your home, as Ceiling Doctor and the author recommend, you save a tremendous amount of start-up costs. Here are two estimates of your total start-up costs; Ceiling Doctor's appear to be low, while the author's estimate tends to be generous.

Expenditure	Ceiling Doctor (Low)	Ceiling Doctor (High)	Probable
Franchise fee	$20,500	$	$20,500
Additional territory	0		1,650
Van lease[a]	300	600	1,000
Premises lease[b]	0		0
Prepaid insurance	500		750
Training expenses[c]	(Varies)		2,000
Miscellaneous[d]	100		1,000
Working capital[e]	2,500		5,000
Total	$23,900	$24,200	$31,900

a. First and last month's payments.
b. Assumes office at home. This is good advice; heed it.
c. Travel and expenses for 10 days in Toronto.
d. This covers business telephone, deposits, occupational licenses, and the like.
e. The author adds living expenses for at least a month, that is, until you can generate a minimal salary and cash flow.

Royalty and Ad Fees

Ceiling Doctor also charges a reasonable 6 percent monthly royalty fee and a 2 percent advertising fund fee. The fund is used for national advertising in magazines, such as *Management and Maintenance,* a prominent trade journal for commercial building managers, Ceiling Doctor's primary customers. And you are required to spend at least 3 percent per month on local advertising, including the Yellow Pages.

One good point about Ceiling Doctor's ad fees is this: unlike some companies, Ceiling Doctor does not require you to pay royalties on the value of any discount programs, coupons, vouchers, or the like, that the company requires you to offer to your customers.

Required Purchases

After you receive your initial equipment and cleaning chemicals and supplies package, you are required to buy any additional company cleaning units and accessories and, most importantly, the company's unique cleaning chemicals. However, these supplies will only cost you about 4 percent of your gross revenues per year.

With these required fees and payments, you can expect your gross margins to fall into the 70 to 80 percent range if you work from home.

Financing Available

You can save $10,500 in initial cash payments by financing that amount. In late 1989, Ceiling Doctor agreed on a financing package with Donnelley Financing in the U.S. and Dun & Bradstreet in Canada. You make a $10,000 down payment, and either of the two financing companies will finance the remaining $10,500 of the franchise fee at rates equal to the prevailing market interest.

If you can borrow from the bank, take out a home equity loan, or arrange financing for your other cash start-up costs, you can save thousands more. However, as this author has noted throughout the book, be very careful about assuming too much debt. Monthly loan and lease payments can sap all your profit and make it difficult to meet even normal living expenses.

What You Get

Ceiling Doctor provides a comprehensive program. A significant advantage comes from the company's unique, environmentally safe cleaning chemicals. With growing concern about industrial pollution, toxic and hazardous chemicals, and the like, acting responsibly can not only protect your health and the health of those in the offices you clean but it can also mean good business.

Ceiling Doctor provides a very comprehensive 10-day training program with both classroom work and on-site, hands-on training at a working location.

Company executives emphasize that they believe "close communication is the key to success both for our franchisees and ourselves. We even have a 'buddy system' in which established franchisees work with new ones to share their experience. And we have 'bitch' sessions, so franchisees can air their complaints."

Field consultants speak with franchisees once or twice a week. They visit you at least twice a year, and more often if you need help. The company has an advisory council that reviews company advertising programs and discusses problems and strategies. It also makes advice available by telephone; it holds annual conventions; it will begin holding regional conventions as the company grows; it sponsors reward and recognition programs; it encourages a suggestion program; and it publishes a franchisee newsletter. In addition, it provides business and operations guidance to support its operations manual.

After you work from your home for two years, the company will help you find space in an executive business center as "you enter you next growth wave," the company executives say.

You also receive an exclusive territory that Ceiling Doctor helps you guard zealously. You cannot solicit or accept business outside your own territory boundaries, and you must refer outside inquiries to headquarters so that the company can refer them to the appropriate franchisee. You may accept the new business inquiries if no one owns the franchise for that area. Ceiling Doctor sets its territory boundaries by city and county borders and zip codes in major metropolitan areas.

Although the initial franchise agreement is only five-years long, the contract does guarantee additional *seven* renewals at five-year terms for a total of 40 years. Few people will own their franchises for that long, but the options do give you a chance to build equity and sell out in 10 to 15 years.

How Much Can You Make?

Ceiling Doctor does not publish any earnings estimates, but it appears that all established U.S. franchisees in business two or more years bring home net incomes "in the six figures," that is, at least $100,000 per year. The average franchisee's gross income rapidly escalates during the first three years:

Year	Per Week	Per Year
First	$ 500	$ 25,000
Second	$2,000–$3,000	$100,000–$150,000
Third	$5,000	$260,000

This is not an unreasonable expectation because the gross revenues of Ceiling Doctor's company-owned service in Toronto exceeded $200,000 during 1988, its fourth year in operation.

With gross margins in the 60 to 80 percent range, net margins should range between 25 and 45 percent even when one leases additional vans and employs more work crews.

The author examined the company's financial statements and extrapolated the following results from Ceiling Doctor's reported franchise fee receipts and sales of required supplies to franchisees: during 1988, the *average* Ceiling Doctor franchisee earned a gross income in excess of $60,000. This average includes about 10 start-up franchisees with very low initial sales during their first few operating months. If you remove the influence of the new franchisees, you can see that franchisees in their second year appear to easily reach and exceed gross incomes of $100,000.

In fact, Ceiling Doctor's franchise agreement requires most franchisees to reach a minimum annual gross sales of $75,000 by the end of their second year. If you meet this requirement, you can expect to take out of the business as salary and profit an amount between $30,000 and $45,000, almost doubling your cash investment.

Ceiling Doctor has two quota plans, depending on territory size. *Part I* requires minimum gross sales of about $75,000 per year in a 500,000-population territory, depending on local population, demographics, available customer base, and the like. *Part II* requires minimum gross sales of about $25,000 per year.

The difference appears to result not from population, but from available business and customer demographics. Ceiling Doctor appears to discourage Part II franchisees.

To meet these quotas and reach these income levels quickly requires hard work and good business sense, so Ceiling Doctor's executives choose their franchisees very carefully. They want people with business, management, sales, or administrative backgrounds and with an ability to communicate well with people, especially customers such as building and maintenance managers.

If you meet these qualifications, Ceiling Doctor provides an excellent low-cost—especially with financing—franchise with significant ROIs and long-term growth potential.

MONOGRAMS PLUS

Monograms Plus
3630 Interstate 35 South
Waco, TX 76702
(817) 662-5050

Monograms Plus combines the service business of adding monograms quickly to practically any apparel or gift item and the retail business of selling leisure-wear apparel and gifts in one relatively inexpensive kiosk, which is a small free-standing unit placed in the aisle of a shopping mall. With an attractive design, Monograms Plus has elevated the shopping-mall kiosk to a new level and one that has attracted strong interest of mall developers around the country, say the franchise executives.

Compared to most regional mall franchises, Monograms Plus costs very little and has a very high profit potential, with net after-tax margins in the 25 to 35 percent range by the end of the second year. Monograms Plus offers very attractive high sales volume, high customer traffic and high-quality location of regional malls, plus a limited inventory of retail apparel, leisure-wear, and gift items. Its monogram service business is based on a high-tech Meister-gram machine.

And Monograms Plus takes advantage of a rapidly growing and apparently insatiable market for everything monogrammed. Company executives say the custom monogram leisure-wear apparel market is growing at 35 percent per year, by far the fastest growing segment of the apparel market.

By the end of 1989, Monograms Plus had more than 80 operating kiosks around the country and had plans to open about 25 to 30 more during 1990. As important as its growth rate, Monograms Plus is part of the T-Shirt Plus family, which is rated as one of the financially strongest franchise companies.

During 1989, Monograms Plus franchisees' total income more than tripled to almost $9 million from $2.5 million during 1988. Much of this growth occurred when Monograms Plus purchased and converted into franchises its largest competitor, Monograms Today, which was based in Houston. Its average franchise earned a gross income of more than $135,000, with net after-tax incomes of more than $40,000.

How Much It Costs

The franchise fee equals $25,000, and the company's estimated start-up costs range from $51,850 to $84,100. Monograms Plus offers two franchise programs: one for an individual kiosk in one mall, and one for area developers who want to open five or more locations within an area.

The company charges a sliding scale of fees for second and subsequent stores:

First location	$25,000
Second	23,000
Third	21,000
Fourth and subsequent	19,000

Under its agreement, Monograms Plus may offer you a store location in a neighboring regional mall. You can accept the right to open that store or forfeit it. If you forfeit the right, the company can sell to another prospect. If you accept, you pay the reduced fee and move to open the new store. You must open a second location within 12 months of your first store opening, the third within 18 months, the fourth within 24 months, and each additional location within six-month increments.

With several stores or more, you can achieve significant economies of scale for your advertising, operational, and management costs.

Initial Start-Up Costs

Your initial costs will average somewhat more than the company's UFOC (Uniform Franchising Offering Circulars) estimates. In the following table, the author adds several cost categories that Monograms Plus does not include:

Category	Low End	High End
Franchise fee	$25,000	$25,000
Initial inventory	5,500	9,600
Display fixtures	2,300	3,000
Construction	14,000	39,700
Build-out management fee[a]	0	3,000
Cash register	3,000	3,000
Grand opening advertising	1,000	3,500
Insurance[b]	500	1,000
Training travel[c]	750	2,000
Lease deposits	1,500	3,500
Working capital[d]	5,000	6,500
Total[e]	$58,550	$99,800

a. Fee if you hire Monograms Plus to manage the construction of your kiosk.
b. Deposits for various required policies.
c. Five business days or more expenses in Waco, Texas, at the company headquarters.

d. Initial employee's salaries, your own living expenses for three months, utility deposits, business license fees, and miscellaneous costs.
e. Company officials say the average start-up investment equals $61,000.

Cash requirements range from as low as $32,800 to as high as $50,000. You can lease the Meistergram monogram machine, and you may be able to finance certain other costs, but Monograms Plus does not offer financing itself.

Other Fees and Costs

You pay a 6 percent weekly royalty fee and a 1 percent weekly advertising fund fee to the company. And you must spend at least 2 percent of your gross revenues on your own local advertising and promotional campaign each quarter.

You are also required to purchase or lease the Meistergram Model 800 XLC electronic monogram machine from the company and a TEC cash register. You can expect the cash register to cost about $3,000 and the lease to cost several hundreds of dollars a month.

You must buy your inventory of apparel and gift items through Monograms Plus, and you can expect to spend at least $13,500 or about 10 percent of your gross sales on inventory purchases each year.

What You Get

Monograms Plus offers one of the best training, service, and support programs in franchising:

Territory. The company agrees to put only one Monograms Plus kiosk in each regional shopping mall, and you have the right of first refusal on any location within a mile of the mall. Territory rights outside the mall are not that important in this business.

Site selection and lease negotiation. Monograms Plus helps you locate appropriate shopping malls and negotiate leases. Company executives say that Monograms Plus franchises are in great demand and have negotiated favorable terms.

Monograms Plus College. A complete week-long training program, both with classroom and on-site work in the company's store in Waco, Texas.

Construction management. For the $3,000 fee, the company will supervise your kiosk construction.

Inventory merchandising. Before your grand opening, company merchandising specialists will stock your store and teach you how to manage the inventory.

Warehouse facilities. As the wholesaler, Monograms Plus provides 57 different gift items and various kinds of apparel at the best available discounts.

Advertising and promotional support. You receive a grand opening package and on-going ad and promotional materials for seasonal sales.

Awards programs. The company holds a national convention at which leading franchisees are honored with prizes and incentives, such as vacations, and the like.

Group sales training. The company shows you how to make group sales to groups, teams, organizations, and corporations.

Custom software and systems. With the monogram machine, you get custom software with which you can offer many automated designs to appeal to your market and geographic region.

On-going support. The company also offers continuous support through hot lines, field representatives, and constant communications with headquarters.

How Much Can You Make?

Company executives say that Monograms Plus generates very high ROIs very quickly. Your net margins on your monogramming service averages 85 percent and makes up 60 percent of your sales volume; your gross margins on your retail apparel and gift items average 50 percent and makes up 40 percent of your gross volume, a very high-profit two-tier structure. Your net after-tax margin ranges from 25 to 35 percent. Company executives say they are disappointed if a franchisee does not breakeven within 10 to 12 months. You can expect to earn 100 percent ROIs within 18 to 24 months, or about $60,000 a year after taxes.

Monograms Plus is a clean, relatively low-cost retail franchise, as well as one of the least expensive ways to establish a shopping-mall location in a world in which it is increasingly more expensive to open mall retail stores.

GENERAL BUSINESS SERVICES, INC.

General Business Services, Inc.
The GBS Building
20271 Goldenrod Lane
Germantown, MD 20874-4090
(301) 428-1040
(800) 638-7940

General Business Services (GBS) is the largest small business counseling, bookkeeping, management consulting, record-keeping, and tax preparation franchise in the country. By the end of 1989, it had more than 600 franchised business counselors in the U.S. Founded in 1962, it is the oldest business consulting franchise as well. It is consistently rated by *Entrepreneur* magazine as a Top Five business services franchise; it is also an excellent opportunity for women and minorities. The perennial winner of GBS' award for the most clients is a black businessman from Richmond, Va.

GBS franchisees, called *business counselors,* do not need to be certified public accountants (CPAs)—although many are—financial planners, or the like. GBS provides training in all of the skills you need to work with your clients: small businesspeople. GBS franchisees aim their services exclusively at the more than 18 million small businesses and self-employed professionals in the U.S. According to U.S. government definitions, small businesses are those with annual revenues under $5 million.

Although your types of clients will vary according to your local situation, GBS's ten leading categories of small business clients include auto-repair and after-market shops, food stores, general contractors, restaurants, furniture and home furnishing stores, small manufacturers, professionals (doctors, dentists, and lawyers), printers, beauty shops, and clothing and apparel shops. Others include construction trades, such as plumbers, electricians, and heating and air conditioning companies.

To work as a GBS counselor, you sell your services to these small businesses, primarily the owners or their office managers or bookkeepers, and then provide those services. You usually begin working from an office at home, and then as you grow, you rent a small office. You need a business telephone line and professional answering service or, eventually, an assistant. If your practice becomes large—more than one hundred clients—you may need to hire a part-time bookkeeper or even a second counselor.

Many types of people have become GBS franchisees, but they are usually retired military officers, business executives, middle managers, engineers, CPAs, financial planners, management information system managers, and insurance agents. Clearly, you do not act simply as a bookkeeper or accountant in this position; more often than not, you advise your clients on serious business management and tax issues.

How Much It Costs

Fortunately, beyond the franchise fee, this is a very low-investment business which allows you to breakeven during your first year and start earning 100 percent-plus ROIs by the end of the second year.

The franchise fee is $25,000, which gives you the right to use the GBS name and logo, all available materials, and a strong panoply of training and support services. If you start working from your home or a small executive office, as GBS suggests, your additional start-up costs should not exceed $10,000, beyond your living expenses. GBS is very forthright about its advice that you have up to six months' living expenses in the bank before you begin. That amount, of course, varies with your requirements (car payment, mortgage, utilities, etc.), or whether or not your spouse works and will help carry the load until you get on your feet. Perhaps, you have a retirement plan (ex-military, for example) or a large severance payment from a former employer you can use to help you get through the transition.

GBS is one of the few franchises that pays for your travel training expenses—a superior benefit.

The following table reflects both GBS's and the author's estimates of your total start-up costs:

Category	Low End	High End
Franchise fee	$25,000	$25,000
Working capital[a]	1,000	5,000
Miscellaneous[b]	4,000	5,000
Training travel[c]	100	500
Living expenses[d]	5,000	18,000
Total	$35,100	$53,500

a. Initial support services—legal fees—and products from GBS or approved suppliers.

b. Telephone deposits, advertising (Yellow Pages, direct mail), office equipment, office supplies, etc.

c. Two and a half weeks at GBS headquarters in Germantown, MD. GBS pays most of the cost of travel, training, meals and lodging, an excellent benefit.

d. From three months at $1,667 per month, to six months at $3,000 per month; it varies according to your needs.

Special Franchise Fees

GBS has a special and very low franchise fee of $4,750 for any spouse of a franchisee who wants to work actively in the business. GBS calls this person an "associate spouse." About 10 percent of GBS franchisees work with their spouses, company experience shows.

And GBS employees may receive a discount of the franchise fee equal to 5 percent for each year of service with the company; the maximum discount is 50 percent and is based on seniority with the company.

Other Fees and Costs

GBS charges several kinds of fees, but works a complicated rebate program which minimizes the impact on your bottom line. The program encourages you to increase the number of clients rapidly.

Continuing support fee. GBS charges a 7 percent of monthly gross receipts, with a $75 monthly minimum for the first 12 calendar months. The minimum increases $25 for each 12-month period thereafter; adjustments to future minimum payments may be made according to increases in the Consumer Price Index of the U.S. Bureau of Labor Statistics.

Client maintenance fee. Under a complex sliding scale plan based on annual gross receipts, GBS charges a client maintenance fee which you pay as compensation to GBS for registering and maintaining your client's records in its automated systems. GBS arranges a maximum royalty you must pay based on your annual gross receipts. It combines the 7 percent support fee and, with a sliding scale, either adds an additional percentage if your gross receipts fall below $60,000 per year or gives you a rebate if your gross receipts exceed $60,000 a year.

The sliding scale ranges from a *cost* of 4.5 percent of your first $20,000 in gross receipts to a *rebate* of 5.45 percent if your gross receipts exceed $180,000 per year. The following table shows the details of this program as it was structured in late 1989. In short, the more money you make, the less you pay, a very strong incentive for you to do very well.

General Business Services' Royalty Payment Structure

Annual Gross Receipts ($)		Monthly Support Fee (%)	+	Client Maintenance Fee (%)	=	Maximum Amount ($)
to $ 20,000		7		4.50		$2,300
Next 20,000 to 40,000		7		3.50		2,100
Next 20,000 to 60,000		7		1.50		1,700
Next 20,000 to 80,000		7		−2.00		1,000
Next 20,000 to 100,000		7		−3.50		700
Next 20,000 to 120,000		7		−4.75		450
Next 20,000 to 140,000		7		−5.00		400
Next 20,000 to 160,000		7		−5.25		350
Next 20,000 to 180,000		7		−5.35		330
Receipts above $180,000		7		−5.45		

GBS knows, however, that the more money you make the more tax returns and business accounts that it will process for you.

Tax Entitlement Account. GBS also charges new franchisees a 4 percent tax entitlement fee which GBS credits to the costs of the income tax preparation services that GBS provides for you during tax season. In effect, you pay GBS up-front to have automated tax preparation systems ready to handle your accounts during annual tax time and to prepare quarterly tax returns, a necessity for most small businesses. GBS does make a profit on this service.

In sum, at worst, your total royalty and fee payments to GBS will equal 15.5 percent of your gross; at best, that will fall to 9.55 percent.

What You Get

You receive a wide variety of training and support programs, including two and a half weeks at GBS's Basic Training Institute, plus a week's field training after you begin. As noted, your fee includes the cost of travel training for up to two people.

Your fee also pays for a beginning advertising and promotional package, a client tax advisory and research service, its income tax preparation service, and a bulletin or newsletter service. The latter demonstrates your professional status to your clients and keeps your name in front of them each month.

You also receive a somewhat exclusive territory that appears to be like being a "little pregnant." You receive a "primary marketing area" with about 1,2500 to 1,500 potential small business clients and a total population ranging from 20,000 to 30,000. Of course, look for areas where you can find numerous small businesses in the major client categories.

Although GBS promises it will not assign any new franchisees to your area for 24 months, you must have at least 30 registered clients at all times, or GBS retains the right to assign new franchisees to exploit the same territory. This works essentially as a quota system; still, it does encourage you to generate new business.

However, in some large metropolitan areas, GBS will assign franchisees to that area based on 25,000-people segments. Even worse, GBS does not prevent its franchisees from competing in each other's territory, although you must locate your office within your own territory. In one way, this makes sense because Yellow Pages ads almost always cover large areas, and most people will get in touch with the GBS counselor closest to their business. It eliminates any corporate hassles and any need to set up a complicated referral system.

The initial term of the agreement is five years with five-year renewals. GBS charges a renewal fee equal to 3 percent of the then-current franchise fee ($750 in 1989).

By the same token, GBS gives its franchisees a very liberal drop-out provision; you can leave the system with only 90 days' notice, one of the better termination clauses among franchise companies.

All in all, GBS offers a very strong training and support program, certainly the best among business-related franchises.

How Much Can You Make?

A GBS newsletter reported that the most successful franchisee of 1988 grossed more than $556,000; the GBS franchisee with the largest number of clients had more than 310 clients. Moreover, the newsletter indicated that an average GBS franchisee grosses between $80,000 and $100,000 a year.

But you can expect to earn very high gross and pre-tax net margins. If you work from your home or a small office, you can expect to earn gross margins in the 65 to 80 percent range. After all, you sell your knowledge and your skills, not physical products or services. Your net pre-tax profit should range from 35 to 65 percent, depending upon how well you manage your expenses. So, during your first full year, you should breakeven, pay back your start-up costs, and earn a small salary. By the end of your second year, you could earn between $50,000 and $80,000 per year.

GBS has a very good success rate. Between 1985 and 1989, it terminated less than 3 percent of its franchises per year, with the vast majority terminated for not paying royalties that they owed. GBS notes with pride that it has never refused to renew an agreement unless the franchisee as violating the agreement, and it has never repurchased a franchise. These statements indicate that GBS franchisees tend to succeed very well and are generally happy with the GBS system. The UFOC does show that, over the past eight years, some franchisees have sued GBS, but it has either won all of the suits or settled out of court for small payments. These results show that GBS manages its system very carefully. In short, GBS offers white-collar professionals an excellent low-investment business-services franchise.

UNIGLOBE TRAVEL INTERNATIONAL, INC.

Uniglobe Travel International, Inc.
U.S. Headquarters
Bay Vista Building
2815 Second Ave.
Suite 200
Seattle, WA 98121
(206) 443-1965

World Headquarters
The Uniglobe Building
900-1199 West Pender St.
Vancouver, B.C.
Canada V6E 2R1
(604) 662-3800

Uniglobe Travel is the leading travel agency franchise in both the U.S. and Canada and has a corporate mission of being the largest travel agency in the world. It was the Number One Canadian franchise and has been listed consistently among the fastest growing franchises and Top 100 franchises in *Entrepreneur* magazine. By the end of 1989, it had more than 750 franchises sold, with about 650 operating franchises in the U.S. and Canada, a two-year increase of more than 36 percent. It projects more than 1,250 franchises by the end of 1991 and 2,500 worldwide by 1997. It claims a 3 percent share of the total retail travel market, with a 1991 goal of doubling that.

Uniglobe has adopted this corporate mission statement to carry it into the mid-1990s: "The mission of Uniglobe Travel is to develop the largest travel agency organization in the world which sets the standard in the industry for professionalism and reliability to the consumer. This will result in consistent profitability for its agencies, the Uniglobe regions, and the Uniglobe international organization."

Uniglobe pursues a very strong sales and marketing philosophy that emphasizes direct sales: first, to corporate and commercial accounts; and then, to the personal vacation and leisure travel market. You achieve this goal by working with a two-step process: first, you aggressively seek out commercial/corporate travel accounts with direct sales pitches; second, when you have a strong base, you move into vacation leisure sales. Your initial sales should be divided 75/25 percent commercial/vacation, and your eventual goal should be to reach a 50/50 division. It also pays to even the split because the vacation and leisure segment shows more growth potential than a corporate marketplace beset by discount fare wars and intense competition.

Uniglobe also differs from other travel agencies in that it works with a limited number of preferred travel supplies, such as Hertz, Alamo, United Airlines, Eastern Airlines, Carnival Cruise Lines, Holland America Cruises, and Canadian Pacific Airlines. You obtain better discounts for your clients and higher commissions, in percentage and volume, if you do not try to deal with every airline, car rental agency, cruise line, or hotel.

Uniglobe relies on a 19-region master franchise program that permits aggressive sales of new franchises, conversions of existing travel agencies, and strong support from the regional staff. Each regional center has a business development manager that is personally responsible for the training, support, and growth of each franchise in the region.

Unlike many franchise companies, its executives have stated that they do want to weed out poorly performing franchisees. For example, during 1985, a rough year in general for independent travel agencies, although Uniglobe added 158 franchises, some 93 others closed, primarily because of the intense competition and market turndown, but also because Uniglobe does not want to prop up poor performers. In fact, during 1987, the company instituted a performance quota which franchisees must meet or lose their license. This move apparently came out of a 1985 President's Club (the select group of top franchisees with the most sales) meeting in which the top performers demanded these standards for the organization.

During 1989, the result of this process has been renewed aggressive franchise sales and much better financial results for the stronger franchisees.

Franchisees benefit from Uniglobe's program as it seeks to become the "brand-name" image in retail travel services. You benefit from the strong, internationally known image, professional sales training, on-going business development assistance, and support services.

All of these factors are fairly new—at least the excellent execution of the principles is new—to the retail travel industry. They were brought to the industry by Uniglobe's chairman, who learned the methods as the co-owner of the $2-billion-a-year Century 21 master franchise for *all* of Canada. He borrowed Century 21's success techniques (described in a different section of this book) and applied them to the travel industry.

How Much It Costs

Although the company did not provide this author with its UFOC, the basic franchise fee is $39,500, but conversion franchises can avoid a portion of that fee. The company does not provide financing. Start-up costs raise the total initial investment to between $80,000 and $100,000 for a two- or three-person office. Of course, if you already own a travel agency, or have significant travel agency experience, you can sharply reduce these costs. Beyond the fee, the types of costs are those normally associated with opening a professional service franchise: lease deposits; telephone/utility deposits; office furniture and machines; telephone systems; computer terminals, which are essential to a modern travel agency; living expenses; travel and training expenses; insurances; permits and licenses; wages and salaries for employees; and so forth.

You pay a low royalty of two-thirds of 1 percent to 1 percent of total sales, not your total commissions. In the travel business, as in the real estate business, the term "total sales" refers to the total cost of the travel, i.e., a $500 air fare is considered a $500 sale. Your commission would be a percentage of that total, but the royalty would be between $3.35 and $5 on that ticket.

The advertising fee is a flat monthly rate which may increase from year to year. You also pay an enrollment fee for your training at its international management academy, but that fee includes hotel rooms, two meals a day, training program materials, transportation to and from the airport, and more.

What You Get

For this fee and start-up costs, you receive one of the most comprehensive and demanding program in the retail travel franchise business:

Term of agreement. The initial agreement runs five years, with additional five-year terms available at a small renewal fee.

Territory. You receive a somewhat exclusive territory in that the company promises not to open an office in the same general area.

Training. Uniglobe offers a travel academy program. The initial program can last as long as four weeks for novices, but currently licensed and ASTA-approved travel agents need only take the business development, sales, and management part of the program. The company also offers an extensive, continuing training program through both the academy and its regional offices.

Advertising support. Uniglobe does national and regional television advertising and provides quality materials for your own local advertising program on radio and in-print media. You also are expected to make heavy use of a direct marketing and mail program to corporate clients.

Uniglobe does have a broad-based support program with more than 250 national and regional staff members to serve its 650-plus operational franchises, a very high ratio in any franchise.

How Much Can You Make?

Company officials state that an average office in business for somewhat longer than 18 months is performing at a more than $1.4 million annual sales level. And the company anticipates that an average franchise in business for five years should have gross sales of $3 million. During 1989, the leading U.S. franchisee had more than $7 million in gross sales. And Uniglobe Advance Travel Ltd. in Vancouver, B.C., Canada, reported the organization's first $1 million sales month in May, 1989. The company's July, 1989, newsletter showed that 12 franchisees exceeded $5 million in annualized sales during fiscal 1989. Even Uniglobe President Charlwood's oldest son reported a sales rate of more than $2.5 million a year during the same period. And the leading new franchise operated at an annual rate of $1.2 million in gross sales during the same year.

Reports from actual franchises show that you achieve success with Uniglobe with aggressive selling, patience, and persistence, as well as by strictly following the company's marketing advice. Franchisees agree. The franchisee for Billerica, Massachusetts, grosses $9 million a year with two offices after six and a half years; the two-year-old franchise in San Jose, California, grosses more than $5 million a year; the franchisee in Federal Way, Washington State, reached $4 million volume in two and a half years. And graduates of advanced travel sales management classes aim to reach $20 million a year in sales.

But gross sales tell only part of the story. Agency commissions on these sales range from 8 to 15 percent, so agency gross incomes should average between $150,000 and $300,000 after about a year and a half to two years in business. The franchisee should net 25 to 35 percent before taxes, for a net income ranging from a low of $37,500 to a high of $90,000, a significantly higher figure than the average independently owned travel agency. The leading franchisees clearly net several times that.

Within five years, the company's figures show that you can expect your net income to range from $100,000 to $175,000 per year. This income and all of the delightful benefits of free and discount travel you can muster are available through this or a similarly well-run travel franchise. Uniglobe appears to be an excellent prospect for ambitious travel agents who want to increase their success and novices who want to work with the best in the travel industry.

PROFUSION SYSTEMS, INC.

ProFusion Systems, Inc.
2851 South Parker Road
Suite 650
Aurora, CO 80014
(303) 337-1949
(800) 777-FUSE

ProFusion Systems used to be known as Western Vinyl Repair, but with master franchises in Japan, the Netherlands, and Canada, Western Vinyl Repair no longer seemed an accurate name. ProFusion Systems also illustrates how Chairman William Gabbard and his staff have truly turned the fly-by-night vinyl repair business into a professional, quality- and service-oriented industry. Before ProFusion Systems perfected a permanent, unnoticeable method of repairing vinyl, leather, velour, and Naugahyde®, vinyl repair businesses were limited to mail order kits which sometimes did, but often didn't, perform as well as promised. However, ProFusion Systems is the only company that offers a 100 percent money-back lifetime guarantee on every repair, a very important marketing and strategic advantage in this business.

Backed with chemical laboratory research and the leadership of experienced franchisors, ProFusion Systems offers an excellent, low-cost, high-profit opportunity. Its products, current and future, are protected by patents pending and patent applications, and the company is researching how to perform similarly quality repairs on nonmetal, natural, and man-made fibers. During early 1990, it introduced a new repair process that reduces the already low cost and expands the markets for this service.

By late 1989, ProFusion Systems had more than 144 franchises, triple the number in 1987. It was rated as the top vinyl repair franchise by *Entrepreneur* magazine and ranked in that magazine's Top 40 fastest growing franchises.

Almost 85 percent of your business would come from a vast variety of commercial accounts. Most vinyl repair companies advise their kit buyers to concentrate on auto dealerships, but ProFusion Systems has expanded its marketing to include any commercial establishments with any product made of or covered with vinyl, leather, velour, and Naugahyde®. These include, in a rough order of success, the following: fast-food restaurants; regional or area restaurant chains; auto dealerships; commercial, public, and school bus companies; bars; hospitals; offices; used car dealers; churches; child care centers; public auditoriums; airlines; leather or upholstery shops; medical and dental offices; hotels and motels; boat and motorcycle shops; golf carts, etc.

ProFusion Systems has organized its franchise so that it appeals to husband-and-wife teams. Both are expected to manage and sell the service, while they farm out the actual repair work to independent contractor/technicians whom they have trained. One successful franchise works like this: the wife sells large accounts, the husband sells mom-and-pop accounts and manages five technicians, and an additional female salesperson sells public and non-profit organizations. The company recommends that you plan to quickly have three or four technicians in the field. Although you can start out of your home, you are required to open a retail-type location within six months.

How Much It Costs

ProFusion Systems is reasonably priced, with a minimum fee of $20,500; of that, $10,500 covers your initial training, technical fee, and grand opening costs; and $10,000 pays for your franchise fee granting you an exclusive territory with between 70,000 and 100,000 people. You can add additional populations in groups of 100,000 for just $5,000 each. The territories are usually organized along county or city boundaries, or zip codes within major metropolitan areas. For example, a city with about 400,000 people would cost $35,500.

You also pay a 6 percent royalty on gross sales and a 1 percent advertising fee administered through an ad fund by an advisory council. You are also required to spend 5 percent of gross revenues on local advertising and direct promotions.

Additional start-up costs are relatively low, as you will start out of your home. ProFusion Systems lists types of start-up costs without putting a dollar estimate on them: two telephones; rental of 400 to 1,200 square feet in warehouse-type space (after 6 months); stationery; $500,000 to $1 million in liability insurance; chemicals and supplies inventory; auto expense and mileage; advertising; and salespeople's and technicians' commissions. An estimate of your additional start-up expenses is shown on page 276.

Within six months, however, you face the substantial costs of opening a retail location. You do not have to have a Main Street storefront; an inexpensive warehouse-type location may suffice, but you will have to pay rent

Telephone deposits	$ 100	to	$ 300
Printing	40	to	200
Liability insurance	400	to	1,000
Supplies	100	to	200[a]
Auto expenses	100	to	200
Miscellaneous	100	to	200
Initial commissions	200	to	1,000[b]
Working capital	2,500	to	3,500
Total	$3,140	to	$6,600

a. You do receive all start-up supplies and equipment from the company, but you may need more after you train your technicians. And you do have to buy them from the company because it is the only source.
b. Based on ProFusion Systems' working capital estimates.

deposits, leasehold improvement costs, utility deposits and bills, and for the purchase or lease of some office furniture and equipment as well. If your operation does well, you may be able to finance your expansion out of your cash flow and income, but you may want to preserve your cash and borrow the money.

Here are estimated expansion costs:

Rent deposits	$ 500	to	$2,500[a]
Leasehold improvements	4,500	to	6,500[b]
Utility deposits	250	to	500
Business licenses	100	to	1,000[c]
Grand opening expenses	500	to	3,000[d]
Total	$5,850	to	$13,500

a. One to three months' rent for adequate office space.
b. ProFusion Systems' estimate for signage and leasehold improvements. You have to buy the signage from the company or an approved supplier.
c. The high end includes the cost of incorporating your business.
d. Depends directly on how much you plan to spend on initial advertising materials and placements.

So, you can expect your total six-month start-up costs to range from about $29,490 to about $45,600 for one franchise. You may be able to finance at least half of this amount through equity loans from a bank, and you can pay for many of your warehouse start-up expenses with cash flow from your current operations, reducing your capital outlay significantly. But, you must add the cost of travel and room and board to the company's Denver, Colorado, headquarters for the training session.

What You Get

In return for this investment, you receive the following:

Exclusive territory. Your territory will be based on population and county boundaries or zip codes, but aim for territory with lots of fast-food restaurants, restaurant chains, auto dealerships, bus companies, and public institutions with lots of vinyl chairs, such as hospitals.

Training. You receive 10-days training, including a technical, how-to-do-it section and a management section that concentrates on sales, advertising, promotions, bidding and estimating procedures, and the like. You, in turn, must train your independent contractors.

Start-up visit. An experienced sales trainer will spend three days with you to help you start making sales calls and signing contracts.

National accounts. ProFusion Systems seeks out national accounts with restaurant chains, and the like, and refers all business to the local franchise. It does not operate any company franchises.

Use rights. The right to use the company's exclusive processes and repair chemicals for the ten-year term of the agreement. If and when these processes become patented, they will become very important assets on which you can build equity in your franchise.

On-going research. ProFusion's consulting lab, Hauser Laboratories, continues to investigate new processes for different materials. You also receive the usual package of manuals, supplies, samples, and the like.

How Much Can You Make?

Most of your gross income turns into gross profit. The cost of materials for each repair is minimal, usually less than $1 per chair. After you pay the 6 percent royalty, the company estimates that you will spend your gross income in these percentages:

- 5 percent on required advertising and direct promotion expenses,
- 15 percent commissions for your salespeople. (If you do the selling, you keep the commissions as your salary.)
- 20 percent commissions to the independent repair technicians, and
- 20 to 30 percent overhead expenses.

Your net profit will range from 30 percent to 40 percent of your gross income.

You charge for your repairs based on several factors. Normally, you should expect to save a customer 90 to 95 percent of the cost of a new item, such as a chair, restaurant booth, or the like. If a chair costs $200, you would charge about $20 for the repair. If you bid on a contract to do all the chairs in a hospital, your per-chair price will be much lower, but you will increase your profits with much greater volumes of work.

Your gross income should grow quickly. One franchise in the Denver area reported a second-year income of more than $300,000, with a likely net profit between $50,000 and $100,000, a significant return on investment in the hundreds of percent.

A significant indicator of how much you can make was included in an article about ProFusion that appeared in a Japanese publication. It stated that ProFusion Systems' executives had said (as they can in Japan, but not in the U.S.) that franchises have gross salaries ranging between $8,000 to $40,000 per month, or $96,000 to $480,000 per year. An average amount of success should bring in $40,000 to $75,000 in net profits—more if you include your salary from the sales commissions that you could pay yourself.

ProFusion Systems is looking for franchisees in the East, Midwest, and California. Its franchise provides a significant and rapidly growing opportunity in yet another market where the need for basically unskilled labor continues to grow, but is not being fulfilled.

PRESS BOX NEWS

Press Box News Drive-Thru Newsstand
2600 Columbia Ave.
Lancaster, PA 17603
(717) 291-9649

Everyone today runs in and out of convenience stores at least once or twice a day. When you are commuting to or from work, however, you may find that the lines in convenience stores are getting longer and longer and longer. You only want to buy a newspaper and a cup of coffee, but the guy in front of you wants a slab of pizza, 10 lottery tickets, and microwaved nachos. Perhaps, convenience stores aren't so convenient anymore!

The founders of Press Box News Drive-Thru Newsstand realized this and have developed an interesting new convenience operation concept designed to attract the working commuter that now dashes in and out of the corner 7-Eleven.

Press Box News Drive-Thru Newsstand has created a relatively inexpensive opportunity to offer to commuters the same quick service methods pioneered by many dairy chains and photo-finishing services. Press Box News offers the commuter a chance to stay in his or her car, yet buy that quick cup of coffee, a newspaper, and a snack in less than 30 seconds.

Company executives, with a combined total of more than 20 years experience in regional newsstand operations and franchising, note that up to 75 percent of all convenience store customers drive, so they believe that a significant proportion of those customers will choose to avoid getting out of their cars and, instead, drive by your free-standing building placed strategically on major thoroughfares.

Press Box Drive-Thru Newsstand is a marvelously simply operation: a small, 100-square-foot free-standing building placed on the extra space in the parking lot of a service station, bowling alley, or similar high-traffic spot. One person—you, a family member, or a part-time employee—sells newspapers, coffee, snacks, soft drinks, lottery tickets, photo finishing, and magazines to commuters. No milk, no bread, no nachos, no hot pizza! Just the average commuter's basic morning pick-me-up's.

You make an average sale of about $2 every 20 to 30 seconds, with as many as 60 to 70 cars passing through during the rush hours. Press Box News requires very little inventory. It offers very low overhead costs—as little as $12 per day, and all of the sales are cash.

At the end of 1989, Press Box News had only eight operational franchises in two states, but it had commitments to build up to 65 more in New Jersey and Pennsylvania during the next five years. It was actively seeking franchisees throughout the Northeast and Southeast. The company is included in this book because, as an emerging franchise, it offers you a ground-floor opportunity. It offers a very simple, low-cost operation, which a husband and wife or family group can easily manage. It appears ideal for semi-retired couples. And it is an all-cash business, one of the few remaining among franchises.

How Much It Costs

For a flat franchise fee of $49,995, you receive a complete turnkey operation, including the 100-square-foot free-standing building, an initial inventory, all of the equipment, such as coffee makers and display stands, a week's training, and more.

Press Box executives provide a very good estimate of total start-up costs and an accurate list of additional costs you can expect to pay. The author adds costs to some categories to reflect more accurately actual experience in related fields:

Category	Low End	High End
Franchise fee[a]	$49,995	$49,995
First month's rent	250	1,000
Lease security deposit	250	2,000
Insurances[b]	300	2,000
Training travel	750	1,500
Professional fees	250	1,000
Utility deposits	300	800
Office supplies	100	300
Working capital	3,500	8,000
Total	$55,695	$66,595

a. Includes building, leasehold improvements, equipment package, opening advertising and promotion, training, and initial inventory.
b. Ranges from initial down payments to total annual premium payments on franchise-required coverage.

Other Fees and Charges

You also must pay a graduated royalty fee, which helps you increase your profits during your first year in business. You pay a small 2 percent weekly royalty during your first six months, 3 percent during your second six months, and 4 percent, thereafter. You pay a 1 percent advertising fund fee each week as well.

You may, but are not required to, buy your supplies through Press Box News, although it offers a wholesale warehouse operation. One of the company founders owns one of the largest newsstand chains in Pennsylvania and has the facilities to provide this service. The company, of course, profits from these supply sales under marketing contracts with the vendors.

What You Get

Press Box News provides many essential services that other companies do not:

Site location. Press Box finds a suitable location for your building. However, you must approve the location before you sign the franchise agreement. Remember that in this franchise, location is *everything*. Without a prime location and very easy and quick in-and-out access, you will have few customers. Prime locations include gas stations, diner parking lots, strip shopping center parking lots, bowling alley parking lots, or any large parking lot on main commuter highways.

Lease negotiation. Press Box executives negotiate the lease for you—with your ultimate responsibility and approval.

Construction. The company manages the construction process at no cost.

Exclusive territory. You also get an exclusive, but small, territory. Although the franchise UFOC is vague on this point, executives have said in an interview that they do not plan to put competing newsstands within a mile or two of each other. The UFOC says the exact territory varies with population, traffic density, and third-party competition in the area.

Agreement term. The initial agreement lasts 10 years and has a one 10-year renewal option with no additional franchise fee. This 20-year potential offers a good chance to take out substantial salaries and build a little equity. The value of your franchise depends on your lease terms and your location.

As noted, you also get the complete turnkey operation. The company has designed its program so that all you have to do is approve a location and a lease, take the training, and go to work.

How Much Can You Make?

Press Box News executives have been quoted in several newspaper articles and one telephone interview as saying that you can gross $250,000 to $400,000 per year with this franchise. That range should perhaps be considered a second- or third-year goal.

A more conservative estimate shows that you can expect to gross between $145,000 and $200,000 during your first year. The low estimate means that you should gross about $400 per day (200 or more cars per 13-hour operation—6 a.m. to 7 p.m.), seven days a week, and 52 weeks a year. The following table shows anticipated expenses and a net profit figure for a conservative first year:

Category	Annual Expense
Cost of goods (50%)	$ 72,500
Loan payments[a]	12,000
Overhead[b]	11,000
Part-time labor[c]	10,000
Royalties[d]	3,800
Total Expenses	$109,300
Gross Income	$145,000
Net Pre-Tax Income[e]	$ 35,700

a. Assuming you borrow $50,000 for five years at conventional interest rates.

b. Ranges from as low as $12 to as high as $50 per day. This number falls in between at about $30 per day.

c. Assumes you and/or your spouse or family work full-time or share working hours.

d. Remember the lower first-year royalty fees.

e This is a conservative estimate; you are likely to do substantially better with a good location and reasonably effective advertising, merchandising, and cost controls. If you do not borrow money, or borrow less than $50,000, you add about one-third more to your net profit.

Clearly, you can breakeven during the 12 to 18 months and earn a 100 percent ROI by the end of your third year, even with a conservative estimate. Press Box Drive-Thru Newsstand offers an excellent all-cash, low-overhead, simple franchise.

DYNAMARK SECURITY CENTERS, INC.

Dynamark Security Centers, Inc.
P.O. Box 2068
Leitersburg Pike
Hagerstown, MD 21742-2068
(301) 797-2124

During 1986, with a 525 percent growth rate, Dynamark Security Centers was the fastest growing franchise in the U.S.; it succeeded with an aggressive program to turn independent security systems dealers and operators into its franchisees. Between 1977 and 1984, Dynamark had sold its security systems through dealerships, but its main competitors, such as Sonitrol and Alliance Security Systems, had begun a new trend toward franchised security companies. Therefore, Dynamark, with a low franchise fee and good support services, established itself as a strong alternative to its competitors.

Dynamark offers a professional, unique, and (potentially) highly profitable system of designing, marketing, installing, servicing, and monitoring residential and light commercial security and fire protection systems. The company does not manufacture its systems, but works with high-quality manufacturers to offer the most innovative electronic security devices. It emphasizes systems integration, unlike other firms that mix and match components from different vendors.

Dynamark and its competitors sit in the middle of the boom stage of franchising the security industry. At present, the residential market is scattered among as many as 15,000 independent businesses that offer security systems of vastly different quality. Security systems consumers—homeowners and small businesspeople—do seriously need relatively inexpensive, 24-hour-a-day, high-quality security protection. A franchise's uniform and consistent methods may more readily fulfill their requirements.

At the end of 1988, Dynamark reported that it had a 1 percent market share in this scattered, but dynamic, market. Its goal for the mid-1990s is to capture a 20- to 25-percent market share. This growth is possible because only about 14 percent of the residential market has installed security systems. And those that already have security systems often change services when the quality of their current service declines. Dynamark executives assume that about 60 percent of all residences are candidates for security service, so the market can quintuple before it reaches saturation.

As the number of households continues to expand, so does the security market. The number of single-family residences and light commercial businesses grows about 3 and 5 percent per year, respectively, so the long-term potential appears excellent.

How Much It Costs

For existing security dealers, Dynamark offers a reduced franchise fee to encourage conversions and because these dealers bring their expertise in installation and general security business practices to their franchises. However, both existing dealers and new franchisees must buy a $10,000 equipment, marketing, and sales-aids package.

If you are new to the security industry, your franchise fee equals $25,000. You must also purchase the $10,000 equipment and supplies inventory and have a minimum of $15,000 operating capital.

Start-Up Costs

The following table applies only to new franchisees. An existing dealer's total investment should not exceed $15,000, and you may be able to borrow most of that from a financial institution if your current business has a good credit rating. Dealers literally may be able to become Dynamark franchisees with no cash investment.

For new franchisees, your total start-up costs will include the following:

Category	Low End	High End
Franchise fee	$25,000	$25,000
Opening package	10,000	10,000
Working capital[a]	15,000	25,000
Total[b]	$50,000	$60,000

a. Includes real estate leases, travel expenses, insurance deposits, fees to local police departments, and the like.

b. The total investment of most Dynamark franchisees is closer to the low investment.

Note: Dynamark encourages you to get the least expensive space available: warehouse-type space is more than adequate for this operation.

Helpful Royalty Fee Arrangement

The royalty fee is a low 3 percent per month, or a $100 monthly minimum, but Dynamark offers a very helpful royalty credit based on your purchase volume per month, that is, how many security systems you buy from them for your new customers.

Monthly Purchase Volume	Royalty Fee (%)
$ 0 to $ 5,000	3
$5,001 to $ 7,500	2
$7,501 to $20,000	1
$20,001 and up	0

These are very attractive royalties because Dynamark primarily works as an equipment sales company.

Advertising Fee

You also pay 1 percent or $50 per month minimum fee to the franchisees' Advertising and Promotion Fund. Franchisees approve annual expenditures from this fund.

Other Requirements

Most importantly, you must buy all of your security equipment through Dynamark and offer only the company's DynaWatch national alarm-monitoring services. Dynamark, of course, makes most of its income from equipment sales and service revenues. After you start, you are obligated to purchase between 75 and 100 percent of all your equipment and services from the company, including the following: master controls, transmitters, accessories, advertising materials, signs, sales aids, business forms, etc. You must also have, in force, the usual alarm-industry insurance coverages. And you must pay for all training travel expenses.

Regional Franchise Program

To existing franchisees with a six-month record of what it calls Class I status (have fulfilled their sales quotas), Dynamark also offers the opportunity of their becoming regional franchisees. The regional territories usually cover one Congressional district, but the company will not grant a regional territory in a district in which a franchise already exists. In a regional territory, you sell to and contract with individual dealerships; they, in turn, purchase their Dynamark equipment through you. In effect, you act as a sizable Dynamark distributor. If you meet regional purchase quotas, you do not have to pay royalties, so you pocket this profit. Like all other franchisees, you still must pay monthly ad fees.

What You Get

Dynamark offers you a complete and aggressive marketing program that targets the residential and light commercial segments. Its proven program uses customers to generate referrals, and low-cost advertising and promotion to create leads. Other elements of Dynamark's program include:

Agreement term. Dynamark has increased its initial term from three to five years, with five-year renewals. Dynamark appears to use this term to separate the wheat from the chaff, so it can refuse to renew poor performers, but reward good ones. If you succeed during your first term, you could add substantial resale value and equity during your second and subsequent terms.

Basic training. You receive five days of training for as many people as you want to bring. Of course, you or they have to pay their expenses. You receive on-going training at your location and through video tapes, newsletters, bulletins, and headquarter's seminars.

Cause-related marketing. Dynamark's Child Seekers® program uses Teddy Ruxpin, the popular toy and official "spokesbear," to encourage franchisees to distribute posters of missing children and help raise funds locally for the National Center for Missing and Exploited Children.

Advertising materials. Dynamark continually updates its advertising, sales promotion, and public relations programs. It also provides sales kits for on-site demonstrations.

Group purchasing programs. They help reduce costs of supplies, insurance, and inventory.

Research and Advisory Board. Active franchisees work with headquarter's staff to approve new products, such as CCTV, central vacuums, intercom and stereo systems, and automobile alarms.

Other support programs. Dynamark also provides staff marketing assistance, field visits, technical assistance, a national training school for installers, DSC workshops, and a national annual convention.

How Much Can You Make?

Fortunately, very good numbers of your potential earnings are available from the time that Dynamark dealt only with dealers. The secret to this franchise is an incredibly profitable concept: you receive profits from your initial equipment installation; profits from recurring monthly income; and profits from annual service contracts. Every time you install a system, you offer to sign the customer to a monthly monitoring service and a maintenance agreement. DynaWatch provides the monitoring service, not you, so after you pay a percentage (30 percent) to Dynamark, your income from the monthly fees is pure profit, and with almost no overhead costs.

For example, the average monthly fee for security monitoring systems is $20. Of that amount, you pay DynaWatch $6. You keep the $14 difference as pure profit, minus a few cents for billing charges. You can cover your billing costs by imposing a monthly late charge in states that allow it.

If you sell eight systems per month, that brings 96 systems on-line per year. At the end of your first year, in addition to your systems sales and installation profits, you will earn a minimum monthly profit of $1,344. Repeat this process each year, and at the end of five years, your minimum monthly profit from monitoring services will equal $6,720.

One caveat: Not every person will continue the monitoring service; people move, and you must sell the service to often reluctant buyers. You should expect an annual turnover of 10 to 15 percent. Therefore, in reality, you need to sell about 115 systems per year to reach that projected income level.

This is just the first way you profit. Other ways include the following:

Equipment and installation. Charges range from $500 to $3,000 or more. You should net at least 25 percent, or $500 on an average $2,000 sale, even after you pay your installers about $7 or so an hour and cover your overhead. You can negotiate your prices and make them very competitive to obtain the recurring monthly monitoring-service agreement.

Service contracts. You also sell service contracts on which you net about 50 percent because your existing installers do the maintenance. Service calls not under contract are billed at between $28 and $50 per hour for labor, and you can sell replacements for equipment not covered by warranties.

Equipment upgrades. If someone begins with a basic system, you can sell equipment upgrades and add-ons and earn the same net profit margins (30 percent) that you receive on initial equipment sales.

Frankly, it appears that an existing dealer should greatly expand his or her business during the first year. A new franchisee can easily recoup cash investment in the first six months and the complete investment within two years.

If you have sales and marketing skills, or if you are an existing security systems dealer, Dynamark provides an amazing range of profit opportunities from a product and a service in great and growing demand.

Bibliography

Books

Dixon, Edward L., Jr., Ed., *The 1989 Franchise Annual Handbook and Directory,* Lewiston, NY: Info Press, Inc., 1988.

International Franchise Association, *Directory of Membership, 1989–1990,* Washington, D.C.: International Franchise Association, 1989.

Rausch, Edward N., *Financial Keys to Small Business Profitability,* New York: AMACOM, 1982.

Webster, Bryce, *The Insider's Guide to Franchising,* New York: AMACOM, 1986.

Magazines

Entrepreneur, "The Annual Franchise 500," January, 1989; *Address:* Entrepreneur Group, Inc., 2311 Pontius Avenue, Los Angeles, CA 90064.

Franchising Opportunities World, bi-monthly; *Address:* International Franchise Association, 1350 New York Avenue, NW, Suite 900, Washington, DC 20005.

Income Opportunities, January–July, 1987; *Address:* Davis Publications, 380 Lexington Avenue, New York, NY 10017.

The Info Franchise Newsletter, Info Press, Inc.; *Address:* Info Press, Inc., 736 Center Street, Box 550, Lewiston, NY 14092.

Venture, "The Franchisor 100," November, 1989; December, 1988; November, 1987; November, 1986; and September, 1985; *Address:* Venture Magazine, 521 Fifth Avenue, New York, NY 10175-0028.

Index

A

AAA Employment Franchise, Inc., 146–149
  advantages of, 147
  costs, 148
  earnings estimates, 149
ADIA Personnel Services, 202–208
  costs, 204–207
  divisions of, 203
  earnings estimates, 207
  territory policy, 206
Advertising
  American Advertising Distributors,
    Inc., 246–251
  Bingo Bugle, 66–76
  Homes and Land Publishing, 159–162
  Tri-Mark Publishing Co., Inc.,
    234–240
Almost Heaven Hot Tubs, Inc., 50–53
  competition, approach to, 52–53
  costs, 50–51
  earnings estimates, 51–52
American Advertising Distributors, Inc.,
  246–251
  costs, 247–249
  earnings estimates, 250
Apparel, Monograms Plus, 262–265
Auto rental, U-Save Auto Rental, 106–110

B

Bathcrest Porcelain Resurfacing, 60–66
  costs, 61–63
  earnings estimates, 65–66
  payment method, 63
  pricing of services, 64–65
  start-up, 61

Bingo Bugle, 66–76
  costs, 67–69
  earnings estimates, 67, 70
  1987–1989 revenues, 71–76
Bio-Care, Inc., 208–214
  costs, 211–213
  earnings estimates, 214
  as speculative service, 210–211
Bloc franchises, 223
Brand name franchises, 3
Breakeven analysis, 25–27
Business format franchises, 3–5
Business plan, outline for, 27–30
Business services, General Business
    Services, Inc., 265–270

C

Carpet cleaning
  Chem-Dry Carpet Cleaning, 91–96
  Duraclean International, 96–101
  Rainbow International, 136–141
  Rug Doctor Pro, 82–81
Carpet dyeing, Rainbow International,
    136–141
Car wash, Sparky Washmobile, 57–59
Ceiling Doctor, 257–261
  costs, 258–259
  earnings estimates, 260–261
Ceiling maintenance
  Ceiling Doctor, 257–261
  Coustic-Glo International,
    114–118
Century 21, 175–178
  advantages of, 175–176
  costs, 176
  earnings estimates, 177–178

Chem-Dry Carpet Cleaning, 91–96
  costs, 93–94
  deferred payments, 94–95
  earnings estimates, 95–96
  territory policy, 92
Cleaning services
  Jani-King, 122–127
  Maids International, 141–146
  Merry Maids, 194–197
  Mini Maid, 119–121
  Molly Maid, 150–158
  Servpro Industries, 162–167
Convenience stores, Press Box News,
    278–282
Cost Cutters Family Hair Care Shops,
    226–229
  costs, 227–228
  earnings estimates, 228–229
  projection models, 229
Coustic-Glo International, 114–118
  advantages of, 117–118
  costs, 115–117
  earnings estimates, 118
CutCo Industries, Inc., 222–226
  costs, 223–225
  earnings estimates, 225

D

Decorating Den, 179–185
  costs, 180–183
  earnings estimates, 185
  franchise packages offered, 180–181
Dial-A-Gift, Inc., 77–82
  costs, 79–80
  earnings estimates, 81–82
Direct mail, American Advertising
    Distributors, Inc., 246–251
Drain cleaning
  Bio-Care, Inc., 208–214
  Mr. Rooter, 110–114
Duraclean International, 96–101
  costs, 97–99
  earnings estimates, 100–101
  franchise packages, 97–98
Dynamark Security Centers, 282–287
  costs, 283–284
  earnings estimates, 286–287
  regional franchise arrangement,
    285

E

Employment services
  AAA Employment Franchise, Inc.,
    146–149
  Adia Personnel Services, 202–208
  Management Recruiters International,
    Inc., 185–193
Exercise, Jazzercise, Inc., 34–38

F

Federal Trade Commission (FTC), on
    earnings claims, 21
Financial aspects
  analysis of, 21–28
  breakeven analysis, 25–27
  business plan, 27–30
  financial warning signs, 22–23
  locating appropriate information, 23–24
  net income, 19–20
  net margin, 20
  net profit, 20
  return on investment (ROI), 19–21
  rough rate of return, calculation of, 24–25
Food, Subway Sandwiches & Salads,
    101–106
Four Seasons Greenhouses, 230–233
  costs, 231–232
  earnings estimates, 233
Franchises
  advantages of, 12–13
  controls/restrictions related to, 31–32
  costs involved, 14–15
  failure, reasons for, 6–7
  financial aspects, 19–30
  franchisees, skills/qualities required,
    16–18
  future trends for, 8–10
  site selection, 31
  termination of contract, 32–33
  types of, 3–5, 8
Franchising, basic concept in, 1–3, 11–12

G

General Business Services, 265–270
  costs, 266–268
  earnings estimates, 269–270

Gifts, Dial-A-Gift, Inc., 77–82
Greenhouses, Four Seasons Greenhouses,
    230–232

H

Hair care
    Cost Cutters Family Hair Care Shops,
        226–229
    CutCo Industries, Inc., 222–226
Homes and Land Publishing, 159–162
    costs, 159–160
    earnings estimates, 162
    factors in success of, 162
Hot tubs, Almost Heaven Hot Tubs, Inc.,
    50–53

I

Interior design, Decorating Den, 179–185

J

Jani-King, 122–127
    costs, 123–125
    earnings estimates, 126–127
    franchise packages offered, 123–124
    territory policy, 126–127
Jazzercise, Inc., 34–38
    costs, 35–36
    earnings estimates, 37–38
    expenses, 36–37

M

Maids International, 141–146
    costs, 142–143
    earnings estimates, 145–146
    support services, 144–145
    territory policy, 142, 144
Mail Boxes Etc. USA, 214–222
    costs, 216–219
    earnings estimates, 220–221
    factors in success of, 221
    territory policy, 215–216
Management Recruiters International, Inc.,
    185–193

Management Recruiters International, Inc.
    (*cont'd*)
    costs, 186–188
    earnings estimates, 189
    1988 operating ratio study, 189–193
    types of franchises, 188
Management systems, Priority Management
    Systems, Inc., 251–256
Master franchise, 8
Merry Maids, 194–197
    costs, 194–195
    net annual profits, 197
    sales quota, 195–196
Mini Maid, 119–121
    costs, 120
    earnings estimates, 121
Molly Maid, 150–158
    average weekly sales, by region,
        155–158
    costs, 151–152
    earnings estimates, 154
Monograms Plus, 262–265
    costs, 263–264
    earnings estimates, 265
Mr. Rooter, 110–114
    costs, 111–112
    earnings estimates, 113–114

N

Net income, 19–20
Net margin, 20
Net profit, 20
Novus Windshield Repair, 41–45
    costs, 42–43
    earnings estimates, 44
    Sears arrangement, 44

P

Packaging/shipping
    Packy the Shipper, 38–40
    Pak Mail Centers of America, Inc.,
        197–202
Packy the Shipper, 38–40
    add-ons to service, 39
    benefits to franchisees, 40
    costs, 39
    earnings estimates, 40

Pak Mail Centers of America, 197–202
   costs, 199–200
   earnings estimates, 202
Perma Ceram, 53–56
   costs, 53–54
   earnings estimates, 56
   market for service, 54–55
   operating expenses, 55
   start-up strategy, 55–56
Porcelain resurfacing
   Bathcrest, Inc., 60–66
   Perma Ceram, 53–56
   Worldwide Refinishing Systems,
      127–135
Postal services, Mail Boxes, Etc. USA,
   214–222
Press Box News, 278–282
   costs, 279–280
   earnings estimates, 281–282
Pressure cleaning, Wash on Wheels, Inc.,
   45–49
Priority Management Systems, Inc., 251–256
   costs, 253–254
   earnings estimates, 255
   profit/loss statement, 256
   territory policy, 254–255
   types of franchises offered, 251
Profusion Systems, Inc., 274–278
   costs, 275–276
   earnings estimates, 277–278
Publishing
   Bingo Bugle, 66–76
   Homes and Land Publishing, 159–162

R

Rainbow International, 136–141
   costs, 137–138
   earnings estimates, 139–140
Real estate
   Century 21, 175–178
   RE/MAX International, 167–171
RE/MAX International, 167–171
   costs, 168–169
   earnings estimates, 170
   fee schedule, 169–170
Return on investment (ROI), 19–21
Rug Doctor Pro, 82–91
   costs, 85–87
   earnings estimates, 90–91
   financing arrangements, 88–89

Rug Doctor Pro (*con't*)
   marketing approach, 84–85
   territory policy, 83

S

Security systems, Dynamark Security
   Centers, 282–287
Selected distribution franchises, 3
Servpro Industries, 162–167
   costs, 164–166
   earnings estimates, 167
   franchise packages offered, 163
   territory policy, 166
Sparky Washmobile, 57–589
   costs, 58
   earnings estimates, 59
   equipment, 57–58
Subway Sandwiches and Salads, 101–106
   costs, 101–102, 103, 104–105
   court actions related to, 103
   earnings estimates, 106
   expenses, 105–106
   territory policy, 104

T

Termination of contract, 32–33
Travel agency
   Travel Agents International, 241–246
   Uniglobe Travel International, Inc.,
      270–274
Travel Agents International, 241–246
   costs, 242–243, 245
   earnings estimates, 245–246
Tri-Mark Publishing Co., Inc., 234–240
   bankruptcy issue, 235–236
   costs, 236–237
   earnings estimates, 238
   national accounts policy, 238
   sales quotas, 238

U

Uniform Franchising Offering Circulars,
   24, 27
Uniglobe Travel International, Inc., 270–274
   costs, 272
   earnings estimates, 273–274

U-Save Auto Rental, 107–110
   costs, 107–108
   earnings estimates, 109

V

Video Data Services, 171–174
   costs, 172
   earnings estimates, 174
   territory policy, 173
Videotaping, Video Data Services, 171–174
Vinyl repair, ProFusion Systems, Inc.,
   274–278

W

Wash on Wheels, Inc., 45–49
   costs, 46–48
   earnings estimates, 49
   services of, 46
Windshield repair, Novus Franchising, Inc.,
   41–44
Worldwide Refinishing Systems, 127–135
   costs, 128–129
   earnings estimates, 130
   pro forma balance sheets, 131–135